3

The Complete Encyclopedia of Cooking

Supercook

Marshall Cavendish · London Sydney New York

Symbols in Supercook

'Low-Calorie' Recipes
The description 'low-calorie' has been given to recipes in *'Supercook'* which contain fewer calories than other comparable recipes in the book. For instance, the pudding recipes marked 'Low-cal' have the fewest calories when compared to other pudding recipes in *'Supercook'*. Some – but not all – of the recipes labelled 'Low-cal' would be suitable for people who are following strict slimming or low-calorie diets. Each recipe should be examined carefully to ascertain whether the ingredients are permitted for a particular special diet.

The labelling 'Low-cal' will be more helpful for those aiming to lose weight slowly by reducing their calorie intake slightly or those who frequently experiment with new recipes but wish to avoid a very high consumption of calories. These recipes can also guide the person entertaining for weight-conscious friends. However,

thought should also be given to what is to be served *with* the 'low-calorie' recipe. An over-enthusiastic combination of these recipes will not guarantee a low-calorie meal!

In deciding which recipes to consider in the 'low-calorie' category, each ingredient needs to be considered for its calorific contribution. Low-calorie ingredients such as vegetables, fruits, white fish and eggs may be combined with a moderate amount of fat or fat-containing foods and still be relatively 'low-calorie'. A generous combination of fats and fat-containing foods will produce a high-calorie recipe. Similarly, recipes which rely heavily on sugar, alcohol, flour or a combination of these foods with or without fat will be excluded from the 'low-calorie' rating.

In some recipes it may be possible to make further reductions in the amount of fats and sugars used, such as substituting low-fat yogurt for cream, or to grill [broil] food and drain off fat rather than frying, although the end results will differ slightly.

The calorie chart under the alphabetical heading CALORIES (p. 302) may be used to work out the approximate calorific value of individual recipes.

Low Cal

This is the guide to the amount of skill needed for each recipe.

Easy	Needs special care	Complicated

This is an estimated guide to the dish's cost, which will, of course, vary with the season.

Inexpensive	Reasonable	Expensive

This is an indication of the amount of time needed for preparing and cooking the dish.

Less than 1 hour	1 hour to 2½ hours	Over 2½ hours

Front Cover: Cheese Soufflé p. 366

Published by Marshall Cavendish House
58 Old Compton Street
London W1V 5PA

This Edition Published 1985

Printed and bound by
New Interlitho Spa, Italy

Cataloguing in Publication Data

Supercook
1. Cookery
1. Cameron-Smith, Marye
641.5 TX717 79-52319

ISBN (for set) 0 85685 534 0
ISBN (this volume) 0 85685 537 5
Library of Congress catalog card number 78-52319.

Recipes in Volume 3

Butter [Dried Lima] Beans

Butter beans are the large, flat, white, dried seeds of a plant grown in Madagascar and South America. They can be stored for several months in a cool, dry place and they are a useful ingredient to have on hand to add to soups, supper dishes or salads.

Before using, butter beans should be soaked for 2 to 3 hours in lukewarm water, drained and then placed in a pan and covered again with warm water. The water is brought slowly to the boil over low heat. Then the pan is removed from the heat and the beans are allowed to soak for 1 more hour.

After soaking, the beans are drained and placed in a pan of boiling water together with 1 onion, 1 carrot, 1 celery stalk and a bouquet garni consisting of 4 parsley sprigs, 1 thyme spray and 1 bay leaf tied together. The pan is covered and the beans simmered over low heat for 1½ to 2 hours, or until they are tender. The beans are then drained and either served plain with butter and parsley or with a light sauce, such as tomato or cheese.

One pound of butter beans will serve four people.

Butter Beans Ménagère

BUTTER BEANS IN CREAM SAUCE

Butter beans can be a little dry, but in this recipe for Butter Beans Ménagère (may-nah-jair) *they are served in a light, creamy sauce. Butter beans are traditionally served with roast or braised mutton, but they go equally well with other meat or egg and fish dishes.*

4 SERVINGS

- **1 lb. butter** [dried lima] **beans**
- **1½ oz.** [3 tablespoons] **butter**
- **4 tablespoons flour**
- **1 tablespoon lemon juice**
- **½ teaspoon salt**
- **¼ teaspoon freshly ground black pepper**
- **2 tablespoons double** [heavy] **cream**
- **1 teaspoon chopped parsley**

COOKING LIQUID

- **2 pints** [5 cups] **water**
- **1 onion**
- **1 carrot, scraped**
- **1 small celery stalk**
- **bouquet garni, consisting of 4 parsley sprigs, 1 thyme spray and 1 bay leaf tied together**

Put the beans in a large bowl and cover them with lukewarm water. Leave the beans to soak for 3 hours.

Drain the beans in a colander, discarding the water, and transfer them to a medium-sized saucepan. Cover the beans again with lukewarm water and place the pan over low heat. Bring the water slowly to the boil, then remove the pan from the heat. Leave the beans to soak again for 1 hour. Drain the beans in a colander, discarding the water, and set them aside.

Put the 2 pints of water for the cooking liquid into the saucepan. Bring the water to the boil over high heat and add the onion, carrot, celery, bouquet garni and beans to the pan. Reduce the heat to moderately low, cover the pan and simmer the beans for 1½ hours or until tender.

When the beans are cooked, drain them in a colander and reserve 5 fluid ounces [⅝ cup] of the strained cooking liquid. Return the beans to the saucepan, cover and set aside.

In a medium-sized saucepan melt the butter over moderate heat. Remove the pan from the heat and with a wooden spoon stir the flour into the butter. Gradually add the reserved cooking liquid, stirring constantly. Place the pan back on the heat and bring the sauce to the boil, still stirring. Cook for 1 to 2 minutes, then stir in the lemon juice, salt and pepper.

Pour the sauce over the beans and stir to coat them with the sauce. Return the pan to low heat and cook for 2 to 3 minutes.

Remove the pan from the heat and stir in the cream. Turn the beans into a serving dish and sprinkle with parsley.

Butter Biscuits

These rich buttery biscuits [cookies] *are easy to make and are ideal to serve with tea or with a simple ice-cream or fruit dessert.*

30 BISCUITS [COOKIES]

- **4 oz.** [½ cup] **butter, cut into small pieces, plus extra for greasing**
- **4 oz. castor** [½ cup superfine] **sugar**
- **1 small egg, beaten**
- **6 oz.** [1½ cups] **self-raising flour, sifted**
- **2 oz.** [½ cup] **lightly toasted almonds**

Preheat the oven to moderate 350°F (Gas Mark 4, 180°C) and position the shelf in the centre of the oven. Lightly grease 2 baking sheets.

To make the biscuits [cookies], melt the butter in a heavy-based saucepan over a low heat. Take the saucepan off the heat and stir in the sugar. Allow the mixture to cool slightly.

Beat the egg into the butter and sugar mixture, then gradually beat in the flour.

Drop in teaspoonfuls on to the baking sheets, spacing about 3 inches apart. Top each with an almond.

Bake for 12-15 minutes until golden. Remove from the oven and allow to firm for 2 minutes, then transfer, with a spatula, to a wire rack to cool.

Butter Beans Ménagère is an unusual and interesting vegetable dish to serve with roast or braised mutton.

Butter Coconut Biscuits

These biscuits [cookies], *with a slight hint of rum, are simple to prepare, attractive and ideal to serve with tea.*

48 BISCUITS

- 8 oz. [1 cup] **butter**
- 6 oz. [$\frac{3}{4}$ cup] **sugar**
- 1 **egg**
- 2 tablespoons **rum**
- 12 oz. [3 cups] **flour**
- $\frac{1}{2}$ teaspoon **salt**
- 4 tablespoons **desiccated** [shredded] **coconut**

In a medium-sized mixing bowl, cream the butter and sugar together with a wooden spoon. Beat in the egg and the rum. Sift in half the flour and the salt and stir to mix. Then sift in the remaining flour and stir thoroughly until the flour is incorporated.

With your hands, lightly form the dough into a roll $2\frac{1}{2}$ inches in diameter. Wrap it in greaseproof paper or aluminium foil and chill in the refrigerator for 4 hours.

Preheat the oven to moderate 350°F (Gas Mark 4, 180°C).

Lightly flour a board. Cut the roll of dough into $\frac{1}{8}$-inch thick slices. Place the biscuits on a baking sheet. Bake in the oven for 10 minutes, or until the biscuits are golden brown.

Transfer the biscuits to a wire rack and sprinkle them with the coconut. Leave them to cool before serving.

Buttercream Icing

Versatile and easy-to-make Buttercream Icing may be used to fill and cover any plain cake. You can flavour it, colour it, and it is ideal for freezing.

TO FILL AND ICE ONE 9-INCH CAKE

- 3 oz. **unsalted butter** [$\frac{3}{8}$ cup sweet butter], **at room temperature**
- 12 oz. **icing sugar** [3 cups confectioners' sugar], **sifted**
- $\frac{1}{8}$ teaspoon **salt**
- $1\frac{1}{2}$ teaspoons **vanilla essence**
- 2 tablespoons **double** [heavy] **cream**

Place the butter in a large mixing bowl, and, with the back of a wooden spoon, cream the butter. When it is smooth, gradually add half of the sugar and the salt. Cream the butter and sugar together until the mixture is pale and fluffy. Mix in the vanilla essence and cream and beat in the remaining sugar.

VARIATIONS

Chocolate Buttercream Icing
Add 2 ounces of melted dark cooking [semi-sweet] chocolate with the cream and vanilla essence to the basic Buttercream Icing.

Orange or Lemon Buttercream Icing
Substitute the grated rind of $\frac{1}{2}$ orange or lemon and 3 tablespoons of orange or lemon juice for the cream in the basic Buttercream Icing.

Butter Curler

A butter curler is a small instrument consisting of a piece of fairly sharp, serrated metal which is attached to a handle. It is drawn over the surface of chilled butter to scrape the butter off in the shape of a curl or shell. After each curl or shell is made, dip the curler into hot water to prevent the butter sticking to it.

Buttermilk

The liquid which is left from churning the cream which has been used in buttermaking, buttermilk consists of about 90 per cent water, 5 per cent milk sugar, 3 per cent casein, or milk protein, mineral salts and lactic acid, which gives it a sour taste. Buttermilk is used with bicarbonate of soda as a raising agent, in the proportion of 10 fluid ounces [$1\frac{1}{4}$ cups] of buttermilk to $\frac{1}{2}$ teaspoon of soda.

Commercial buttermilk is available in cartons and is widely used in recipes, especially in the United States. It also makes a nourishing and refreshing drink.

Buttermilk Doughnuts

These Buttermilk Doughnuts, with their light but spicy taste, will be popular with the entire family. A deep-fat thermometer will ensure that the doughnuts are properly cooked and temptingly fluffy.

36 DOUGHNUTS

- 3 **eggs**
- 8 oz. [1 cup] **sugar**
- $1\frac{1}{2}$ oz. [3 tablespoons] **butter, melted**
- 6 fl. oz. [$\frac{3}{4}$ cup] **commercial buttermilk**
- 1 lb. $2\frac{1}{2}$ oz. [$4\frac{1}{2}$ cups plus 2 tablespoons] **flour**

These American Buttermilk Doughnuts and Scones are easy to make and especially popular with children.

½ teaspoon ground nutmeg
½ teaspoon ground allspice
1 teaspoon bicarbonate of soda [baking soda]
1½ teaspoons baking powder
1½ teaspoons salt
sufficient oil or fat for deep-frying

In a large mixing bowl, use a rotary beater or wire whisk to beat the eggs until they are thick and pale yellow. Gradually beat in the sugar. Then stir in the butter and half the buttermilk.

With a metal spoon, fold the flour, nutmeg, allspice, soda, baking powder and salt into the egg mixture until all the ingredients are well combined and a smooth dough is formed. Add more buttermilk if necessary.

Cover the bowl with a cloth or plate and place it in the refrigerator. Leave the dough to chill for 30 minutes.

Turn the dough out on to a well-floured board. Using a floured rolling pin, roll the dough out until it is about ¼-inch thick. With a floured pastry cutter, cut rounds of the dough 2½ to 3 inches in diameter. Cut a small hole out of the centre of each round.

Heat the oil or fat to 375°F (190°C) in a deep frying-pan.

Fry 2 or 3 of the dough rounds in the hot fat for 3 minutes on each side, or until both sides are golden brown.

With a slotted spoon, remove the doughnuts from the pan and drain on kitchen paper towels. Serve them hot or cold.

Buttermilk Pie

This creamy American pie is an economical dessert and is delicious served with a fruit sauce. To make especially light pastry, it is important to use a good vegetable fat.

ONE 10-INCH PIE

PIE CRUST
6 oz. [1½ cups] flour
¼ teaspoon salt
3 teaspoons sugar
2 oz. [¼ cup] vegetable fat
2 oz. [¼ cup] butter
1 small egg, lightly beaten
1 tablespoon lemon juice
3 to 4 tablespoons cold water

FILLING
4 oz. [½ cup] sugar
¼ teaspoon salt
2 tablespoons flour
2 eggs, separated
2 teaspoons vanilla essence
10 fl. oz. [1¼ cups] commercial buttermilk
2 oz. [¼ cup] butter, melted

To make the pastry, sift the flour, salt and sugar into a medium-sized bowl. Add the fat and butter and cut them into small pieces with a knife. With your fingertips rub the fat into the flour until the mixture resembles coarse breadcrumbs.

Stir the egg, lemon juice and 2 tablespoons of the water into the flour mixture. Mix with a fork and then, using your hands, lightly pat the dough into a ball. Add more water if the dough is too dry. Cover the dough with greaseproof paper or aluminium foil and chill in the refrigerator for 30 minutes.

On a lightly floured board, roll out the pastry to a circle 11½ inches in diameter. Line a 10-inch pie dish with the pastry and decorate the edges by crimping with a fork. Refrigerate it while you are preparing the filling.

Preheat the oven to hot 425°F (Gas Mark 7, 220°C).

Sift the sugar, salt and flour into a medium-sized mixing bowl. Beat the egg yolks lightly with a fork and pour them into the flour mixture along with the vanilla, buttermilk and melted butter. Beat well until the mixture is well blended.

Beat the egg whites with a whisk until they are stiff. Fold them into the egg-yolk mixture. Pour the mixture into the pastry shell.

Bake in the oven for 20 minutes. Then reduce the heat to warm 325°F (Gas Mark 3, 170°C) and cook for a further 40 minutes, or until a knife inserted in the centre of the pie comes out clean. Serve immediately while hot.

Buttermilk Scones

These American scones are easy-to-make. The addition of buttermilk to the batter makes them especially light and fluffy. They are ideal to serve for tea with butter and jam.

18 SCONES

2 oz. [¼ cup] plus ½ tablespoon butter
12 oz. [3 cups] flour
1 teaspoon salt
1 teaspoon baking powder
½ teaspoon bicarbonate of soda [baking soda]
10 fl. oz. [1¼ cups] commercial buttermilk

Preheat the oven to hot 425°F (Gas Mark 7, 220°C). Grease a baking sheet with ½ tablespoon of the butter.

Sift the flour, salt, baking powder

and soda into a medium-sized mixing bowl. With your fingertips, rub the remaining butter into the flour mixture until the mixture resembles coarse breadcrumbs. Using a fork, stir in enough buttermilk to make a soft dough.

Turn the dough out on to a lightly floured board. Knead it gently for 30 seconds. Roll out the dough to $\frac{1}{2}$-inch thickness. With a 2-inch round pastry cutter, cut out the scones and place them on the prepared baking sheet.

Bake the scones in the oven for 15 minutes, or until a skewer inserted in one of the scones comes out clean. Serve hot or cool.

Butter Paddles

Small, rectangular, bat-shaped pieces of wood scored on one side and with a handle, butter paddles are used to make butter balls. Chilled butter is cut into small squares and these squares are then rotated between the two paddles until they are round.

Butterscotch

A rich flavouring of brown sugar and butter, butterscotch is also the name of a hard toffee or candy.

Butterscotch Brownies

NUTTY BUTTERSCOTCH CAKES

Simple to make, Butterscotch Brownies are equally popular with children and adults. They are best when slightly moist and chewy, so they should not be overbaked. They may be served with tea or with an ice-cream or fruit dessert.

ABOUT 16 BROWNIES

4 oz. [$\frac{1}{2}$ cup] butter
5 oz. [$\frac{5}{8}$ cup] light soft brown sugar
2 eggs
$\frac{1}{4}$ teaspoon salt
4 oz. [1 cup] self-raising flour
1 teaspoon vanilla essence
2 oz. [$\frac{1}{3}$ cup] chopped walnuts or hazelnuts

Preheat the oven to moderate 350°F (Gas Mark 4, 180°C). Grease an 8-inch baking tin.

Mix all the ingredients together thoroughly in a large bowl using a wooden spoon.

Pour the mixture into the prepared baking tin and bake for 25 minutes.

Cut the brownies into squares while warm, then leave in the tin until cold. Butterscotch Brownies can be stored in an airtight tin for 2-3 days.

C

Cabbage

One of the oldest known vegetables, the cabbage is of European origin. It is cultivated in many varieties and belongs to the same family as CAULIFLOWER, BRUSSELS SPROUTS, KALE and BROCCOLI, all of which are descended from the wild cabbage. The two main kinds of cabbage are those with curled leaves and those with smooth leaves.

Cabbage grows best in a mild or cool climate and will tolerate frost. It is available all year round. Spring cabbage is the name for young cabbage regardless of season. Savoy cabbage, in season from September to March, has wrinkled leaves and tends to be milder in flavour than smooth-leaved winter cabbage.

Cabbage contains Vitamin A, iron, calcium and varying amounts of Vitamin C. It may be eaten as a raw vegetable, used in salads and cooking and for making sauerkraut. Savoy cabbage makes very good shredded cabbage salad, or COLE SLAW. Red cabbage, another variety, is used chiefly for pickling, although it is also delicious braised.

Cabbage should be washed well before being used. To prepare a cabbage for boiling, using a sharp knife cut the cabbage into quarters. Remove the coarse outer leaves and the hard core. Soak the cabbage in cold salted water for 10 minutes. Drain the cabbage thoroughly in a colander.

Put enough water into a medium-sized saucepan to make a 1-inch layer. Bring the water to the boil over high heat and add 1 teaspoon of salt. Drop the cabbage into the boiling water, reduce the heat to moderately low, cover the pan and cook the cabbage for about 10 minutes, or until it is tender but still crisp.

Drain the cabbage in a colander and then press it between 2 plates to remove any excess moisture.

Slice the pressed cabbage into rectangles and place it on a serving dish. Keep it warm.

Melt 2 tablespoons of butter in a small saucepan over moderate heat. Stir in a few drops of lemon juice and 1 tablespoon chopped parsley. Pour the flavoured butter over the cabbage.

Serve at once.

Cabbage Braised in Stock

Braised cabbage may be served as a vegetable dish, or, if the quantities are doubled, as a light main dish.

4 SERVINGS

1 medium-sized green cabbage
$\frac{1}{2}$ lb. streaky bacon slices, rind removed
1 onion, sliced
1 large carrot, scraped and cut into quarters
$\frac{1}{2}$ teaspoon mixed dried herbs
$\frac{1}{2}$ teaspoon salt
$\frac{1}{4}$ teaspoon freshly ground black pepper
$\frac{1}{4}$ teaspoon grated nutmeg
3 to 4 fl. oz. [$\frac{3}{8}$ to $\frac{1}{2}$ cup] beef stock

Low Cal

Preheat the oven to moderate 350°F (Gas Mark 4, 180°C).

Using a sharp knife, cut the cabbage into quarters. Place it in a colander and wash it under cold running water. Drain well. Break up the cabbage leaves and remove the thick portions of the stem.

Arrange half the bacon on the bottom of a flameproof casserole. Put the cabbage leaves with the onion, carrot and herbs on top. Season with the salt, pepper and grated nutmeg. Pour in the stock and cover the mixture with the remaining strips of bacon.

Put the casserole over moderate heat and cook uncovered for 10 minutes. Cover the pan. Place it in the oven and braise for 1 hour.

Cabbage in Orange Juice

An unusual and interesting way to prepare cabbage, Cabbage in Orange Juice goes well with most meat dishes.

4 SERVINGS

2 oz. [$\frac{1}{4}$ cup] butter
1 medium-sized green cabbage, coarsely shredded
2 tablespoons sugar
2 tablespoons lemon juice
1 teaspoon salt
$\frac{1}{2}$ teaspoon white pepper
8 fl. oz. [1 cup] orange juice

In a large frying-pan melt the butter over moderate heat. Add the shredded cabbage. Stir and toss until all the cabbage

A warming, winter dish, Cabbage and Lamb Hot Pot is tasty, economical and ideal for a family lunch or supper.

is coated with the butter. Add the sugar, lemon juice, salt and pepper. Stir to mix well and then add the orange juice.

Reduce the heat to low and simmer slowly, uncovered, stirring occasionally, until the cabbage is tender but still crisp. Taste and add more salt and pepper if necessary. Turn the cabbage into a warmed serving dish and serve immediately.

Cabbage and Lamb Hot Pot

This tasty, easy-to-make Cabbage and Lamb Hot Pot is a satisfying dish to serve for a family lunch or supper. It may be accompanied by boiled rice or new potatoes.

4 SERVINGS

1 tablespoon vegetable oil or butter
4 large lamb chops
1 medium-sized green cabbage, coarsely shredded
1 teaspoon salt
¼ teaspoon freshly ground black pepper
½ teaspoon dried rosemary
5 oz. canned tomato purée
2 fl. oz. [¼ cup] water

Low Cal

In a large saucepan, heat the oil or butter over moderate heat and brown the chops for 3 minutes on both sides. When they are browned, add the shredded cabbage, salt, pepper, rosemary, tomato purée and water and stir well.

Reduce the heat to low and cook for 45 minutes, or until the meat is tender when pierced with a fork and the cabbage is translucent.

Serve immediately.

Cabbage and Pepper Salad

This tasty and attractive cabbage and pepper salad is ideal to serve with meat or chicken when salad greens are not available.

8 SERVINGS

- 1 red pepper, white pith removed, seeded and finely sliced
- 1 green pepper, white pith removed, seeded and finely sliced
- 6 to 8 spring onions [scallions], finely chopped
- 1 cucumber, cut into ½-inch cubes
- 1 lb. tomatoes, finely sliced
- ½ white cabbage, coarse outer leaves removed, washed and finely sliced
- 2 tablespoons clear honey
- juice of 1 lemon
- 8 tablespoons oil
- 4 tablespoons vinegar
- 2 teaspoons salt
- 1 teaspoon black pepper

Low Cal

Combine the peppers, spring onions [scallions], cucumber, tomatoes and cabbage in a large salad bowl.

Put the honey, lemon juice, oil, vinegar, salt and pepper into a screw-top jar and shake it until the dressing is well mixed.

Pour the dressing over the salad just before serving and toss well.

Cabbage and Pineapple Salad

This delightful mixture of cabbage and pineapple with cream cheese can be served as a first course or a salad to accompany cold meats.

6 SERVINGS

- 1 small white cabbage (about ½ lb.) coarse outer leaves removed, washed and finely sliced
- 12 oz. canned pineapple chunks
- 3 oz. cream cheese
- 1 tablespoon chopped chives

Place the cabbage in a medium-sized salad bowl.

Drain the pineapple chunks and reserve the liquid. Add the pineapple to the cabbage and toss together.

Place the bowl in the refrigerator and chill the cabbage-and-pineapple mixture for 30 minutes.

In a small mixing bowl, with a fork or wooden spoon, beat the cream cheese until it is soft and smooth. Beating continuously, slowly add 3 tablespoons of the reserved pineapple juice. Continue beating until the dressing is well blended and creamy.

Just before serving add the dressing to the cabbage and pineapple mixture and toss the salad well. Garnish with the chopped chives.

Cabbage Rolls

This Finnish recipe for stuffed Cabbage Rolls is a tasty and substantial main dish to serve for a family lunch or supper. In Finland it is traditionally accompanied by cranberry sauce.

6 SERVINGS

- 1 teaspoon salt
- 1 large white cabbage, coarse outer leaves removed

FILLING

- 4 oz. [⅔ cup] rice, washed, soaked in water for 30 minutes and drained
- 9 fl. oz. [1⅛ cups] water plus 10 fl. oz. [1¼ cups] boiling water
- 1 teaspoon salt
- 1½ oz. [½ cup] dry white breadcrumbs
- 14 oz. minced [ground] lean beef
- 8 fl. oz. single cream [1 cup light cream]
- 1 teaspoon paprika
- ½ teaspoon white pepper
- 1 tablespoon butter
- 2 tablespoons golden [corn] syrup
- 1 tablespoon flour

Preheat the oven to fairly hot 375°F (Gas Mark 5, 190°C).

Cabbage and Pepper Salad is a tasty accompaniment to roast meat.

Apples and cabbage combine with pork sausages to make Cabbage Soup, a warming, satisfying first course.

Half-fill a large saucepan with water and bring it to the boil over high heat. Add the salt and the cabbage, reduce the heat to moderately high and boil the cabbage for 8 minutes.

Drain the cabbage in a colander. Slice off the large outer leaves at the base of the cabbage. Continue cutting the leaves at the base until you reach the small centre leaves. Place the large leaves flat on kitchen paper towels and drain thoroughly.

With a sharp knife, finely chop the small inner leaves and set them aside.

To make the filling, put the rice in a medium-sized saucepan and cover with the cold water. Add $\frac{1}{2}$ teaspoon of salt and bring the water to the boil over high heat. When the rice is boiling vigorously, cover the pan and reduce the heat to very low. After 10 minutes, the rice should be cooked and the water absorbed. If the rice is still damp, leave it on the heat, covered, for 5 minutes.

In a large bowl mix together the breadcrumbs, beef, cream, paprika and rice. Add the finely chopped cabbage leaves to the rice mixture with the remaining salt and the pepper and mix well.

Put 2 tablespoons of the filling at the broad end of each large cabbage leaf and roll the leaf around the stuffing to form a small bundle.

With the butter, grease a large, flameproof casserole. Place the cabbage rolls in it seam side down. Spoon golden syrup over the tops of the cabbage rolls. Place the casserole in the oven and bake the cabbage rolls for 15 minutes.

When the cabbage rolls have browned, pour the boiling water into the casserole and leave the cabbage rolls to cook in the oven for 1 hour.

Using a slotted spoon transfer the rolls to a warmed serving dish. Cover the dish to keep the rolls warm.

Place the casserole on top of the stove over moderate heat. With a wooden spoon, stir in the flour and bring the liquid in the casserole to the boil. Reduce the heat to low and, stirring constantly, cook the gravy for 3 minutes or until it is thick and smooth.

Pour the gravy over the cabbage rolls and serve immediately.

Cabbage Salad

This refreshing, crisp salad may be served with cold meats or as part of a vegetarian meal.

6 SERVINGS

- 1 medium-sized white cabbage, coarse outer leaves removed
- 3 pints [$7\frac{1}{2}$ cups] water
- $1\frac{1}{2}$ teaspoons salt
- 2 tablespoons wine vinegar
- 6 tablespoons olive oil
- $\frac{1}{2}$ teaspoon black pepper
- 1 teaspoon mustard
- 2 teaspoons caraway seeds

Low Cal

With a sharp knife cut the cabbage in half across the middle and cut out the core. Put the two halves in a bowl and cover them with the water, adding 1 teaspoon of salt. Soak for 10 minutes.

Drain off the water. With a sharp knife shred the cabbage very finely and put it in a salad bowl. Mix the remaining salt, the vinegar, olive oil, pepper and mustard together in a cup. Taste and add more vinegar if required. Pour the dressing over the salad. Toss well and refrigerate for at least 2 hours before serving. Add the caraway seeds and serve.

Cabbage and Sausage Casserole

A satisfying main dish for a family lunch or supper, Cabbage and Sausage Casserole is economical and easy to prepare.

4 SERVINGS

- $\frac{1}{2}$ lb. lean bacon, sliced
- 1 medium-sized green cabbage, coarse outer leaves removed, washed, quartered and cored
- 1 onion, sliced
- 1 small turnip, chopped
- $\frac{1}{2}$ teaspoon salt
- $\frac{1}{2}$ teaspoon black pepper
- 8 fl. oz. [1 cup] beef stock
- $\frac{1}{4}$ teaspoon caraway seeds
- 1 lb. pork sausages

Preheat the oven to moderate 350°F (Gas Mark 4, 180°C).

Line a large, ovenproof casserole with the bacon slices. Put the cabbage quarters into the casserole. Add the onion, turnip, salt, pepper, stock and caraway seeds. Place the sausages on top.

Bake the casserole in the oven for 1 hour, or until the cabbage is tender when pierced with a knife.

Cabbage Soup

A satisfying start for a winter lunch or supper, this cabbage soup is an adaptation of a Swedish recipe.

6 SERVINGS

- 2 oz. [$\frac{1}{4}$ cup] butter
- 1 medium-sized cabbage, coarse outer leaves removed, washed and shredded
- 3 pints [$7\frac{1}{2}$ cups] beef stock
- 1 bay leaf
- $\frac{1}{2}$ teaspoon salt
- $\frac{1}{4}$ teaspoon black pepper
- $\frac{1}{4}$ lb. pork sausages
- 1 tart apple, peeled, cored and chopped

In a large saucepan, melt the butter over moderately high heat. When the foam subsides, add the cabbage and cook it for 15 minutes, or until it is lightly coloured, stirring occasionally.

Add the stock, bay leaf, salt and pepper. Reduce the heat to low. Simmer the soup gently for 30 minutes, or until the cabbage is almost tender.

Add the sausages and apple and continue simmering for a further 20 minutes, or until the sausages are cooked.

With a slotted spoon, remove the sausages from the soup and slice them into thin rounds. Return them to the soup. Taste the soup and add more salt if necessary. Remove the bay leaf. Serve very hot.

Cabbage in Sour Cream

Quick and easy to prepare, Cabbage in Sour Cream goes well with simple lamb or beef dishes.

6 SERVINGS

- 3 oz. [$\frac{3}{8}$ cup] butter
- 1 small green cabbage, coarse outer leaves removed, washed and finely sliced
- 1 egg, lightly beaten
- 8 fl. oz. [1 cup] sour cream
- 2 tablespoons sugar
- 1 tablespoon white wine vinegar
- 2 teaspoons caraway seeds
- $\frac{1}{2}$ teaspoon salt
- $\frac{1}{4}$ teaspoon black pepper

In a large saucepan melt the butter over moderate heat. Add the cabbage and cook for 10 minutes, or until the cabbage is tender but not coloured. Stir occasionally to prevent the cabbage sticking to the pan.

In a medium-sized mixing bowl, combine the egg, sour cream, sugar, vinegar, caraway seeds, salt and pepper. Pour the mixture into the saucepan and stir to coat the cabbage completely with the sauce. Cook for 2 to 3 minutes, stirring constantly. Do not allow the sauce to boil. Transfer it to a warmed serving dish and serve immediately.

Cabbage in White Wine

Cabbage cooked in white wine is simple to prepare and makes a rather special vegetable dish.

6 SERVINGS

- 4 oz. [$\frac{1}{2}$ cup] butter
- 1 medium-sized green cabbage, coarse outer leaves removed, washed and coarsely chopped
- 8 fl. oz. [1 cup] dry white wine
- 1 garlic clove, crushed
- $\frac{1}{2}$ teaspoon dried tarragon
- 1 teaspoon salt
- 4 grindings black pepper

In a large frying-pan, melt the butter over moderate heat. When the foam subsides, add the cabbage. Cook it for 10 minutes, stirring occasionally. Add the wine, garlic, tarragon, salt and pepper.

Increase the heat to high and bring the liquid to the boil. Cover the pan and reduce the heat to low. Simmer the cabbage for 5 to 10 minutes, or until it is tender.

With a slotted spoon, transfer the cabbage to a warmed serving dish. Bring the liquid in the frying-pan to the boil. Boil it for 3 to 4 minutes and then pour it over the cabbage.

Cabillaud à la Boulangère

COD WITH POTATOES AND ONIONS

A good, satisfying supper dish, Cabillaud à la Boulangère (kah-bee-yoh ah lah boo-lon-jair) *may be served with grilled* [broiled] *tomatoes and Brussels sprouts to add colour.*

4 SERVINGS

- $\frac{7}{8}$ lb. potatoes
- 4 x 7 oz. cod steaks or fillets
- $\frac{1}{2}$ teaspoon black pepper
- 1 teaspoon lemon juice
- 1 garlic clove, finely chopped
- 1 teaspoon salt
- 2 oz. [$\frac{1}{4}$ cup] butter, plus extra for greasing
- 1 onion, finely sliced then separated into rings
- 1 tablespoon chopped parsley, to garnish

Preheat the oven to moderate 350°F (Gas Mark 4, 180°C).

Blanch the potatoes for 5 minutes to soften them slightly. Drain, cool, slice and set aside.

Meanwhile, lightly grease a large, shallow ovenproof dish. Put the cod in the dish in one layer and then sprinkle with the black pepper, lemon juice, chopped garlic and half the salt.

In a small saucepan, melt the butter. Reserve 4 teaspoons and pour the remainder over the fish.

Arrange the onion rings over the cod, then overlap the sliced potatoes on top. Pour the reserved butter over and sprinkle with the remaining salt.

Bake the fish for 40-45 minutes. Remove the dish from the oven, generously sprinkle the chopped parsley over the top and serve immediately straight from the dish.

Cabillaud Gratiné

COD IN WHITE SAUCE

Poached cod coated with a white sauce and topped with cheese and breadcrumbs, Cabillaud Gratiné (kah-bee-yoh grah-tee-nay) *is a marvellously simple and tasty supper dish. If you like, fresh haddock or whiting may be substituted for the cod. Broccoli or spinach go particularly well with this dish.*

4 SERVINGS

- $1\frac{1}{2}$ pints [$3\frac{3}{4}$ cups] water or water and white wine mixed
- 2 tablespoons cider or white wine vinegar
- 2 carrots, scraped and sliced
- 1 onion, sliced
- 2 celery stalks, chopped
- $\frac{1}{2}$ teaspoon salt
- bouquet garni, consisting of 4 parsley sprigs, 1 thyme spray, 1 bay leaf and 6 peppercorns tied together in a piece of cheesecloth
- $1\frac{1}{2}$ lb. cod fillets, washed and prepared for cooking

SAUCE

- 2 tablespoons butter
- $1\frac{1}{2}$ tablespoons flour
- 5 fl. oz. [$\frac{5}{8}$ cup] milk, warmed
- $\frac{1}{2}$ teaspoon salt
- $\frac{1}{4}$ teaspoon white pepper
- 2 oz. [$\frac{1}{2}$ cup] Parmesan cheese, grated
- 2 oz. [$\frac{2}{3}$ cup] dry white breadcrumbs

Put the water, vinegar, carrots, onion, celery, salt and bouquet garni in a large saucepan. Place the pan over high heat and bring the liquid to the boil. Reduce the heat to low and simmer the court bouillon gently for 30 minutes.

Remove the pan from the heat and allow the court bouillon to cool in the pan to lukewarm.

Place the fish in the court bouillon and return the pan to low heat. Cook gently for 10 to 12 minutes or until the fish flakes easily when tested with a fork.

Remove the pan from the heat and carefully take out the fish. Allow the fish to cool slightly, then with your fingers remove the skin. Place the fish in a warmed, flameproof serving dish. Cover the fish with aluminium foil to keep it hot. Strain the court bouillon into a measuring jug, discarding the vegetables and flavourings. Reserve 5 fluid ounces [$\frac{5}{8}$ cup] of the bouillon.

In a small pan melt the butter over moderate heat. Remove the pan from the heat and with a wooden spoon, stir in the flour. Stirring constantly, gradually add the reserved court bouillon to the butter-and-flour mixture. Then slowly stir in the milk.

Return the pan to moderate heat and cook, stirring, until the sauce boils. Reduce the heat to low and continue cook-

Cabillaud Provençal is an attractive dish of cod steaks with anchovies, olives and green peppers in a delicious red wine and tomato sauce.

ing the sauce for 3 minutes, stirring constantly. Add the salt and pepper.

Preheat the grill [broiler] to high.

Remove the pan from the heat and pour the sauce over the fish.

In a small bowl combine the grated cheese with the breadcrumbs. Sprinkle the sauce-covered fish with the cheese-and-breadcrumbs mixture and place it under the grill [broiler].

Grill [broil] for 3 to 5 minutes, or until the top is browned and bubbling. Remove the dish from the heat.

Serve at once.

Cabillaud Provençal

COD WITH GREEN PEPPERS, ANCHOVIES AND BLACK OLIVES

This is an attractive and exceptionally tasty way of serving cod. Cabillaud Provençal (kah-bee-yoh proh-von-sahl) *may be accompanied simply by rice or boiled new potatoes.*

4 SERVINGS

½ teaspoon butter
2 fl. oz. [¼ cup] olive oil
1 small onion, thinly sliced
1 garlic clove, chopped
1 green pepper, white pith removed, cored, seeded and thinly sliced
2 oz. canned anchovies, drained and chopped
2 oz. [¾ cup] black olives, stoned
⅛ teaspoon fennel seed
8 x 4 oz. cod steaks
3 small tomatoes, thinly sliced
½ teaspoon salt
¼ teaspoon black pepper
2 oz. canned tomato purée
4 fl. oz. [½ cup] dry red wine

Low Cal

Preheat the oven to fairly hot 400° F (Gas Mark 6, 200°C).

Lightly grease a large, shallow baking dish with the butter and set aside.

In a medium-sized frying-pan heat half the olive oil over moderate heat. When the oil is hot add the onion, garlic and green pepper. Cook them for 8 to 10 minutes, stirring occasionally, or until the onion is soft and translucent but not brown. Remove the pan from the heat and stir in the anchovies, olives and fennel seed.

Place four of the cod steaks in the greased dish and spread the anchovy mixture evenly over them. Top each steak with another cod steak. Arrange the tomatoes on top. Using a pastry brush, brush the tomatoes with the remaining oil and sprinkle with the salt and pepper.

In a small bowl, combine the tomato purée with the wine. Pour the mixture over the fish.

Place the dish in the oven and bake for 30 minutes, basting twice with the liquid in the dish.

Remove the dish from the oven and serve at once.

Cabinet Pudding

Cabinet, or Chancellor's Pudding, as it is sometimes called in old English recipe books, is an elegant steamed pudding much beloved by Victorian hostesses for their buffet tables. There is a similar steamed pudding called Lords and Commons Pudding, probably created by the same chef.

4 TO 6 SERVINGS

2 oz. [$\frac{1}{2}$ cup] glacé cherries, halved
12 small pieces angelica, cut into diamond shapes
3 trifle sponges
1 oz. [2 tablespoons] crushed ratafia or amaretti biscuits [cookies]
1 oz. [$\frac{1}{4}$cup] crystallized mixed peel
14 fl. oz. [$1\frac{3}{4}$ cups] milk
2 eggs
1 oz. castor [2 tablespoons superfine] sugar
$\frac{1}{2}$ teaspoon vanilla essence
1 teaspoon orange-flower water
butter for greasing

SAUCE
2 egg yolks
2 oz. [$\frac{1}{4}$ cup] castor sugar
$\frac{1}{2}$ teaspoon arrowroot
2 fl. oz. [$\frac{1}{4}$ cup] dry sherry or an orange-flavoured liqueur

Grease a $1\frac{1}{2}$-pint pudding basin and line the bottom with greased greaseproof [waxed] paper. Arrange 12 cherry halves and 12 pieces of angelica on the bottom of the basin (this will be the top when the pudding is turned out).

Break the sponges into small pieces and mix with the crumbled biscuits, the remaining glacé cherries and the mixed peel. Put the mixture into the prepared pudding basin.

Heat the milk in a small saucepan until warm but not boiling.

Whisk the eggs and sugar together in a bowl until creamy, then add a little of the milk and whisk again. Gradually pour in the remaining milk, in a steady stream, whisking continually, then add the vanilla essence to the mixture.

Stir the orange-flower water into the custard, then pour the custard into the pudding basin. Leave to soak for 15 minutes.

Cover the pudding basin with pleated greaseproof [waxed] paper and tie a cloth round the top of the basin.

Stand the basin on a trivet in a saucepan and pour in boiling water to come two-thirds of the way up the sides. Cover with a lid, turn heat to low and steam gently for 1 hour, topping the pan up with more boiling water, if necessary. Cool completely and chill in the regrigerator for 4 hours.

To serve, ease a palette knife round the pudding and turn it out on to a serving plate, removing the greaseproof [waxed] paper.

Make the sauce 15 minutes before serving. In a bowl, whisk together the egg yolks and sugar until the mixture is thick, fluffy and pale.

Blend the arrowroot with 1 tablespoon of the sherry or orange-flavoured liqueur, then stir into the egg mixture. Gradually add the rest of the sherry or liqueur, whisking all the time.

Bring the water in the bottom half of a double boiler to the boil, turn the heat to low, then put the bowl over the top and whisk for 5-7 minutes until the sauce is thick and creamy.

Pour a little sauce over the cold pudding and serve immediately. The remaining sauce should be handed round separately.

Caccio-Cavallo

Caccio-Cavallo is a hard, smooth Italian cheese made from skimmed cow's milk.

Cacciucco

ITALIAN SEAFOOD STEW

A superb Italian seafood stew, Cacciucco (kahch-OO-choh) *is less complicated to prepare than the French Bouillabaisse. Served in soup bowls, it is a one-dish meal and needs only crusty bread as an accompaniment. A light dry white wine would go well with this dish.*

4 SERVINGS

4 fl. oz. [$\frac{1}{2}$ cup] olive oil
2 garlic cloves, chopped and 1 cut in half
1 red chilli, chopped and seeds removed
8 oz. raw shrimps, shelled, deveined and chopped
8 oz. squid, skinned, cleaned and chopped
4 fl. oz. [$\frac{1}{2}$ cup] dry white wine
3 tablespoons tomato purée
16 fl. oz. [2 cups] water
$\frac{1}{2}$ teaspoon salt
8 oz. cod fillet, cut in pieces
8 oz. haddock, cut in pieces
4 slices bread, trimmed of crusts and toasted
2 tablespoons chopped pimiento

In a large saucepan heat the oil over moderate heat. Add the chopped garlic and the red chilli and cook for 5 minutes, or until the garlic is slightly brown, stirring occasionally with a wooden spoon.

Add the shrimp and squid to the pan. Cover and reduce the heat to low. Stirring occasionally, cook for 30 minutes.

Pour in the wine and continue cooking, uncovered, for 15 minutes. Stir in the tomato purée, water and salt. Add the pieces of cod and haddock to the pan. Cover and simmer for 15 minutes, or until the fish is tender.

While the stew is cooking, rub the toasted bread slices with the garlic halves.

Taste the stew and add more salt and pepper if necessary.

To serve, place a slice of the toast in each soup bowl and spoon the hot stew over it. Sprinkle with the chopped pimiento.

Caerphilly

A white, crumbly, whole-milk cheese, Caerphilly is somewhat salty and has a distinct taste of buttermilk. Originally a Welsh cheese, it it now also produced in the English counties of Somerset, Wiltshire, Devon and Dorset.

Caesar Salad

This unusual salad comes from the United States where it is eaten on its own as a light lunch dish, or served with grilled [broiled] *steak, or fish.*

4 SERVINGS

5 fl. oz. [$\frac{5}{8}$ cup] olive oil
4 thick slices white bread, crusts removed and cut into cubes
1 garlic clove
$1\frac{1}{2}$ teaspoons salt
2 tablespoons wine vinegar
1 teaspoon lemon juice
$\frac{1}{2}$ teaspoon Worcestershire sauce
$\frac{1}{4}$ teaspoon prepared mustard
$\frac{1}{8}$ teaspoon sugar
$\frac{1}{4}$ teaspoon freshly ground black pepper
2 heads cos [romaine] lettuce, washed and dried
6 anchovy fillets, cut in small pieces
1 egg, cooked in boiling water for 1 minute
2 oz. [$\frac{1}{2}$ cup] Parmesan cheese, grated

Heat 2 fluid ounces [$\frac{1}{4}$ cup] of the olive oil in a large, heavy frying-pan over moderately high heat. Fry the bread cubes in the oil for 10 to 15 minutes or until crisp, turning frequently with a spoon.

Cacciucco is an unusual and delicious Italian seafood stew.

Remove the croûtons from the pan and drain them on kitchen paper towels.

Mash the garlic together with the salt in the bottom of a large salad bowl. Add the remaining olive oil, the vinegar, lemon juice, Worcestershire sauce, mustard, sugar and the pepper and mix well.

Tear the lettuce into bite-sized pieces and add to the salad bowl with the anchovy. Toss well with the dressing.

Break the egg over the top of the salad, add the croûtons and Parmesan cheese and toss the salad again. Serve immediately.

Café Brûlot

Café Brûlot (kah-fay broo-loh) *is a delicious mixture of spiced, strong black coffee that is flamed with cognac. It does make a spectacular end to a special dinner party especially if it is prepared at the table in a chafing dish.*

10 TO 12 SERVINGS

2 oranges
1 lemon
1 cinnamon stick
1 teaspoon ground allspice
6 large sugar cubes
5 fl. oz. [$\frac{5}{8}$ cup] Cognac
$1\frac{1}{4}$ pints [$3\frac{1}{8}$ cups] freshly brewed, strong black coffee

Using a sharp, serrated-edge knife, peel the oranges and lemon, being careful not to take any of the white pith with the rind. Cut the rind into wafer thin slivers.

If you want to prepare the Café Brûlot at the table, put the slivers of orange and lemon rind into a chafing dish set over a methylated spirit flame. Otherwise, put the peel into a medium-sized saucepan over very low heat. Add the cinnamon, allspice and sugar cubes and mash the ingredients with the back of a long-handled metal spoon until the sugar is dissolved.

Pour the cognac into a small saucepan and warm it over very low heat. Pour the warmed Cognac into the chafing dish or saucepan and stir it to mix.

Use a match to set the Cognac alight and continue stirring the mixture to dissolve the sugar. Then stir in the hot coffee, pouring it gradually in a steady stream into the chafing dish or saucepan.

Serve the Café Brûlot, as soon as the flame goes out, by straining it into small coffee cups.

Caffeine

The main pharmacological agent in coffee and tea, caffeine acts as a non-intoxicating stimulant.

Cailles avec Raisins en Timbale

QUAIL WITH GRAPES IN A PASTRY CASE

Cailles avec Raisins en Timbale (kuy ah-veck ray-zan on tam-bahl) *is a difficult and time-consuming dish to prepare but the end result is certainly impressive. You can prepare the* fonds lié (faun lee-ay) *several days ahead if it is kept, covered, in the refrigerator.*

If you want to serve this dish in classic French fashion, leave the heads and feet on the quail.

4 SERVINGS

1 lb. green grapes, peeled and seeded
8 tablespoons brandy
1 teaspoon salt
$\frac{1}{2}$ teaspoon black pepper
8 quail, drawn and heads and feet removed
2 oz. [$\frac{1}{4}$ cup] clarified butter

TIMBALE

8 oz. [2 cups] flour
$\frac{1}{2}$ teaspoon salt
4 oz. [$\frac{1}{2}$ cup] plus 1 tablespoon butter
1 egg, lightly beaten
4 to 5 tablespoons iced water

FONDS LIE (THICKENED BROWN SAUCE)

$1\frac{1}{2}$ pints [$3\frac{3}{4}$ cups] rich brown stock
8 tablespoons coarsely chopped mushrooms
4 parsley sprigs
3 tablespoons arrowroot
4 tablespoons cold water
1 oz. [2 tablespoons] unsalted butter, cut into small pieces

Put the grapes in a small bowl and sprinkle the brandy over them. Using a spoon, toss the grapes until they are coated and soaked with brandy. Set the bowl aside for at least 1 hour, stirring occasionally.

To make the pastry case, sift the flour and salt into a medium-sized mixing bowl. Add 4 ounces [$\frac{1}{2}$ cup] of the butter and with a knife cut it into small pieces. Using your fingers, rub the butter into the flour until the mixture resembles coarse breadcrumbs.

Add the egg and 3 tablespoons of iced water to the butter-and-flour mixture. Using a fork, toss the mixture until it is well blended. Gather it into a ball in your hands. If the dough is too dry and crumbly to form a ball, add more water, 1 tablespoon at a time, until the dough is the right consistency.

Wrap the dough in greaseproof paper or aluminium foil and chill it in the refrigerator for 30 minutes.

Preheat the oven to fairly hot 400°F (Gas Mark 6, 200°C).

Place the 1 tablespoon of butter in a small bowl and soften it by beating it with a wooden spoon. Thickly spread the softened butter evenly over the bottom and sides of an 8 to 9-inch square baking tin. Set the tin aside.

Turn the dough out of the bowl on to a lightly floured board, or marble slab. Sprinkle a little flour over the surface of the dough and roll it out into a square, at least 16-inches wide and $\frac{1}{4}$-inch thick.

Roll the dough around the rolling pin to lift it off the board and unroll the dough over the buttered tin. With your fingers, gently press the dough into the tin, being careful not to tear the dough. Press the dough first against the bottom and sides of the tin and then into the corners.

Leave $\frac{1}{4}$-inch of dough hanging over the sides of the tin. With scissors trim off the rough edges. Using your fingers, fold the overhanging dough under the edge of the tin and flute or crimp the dough around the rim.

Cut out two rectangles of aluminium foil the same width as the tin and butter them. Line the pastry with the foil, placing the sheets of foil at right angles to each other. Make sure the foil is pressed securely into the edges of the dough so that the sides of the pastry will be supported. Spread a layer of dried beans over the foil.

Place the tin in the oven and bake for 20 minutes. Remove the tin from the oven and lift off the aluminium foil with the beans. Return the tin to the oven and continue baking for 20 minutes, or until the pastry is golden brown.

Remove the tin from the oven and transfer it to a wire rack to cool for 10 minutes. Then loosen the sides of the pastry. Place the wire rack, inverted, over the tin and reverse the two. The pastry should slide out of the tin on to the rack. Transfer the pastry case to a serving dish and set it aside.

While the pastry case is baking, prepare the *fonds lié*. Put the brown stock, mushrooms and parsley in a medium-sized saucepan over moderate heat. Bring the liquid to the boil. Reduce the heat to low and cook for 15 minutes.

In a cup, combine the arrowroot and water, stirring until the arrowroot dissolves. Using a wire whisk, gradually stir the arrowroot mixture into the saucepan.

Simmer the *fonds lié* for 10 minutes, stirring it occasionally, until it thickens slightly. Pour the *fonds lié* through a strainer into a medium-sized bowl and, using the back of a spoon, press down on the mushrooms and parsley to extract their juices.

Sprinkle the pieces of butter over the surface of the *fonds lié*: When the butter has melted, tip and rotate the bowl so that the butter covers the entire surface of the *fonds lié*.

Increase the oven temperature to very hot 450°F (Gas Mark 8, 230°C).

Season the insides of the quail with the salt and pepper and truss the birds securely.

In a large flameproof casserole heat the clarified butter over high heat. Place the quail in the pot and using a spoon turn the birds until they are coated on all sides with butter.

Lower the heat to moderately high and

An impressive dinner party dish, Cailles avec Raisins en Timbale is complicated but well worth the effort.

cook the quail until they are browned on all sides. Then transfer the casserole to the oven. Roast the quail for 20 minutes, or until they are tender. To test if the quail are cooked, pierce the thigh of one bird with the point of a sharp knife or a skewer. The juices that run out should be pale pink.

While the quail are cooking, prepare the sauce. Drain the grapes, reserving the brandy. Set the grapes aside in a bowl. Pour the brandy into a medium-sized saucepan and bring it to a boil over high heat, stirring constantly with a metal spoon. Pour the *fonds lié* into the saucepan and, still stirring, continue to cook for 4 minutes. Taste the sauce and, if necessary, add salt and pepper.

Strain the sauce into a small bowl or saucepan and keep warm.

When the quail are tender remove the casserole from the oven. Using tongs or a slotted spoon, lift the quail out of the casserole and arrange them in the pastry case. Spoon the grapes over the quail. Pour the sauce over the quail and serve immediately.

Cake Mix

A cake mix is a commercial preparation to which only water, milk or an egg is added before baking. A great variety of cake mixes are available and they generally contain a special type of fat, which will not become rancid, flour, sugar, a raising agent, flavouring, sometimes milk powder, and, occasionally, preservatives.

Cake mixes may be more expensive than home-made cakes, but they save preparation time. They are always successful if the directions are followed exactly.

Cakes

Cake-making is a most satisfying and rewarding job—indeed many people make it their hobby. There is nothing more satisfying than to have a selection of home-made cakes in tins ready to serve to friends when they pop in for a cup of tea or when the children come home from school and want a snack before their evening meal.

If you have a home freezer then you can have a "batch baking" day and the cakes will freeze and may be stored for months.

The variety of cakes is endless, plain "cut and come again" cakes, plain or rich fruit cakes, sponge cakes and rich exotic gâteaux that can also be served as a dessert, to mention only a few.

Every country too has its own favourites. Britain is famous for fruit cakes, Victoria sandwiches and Madeira cake, as well as local specialities such as Bath buns, Richmond maids of honour and Yorkshire curd cakes.

Angel cakes, devil's food cake, brownies and cheese cake are some well known American cakes. Possibly the most famous of all cakes and gâteaux originated in Austria, France and Belgium. Luscious roulades, Linzer and Sacher tortes, madeleines and gâteau St. Honoré, are only a few of the mouth-watering cakes one sees in the bakers' shops.

Cakes are made for special occasions —decorated cakes for weddings, birthdays and anniversaries, as well as for festive occasions.

Cake-Making

For the best results when making cakes have all the ingredients at room temperature (about 75°F).

Preheat the oven to the specified temperature. If the oven is too cool when you put in the cake, the finished cake will have a heavy texture.

Use the correct size tin or pan as specified in the recipe. If the tin is too large, the cake will be thin and heavy. If it is too small, the mixture may overflow as it rises and the cake's texture will be coarse.

Grease and flour the tin or pan before you begin to mix the cake batter. To prepare the tin, spread only a thin film of lard, oil or butter over the sides and bottom of the tin. Sprinkle in the flour and tip and rotate the tin to distribute the flour evenly. Shake out any excess flour by turning the tin upside-down and gently knocking on the bottom.

If the cake is rich and requires a long baking, the tin should be greased and then lined with buttered greaseproof or waxed paper. For a rich fruit cake, tie a band of brown paper around the outside of the tin as well.

If the recipe specifies flour, do not substitute self-raising flour, as the texture will be too open and the cake will rise too much. If self-raising flour is required but is not available, use plain [all-purpose] flour with baking powder in the proportion of 4 level teaspoons of baking powder to 1 pound plain [all-purpose] flour. Flour and other ingredients should always be sifted before use.

Measure the ingredients accurately and blend them together thoroughly. But do not beat the batter after the flour has been added or the cake will be heavy.

Fill the cake tin only one-half to two-thirds full of batter.

Place the tin in the centre of the oven so the heat can circulate around it. In general, small cakes should be baked near the top of the oven, and large cakes in the middle of the oven.

Bake the cake for the length of time specified in the recipe. Before removing it from the oven, test it to be sure that it is done. If not, continue baking for 5 minutes and test again.

To test if the cake is completely baked, insert a metal skewer or thin knife into the centre of the cake. If it comes out clean, the cake is done. Alternatively, lightly press the top of the cake with a fingertip. The cake will spring back if it is cooked.

As soon as the baking is completed, remove the cake from the oven and let it stand for a few minutes. Then loosen the sides of the cake by running a knife between the cake and sides of the tin and place a clean cloth over the top. Turn the cake out on to the cloth and then transfer it to a wire cake rack (place the rack, inverted, on the bottom of the cake and turn it over). The cloth will prevent the top of the cake from being marked by the rack.

If the cake is to be iced or frosted, wait until it has cooled to room temperature.

Methods of Cake-Making

CREAMING

This method is used for richer cakes when the margarine or butter is creamed together with sugar, using a wooden spoon or an electric mixer. The mixture should be beaten until it is light and fluffy, as this incorporates the air and dissolves the sugar crystals.

The eggs are then beaten in, one at a time, and the flour (and other ingredients such as fruit and nuts) are folded into the mixture. If the mixture starts to curdle when the eggs are added beat in a spoonful of the measured flour as given in the recipe.

WHISKING

Cakes made by this method contain no fat. The basic ingredients are eggs, castor sugar and flour. The whisking of the eggs and sugar should be done with a wire whisk or electric mixer so that as much air is incorporated into the mixture as possible to produce a light, fluffy cake.

Flour should always be folded in with a metal spoon, with the side of the spoon acting as a cutting edge. This is done to prevent the air from escaping from the mixture.

Whisked cakes should be eaten as soon as possible because the omission of fat in the recipe gives them a drier texture. If a sponge cake is to be kept for later use, the same method is used with the addition of melted butter or oil. The best known cake made with this method is called a Genoese sponge cake.

RUBBING IN

Plainer cakes, scones and biscuits are made by this method. Usually the proportion of fat is one-quarter to one-half of the flour. The fat is rubbed into the flour until the mixture resembles fine breadcrumbs. Fruit and flavouring are added and then the liquid, generally egg and milk.

MELTING

This method makes moist cakes that keep well. The fat is melted with the sugar, syrup or treacle [molasses] and then mixed into the dry ingredients. Most recipes use plain [all-purpose] flour with the addition of bicarbonate of soda [baking soda], or baking powder as a raising agent. A better result is obtained if moist brown sugar is used, as this gives the cake a rich dark colour and increases its keeping qualities.

Cake Rack

A flat wire rack on which cakes and biscuits [cookies] are placed to cool after they are taken out of the oven, it allows air to circulate all around the cake.

Calamares en su Tinta

SQUID IN ITS OWN INK

Calamares en su Tinta (kah-lah-MAH-rehs on soo TEEN-tah) *is a famous Spanish dish. The thick black sauce is unusual and delicious.*

6 SERVINGS

- 3 fl. oz. [⅜ cup] olive oil
- 3 lb. fresh whole squid, cleaned thoroughly and cut in ½-inch pieces (with the ink sacs reserved)
- 1 medium-sized onion, finely chopped
- 2 garlic cloves, finely chopped
- 1 tablespoon finely chopped parsley
- ⅛ teaspoon ground mace
- 1 teaspoon salt
- ¼ teaspoon black pepper
- 8 fl. oz. [1 cup] cold water
- 2 tablespoons flour

Low Cal

In a large saucepan heat the olive oil over moderate heat. Add the squid, onion, garlic and parsley to the pan. Cook for 6 to 7 minutes, stirring constantly with a metal spoon. Add the mace, salt and pepper. Reduce the heat to low, cover the pan and simmer gently for 20 minutes.

While the squid is cooking, with a wooden spoon mash the ink sacs through a strainer set over a bowl to extract the ink. Pour the water over the sacs and mash again. With a wire whisk, beat the flour into the ink-and-water until the sauce is smooth.

Pour the sauce over the squid in the saucepan and increase the heat to high. Bring the sauce to the boil, stirring constantly. As soon as the boiling point is reached, reduce the heat to very low, cover the pan and cook for 5 minutes. Remove the pan from the heat and leave it, covered, for 5 minutes.

Taste the sauce for seasoning, add more salt and pepper if necessary and serve at once.

Stuffed squid in a rich tomato and wine sauce, Calamari Ripieni is an exotic and unusual dinner party dish.

Calamari Ripieni

ITALIAN STUFFED SQUID

Squid stuffed with a cheese, garlic and parsley mixture and then cooked in a wine and tomato sauce, Calamari Ripieni (kah-lah-MAH-ree rip-YEH-nee) *is an unusual main dish for a dinner party. It may be served with rice and a green salad.*

4 SERVINGS

- 6 large squid, cleaned thoroughly and skinned with the tender parts of the tentacles reserved
- 3 tablespoons fresh breadcrumbs
- 2 tablespoons finely chopped parsley
- 6 tablespoons grated Parmesan cheese
- 2 garlic cloves, finely chopped, plus 4 whole garlic cloves
- 1 egg, lightly beaten
- 2 fl. oz. [¼ cup] olive oil
- ⅛ teaspoon cayenne pepper
- ½ teaspoon salt
- ¼ teaspoon black pepper
- 4 tomatoes, blanched, peeled, seeded and chopped
- 2 teaspoons tomato purée
- ½ teaspoon dried rosemary
- 2 fl. oz. [¼ cup] dry white wine

With a small, sharp knife chop the tentacles finely and place them in a large mixing bowl. Add the breadcrumbs, parsley, cheese, 1 chopped garlic clove, the egg, 1 tablespoon of olive oil, cayenne, ¼ teaspoon of salt and ⅛ teaspoon of pepper to the bowl. Mix well.

Divide the mixture between the squid and spoon it into the bodies. Do not put in too much stuffing as the squid will shrink a little during cooking.

With a thick needle and thread, sew up the openings of each squid.

In a large, deep frying-pan, or saucepan, heat the remaining oil over moderate heat. Add the whole garlic cloves to the pan and cook them for 5 minutes, stirring. Remove and discard the garlic cloves.

Add the squid to the garlic-flavoured oil and brown them lightly on all sides, turning them carefully with 2 spoons. Add the tomatoes, tomato purée, rosemary, the remaining chopped garlic, the wine, and the rest of the salt and pepper.

Reduce the heat to low, cover the pan and simmer gently for 20 to 30 minutes.

With a slotted spoon, remove the squid from the pan and place them on a plate. Remove and discard the thread. Slice the squid and arrange the slices in a warmed serving dish.

Pour the sauce over the squid and serve at once.

Calcium

Calcium is a mineral which is essential in the building of strong bones and teeth. Calcium is available in several foods. Milk, cheese, oily fish, some meat and bread are the major sources.

It is especially important for babies, young children and expectant mothers to have an increased amount of calcium and they should include some of the above foods in the daily diet.

Milk is particularly important and at least 10 fluid ounces [1¼ cups] should be either drunk or used in cooking every day.

Calderete de Jerez

LAMB STEW WITH SHERRY

Calderete de Jerez (kahl-day-RAY-tay d' hare-ezz) *is a well-known, flavourful Spanish dish in which pieces of lamb are marinated in sherry.*

6 SERVINGS

10 fl. oz. [1¼ cups] dry sherry
2 garlic cloves, crushed
3 lb. boned lamb, cut into 2-inch pieces
1 teaspoon salt
½ teaspoon black pepper
1 teaspoon ground cumin
4 tablespoons vegetable oil
2 medium-sized onions, sliced
2 tablespoons flour

Low Cal

Combine the sherry and garlic in a large mixing bowl. Add the pieces of lamb, and mix well. Cover the bowl and leave the meat to marinate for 3 hours, stirring occasionally.

With a slotted spoon remove the lamb from the marinade. Drain well and dry the meat on kitchen paper towels. Reserve the marinade.

Sprinkle the salt, pepper and cumin over the lamb.

Heat the oil in a large saucepan over moderate heat. Add the pieces of lamb and fry them, stirring frequently, until they are brown. Add the onions and fry for 2 to 3 minutes.

Add the flour and mix it well with the lamb and onions. Pour over the reserved marinade and, stirring constantly, bring to the boil. If the sauce is too thick add a little water.

Cover the saucepan and reduce the heat to moderately low. Simmer the stew for at least 1 hour, or until the lamb is tender.

Serve very hot.

Calderete de Jerez is a simple, tasty Spanish lamb and sherry stew.

Caldo de Congrio

CONGER EEL SOUP

This Spanish soup, Caldo de Congrio (kal-doh d' kohn-GREE-oh) *is an unusual first course for a dinner party. If you cannot obtain conger eel, you may substitute any firm, white-fleshed fish.*

8 SERVINGS

1½ tablespoons olive oil
3 medium-sized onions, thinly sliced
1 garlic clove, finely chopped
1½ lb. tomatoes, blanched, peeled, seeded and coarsely chopped
2 teaspoons tomato purée
½ teaspoon dried oregano
1 small bay leaf
1 teaspoon salt
½ teaspoon freshly ground black pepper
1 lb. potatoes, peeled and cut into strips ½-inch wide
1½ pints [3¾ cups] fish stock
1 x 6 lb. conger eel, cleaned and cut into 2-inch steaks
1 teaspoon ground coriander
2 tablespoons finely chopped parsley

In a large saucepan heat the oil over moderate heat. Add the onions and garlic and cook for 6 to 8 minutes, stirring constantly, or until the onions are soft and translucent but not brown.

Add the tomatoes, tomato purée, oregano, bay leaf, salt and pepper to the pan and cook, stirring constantly, for 5 minutes.

Add the potatoes and fish stock and cover the pan. Reduce the heat to low and simmer for 30 minutes.

Stir in the eel and coriander. Cover the pan and cook for a further 12 minutes or until the eel is firm and the potatoes cooked.

Pour the soup into a warmed tureen and sprinkle it with parsley. Serve at once.

Caldo Haba

WHITE BEAN SOUP WITH HAM AND SAUSAGE

An appetizing Spanish soup with white beans, smoked ham and garlic sausage, Caldo Haba (kahl-doh hah-bah), *accompanied by hot crusty rolls, is almost a meal on its own. If it is served as a first course it should be followed by a light main course such as a salad.*

6 SERVINGS

$3\frac{1}{2}$ pints [$8\frac{3}{4}$ cups] water
6 oz. dried black-eye beans
8 oz. Serrano ham, or lean smoked ham, cut into $\frac{1}{2}$-inch cubes
1 medium-sized onion, finely chopped
$1\frac{1}{2}$ teaspoons salt
$\frac{1}{4}$ teaspoon freshly ground black pepper
5 oz. smoked garlic pork sausage
1 small turnip, finely chopped
2 potatoes, peeled and finely chopped

In a large, heavy pan bring the water to a boil over high heat. Add the beans and boil them for 2 minutes. Remove the pan from the heat and leave the beans to soak for $1\frac{1}{2}$ hours.

Replace the pan on the heat. Add the ham, onion, salt and pepper to the beans and bring to the boil over high heat. Using a slotted spoon skim off the scum which rises to the surface of the liquid as it heats.

Reduce the heat to low, partially cover the pan and simmer the soup gently for $1\frac{1}{2}$ hours.

Prick the sausage in two or three places with a fork. Add it to the pan with the turnip and potatoes and cook for a further 30 minutes, or until the beans and potatoes are tender when pierced with the point of a sharp knife.

With tongs remove the sausage from the soup and allow it to cool. Then remove the skin from the sausage and cut it into slices. Return the sausage slices to the soup. Taste the soup and add more salt and pepper if necessary.

Pour it into a heated soup tureen and serve immediately.

Caldo Tlalpeño

MEXICAN CHICKEN AND BEAN SOUP

The ingredients for this Mexican soup may surprise you, but the blend of flavours is quite delicious. Caldo Tlalpeño (kahl-doh tlah-pane-yoh) *is a meal in itself, accompanied by crusty bread and butter or—to be really authentic—hot tortillas.*

4 SERVINGS

1 x 5 lb. boiling chicken
1 medium-sized onion, quartered
1 carrot, scraped and sliced
2 teaspoons salt
4 peppercorns
bouquet garni, consisting of 2 parsley sprigs, 1 thyme spray and 1 bay leaf tied together
5 pints [3 quarts] water
2 green peppers, white pith removed, seeded and sliced
1 large onion, sliced and pushed out into rings
14 oz. canned chick-peas, drained
$\frac{1}{4}$ teaspoon black pepper
8 oz. Wensleydale or any white cheese, cubed
1 avocado, peeled, stoned, sliced and sprinkled with lemon juice

Put the chicken in a large saucepan with the quartered onion, carrot, 1 teaspoon of salt, the peppercorns and bouquet garni. Pour over the water, adding more if necessary to cover the chicken completely.

Place the saucepan over moderately high heat. Bring the liquid to a boil and then reduce the heat to moderately low. Simmer the chicken for 2 hours or until it is tender.

Remove the chicken from the pan. Set it on a board and cover it with aluminium foil to keep it warm.

Increase the heat under the saucepan to moderately high and bring the liquid back to the boil. Boil it for 15 minutes to reduce it slightly. Then strain the liquid, discarding the vegetables and seasonings. Rinse out the saucepan and return the liquid to it.

Bring the liquid back to the boil, using a metal spoon to skim off any fat that rises to the surface. Add the sliced green peppers and onion rings. Reduce the heat to moderately low and simmer for 10

minutes. Then add the chick-peas and continue simmering for 5 minutes.

While the chick-peas, peppers and onions are cooking, cut the chicken into serving pieces. Return the chicken pieces to the saucepan. Add the remaining 1 teaspoon salt and the pepper, and cook the soup for 5 minutes longer or until the chicken pieces are heated through. Stir in the cheese. As soon as the cheese begins to melt, transfer the soup to a warmed tureen. Add the avocado slices. Serve at once.

Caldo Verde

CABBAGE AND POTATO SOUP WITH SAUSAGE

A filling and pungent soup, Caldo Verde (kahl-doh vair-day) *is a national dish of Portugal. It makes an excellent winter luncheon served with crusty bread.*

4 SERVINGS

4 oz. smoked garlic pork sausage
1 lb. potatoes, peeled and thinly sliced
2 pints [5 cups] water
1 teaspoon salt
2 tablespoons olive oil
1 teaspoon freshly ground black pepper
1 medium-sized green cabbage, coarse outer leaves removed, washed and finely shredded

Prick the sausage in two or three places with a fork. Place it in a medium-sized saucepan and add enough water to cover the sausage. Bring the water to the boil over high heat, then reduce the heat to very low. Cover the pan and simmer the sausage for 15 minutes. Drain the sausage in a colander. Allow it to cool and then remove the skin. Slice the sausage thinly and set it aside.

Meanwhile, in a large saucepan boil the potatoes in the water with the salt over moderate heat for about 8 to 10 minutes, or until the potato slices are completely cooked. With a slotted spoon transfer the potato slices to a medium-sized mixing bowl, reserving the cooking liquid. Mash the potatoes to a purée with a fork or potato masher. Return the puréed potatoes to the saucepan containing the cooking liquid. Stir in the olive oil, pepper and cabbage and bring to the boil over high heat, stirring to blend all the ingredients together. Cook the mixture, uncovered, over moderate heat for 5 to 6 minutes. Add the sausage slices to the saucepan and continue cooking for a further 4 minutes. Serve immediately.

Green peppers, chicken and cheese are just some of the ingredients of Caldo Tlalpeño — a delicious Mexican soup.

Calf's Foot Jelly

Calf's foot jelly is nourishing and is easily digested so it is often given to invalids. It takes two days to make since the stock should be made the first day and the jelly finished the second. In hot weather, it may be necessary to add a little gelatine to stiffen the stock.

1 PINT JELLY

2 calf's feet, cut into pieces and thoroughly washed
6 oz. [$\frac{3}{4}$ cup] sugar
5 fl. oz. [$\frac{5}{8}$ cup] sherry
1-inch cinnamon stick
6 allspice berries
4 lemons
2 egg whites and crushed shells

Put the pieces of calf's feet into a large saucepan and cover them with water. Place the saucepan over high heat and bring the water to the boil. Drain the calf's feet in a colander and rinse them well. Return them to the saucepan. Cover the pieces again with cold water, cover the pan and bring the water to a boil. Reduce the heat to low and simmer the pieces for 5 hours.

Remove the pan from the heat and strain the stock into a measuring jug. Leave the stock until it is cold and of a firm jellied consistency.

Skim any fat off the surface of the stock with a metal spoon. Put 1 pint [$2\frac{1}{2}$ cups] of the stock into a saucepan. Add the sugar, sherry, cinnamon and allspice.

Grate the rind of 2 of the lemons and squeeze the juice from all 4 lemons. Add enough water to the lemon juice to make 5 fluid ounces [$\frac{5}{8}$ cup]. Add the grated rind and juice and the egg whites and shells to the stock in the saucepan.

Bring the liquid to the boil over moderate heat. With a wire whisk beat vigorously. The whisking should be done in the reverse of the usual movement or anti-clockwise. This will more thoroughly mix the egg whites into the stock. As soon as the stock boils, stop whisking and allow it to rise to the top of the pan. Remove the pan from the heat and leave it for 5 minutes until the stock has settled.

Slowly strain the stock through a scalded jelly bag or scalded clean cloth into a large bowl. Allow it to strain in its own time—do not squeeze it because this will make the jelly cloudy and do not break the egg white crust.

If the jelly is not clear, repeat the straining process, using a clean jelly bag and bowl.

If the jelly stiffens in the jelly bag before it has all strained through, place a small bowl of hot water in the centre of the jelly to melt it. If the jelly is still too stiff, return it to the pan and whisk and strain again.

When the jelly has been completely strained, refrigerate it and use as required.

Calf's Liver

The livers of calves, oxen, pigs, sheep, poultry and game are all used in cooking, but calf's liver is generally considered to be the best and is the most tender. It is a good source of Vitamin A, the Vitamin B complex, protein and iron.

Calf's liver is usually cut into slices $\frac{1}{4}$- to $\frac{1}{2}$-inch thick. The slices may then be grilled [broiled] or lightly coated with flour and fried in butter or olive oil over moderately high heat. When it is cooked, the liver should be pale brown on the outside and slightly rare in the centre. If it is overcooked, it will be tough. Between $\frac{1}{4}$ and $\frac{1}{2}$ pound of calf's liver should be allowed per person, depending on the method of preparation. It can then be served with bacon and sautéed mushrooms or onion rings.

Calf's Liver with Apples and Onion Rings

Perfect for a light family supper this tasty German dish of liver with apples and onions may be served with French fried or mashed potatoes.

4 SERVINGS

6 oz. [$\frac{3}{4}$ cup] butter
2 lb. tart apples, peeled, cored and sliced into $\frac{1}{4}$-inch rings
4 medium-sized onions, thinly sliced and pushed out into rings
$\frac{1}{2}$ teaspoon salt
$\frac{1}{4}$ teaspoon black pepper
2 oz. [$\frac{1}{2}$ cup] seasoned flour, made with 2 oz. plain flour [$\frac{1}{2}$ cup all-purpose flour], $\frac{1}{2}$ teaspoon salt and $\frac{1}{4}$ teaspoon black pepper
$1\frac{1}{2}$ lb. calf's liver, cut into $\frac{1}{4}$-inch slices

Preheat the oven to very cool 250°F (Gas Mark $\frac{1}{2}$, 130°C).

In a large frying-pan, melt 2 tablespoons of the butter over moderate heat. When the foam subsides, add one-third of the apple rings to the pan. Cook the rings for 3 to 4 minutes or until they are golden brown on both sides.

Using a slotted spoon, transfer the apple rings to an ovenproof plate. Cover with aluminium foil and place the plate in the oven.

Cook the remaining apple rings in the same way, using additional butter as required. Add the rings to those being kept warm in the oven.

Melt another 2 ounces [$\frac{1}{4}$ cup] of the butter in the frying-pan. When the foam subsides, add the onion rings, salt and pepper. Fry the onion rings for 8 to 10 minutes or until they are golden brown. Transfer them to the ovenproof plate with the apple rings.

Sprinkle the seasoned flour on to a plate and coat each slice of liver with the flour, shaking off any excess.

Add the remaining butter to the pan and melt it. When the foam subsides, add the liver slices and fry them for about 2 minutes on each side, or until they are light brown.

Transfer the liver to a warmed serving dish. Remove the apples and onions from the oven and arrange them decoratively on the liver. Serve at once.

Calf's Liver with Mustard and Cream Sauce

An easy main dish to prepare, calf's liver with a tasty mustard and cream sauce may be served with a green vegetable and mashed potatoes.

4 SERVINGS

$1\frac{1}{2}$ lb. calf's liver, cut into $\frac{1}{4}$-inch slices
2 oz. [$\frac{1}{2}$ cup] seasoned flour, made with 2 oz. plain flour [$\frac{1}{2}$ cup all-purpose flour], $\frac{1}{2}$ teaspoon salt and $\frac{1}{4}$ teaspoon black pepper
2 oz. [$\frac{1}{4}$ cup] butter
1 tablespoon chopped parsley

SAUCE

5 fl. oz. [$\frac{5}{8}$ cup] brown stock
5 fl. oz. single cream [$\frac{5}{8}$ cup light cream]
1 tablespoon prepared mustard mashed with 2 tablespoons butter to a smooth paste

Coat the liver slices with the seasoned flour, shaking off any excess.

In a large frying-pan, melt the butter over high heat. When the foam subsides, add the liver slices and sauté them for 2 minutes on each side, or until the liver is a light brown. Remove the slices from the pan and place them in a warmed serving dish. Keep them hot while making the sauce.

Add the brown stock to the pan and bring it to the boil. Boil it for 5 to 7 minutes, stirring constantly. Stir in the cream and simmer the sauce for 1 minute.

Remove the pan from the heat and stir in the mustard-and-butter mixture in

Tripe with tomatoes and onions in a wine sauce, Callos Vizcainos is a tasty Spanish dish.

small pieces. When the mixture has completely dissolved, pour the sauce over the liver, sprinkle with parsley and serve at once.

Calf's Liver Sauté

Quickly and easily prepared, Calf's Liver Sauté may be served with fried onion rings and green peas.

4 SERVINGS

½ teaspoon black pepper
1 teaspoon Worcestershire sauce
1½ lb. calf's liver, cut into ¼-inch slices
6 tablespoons plus 1 teaspoon flour
2 oz. [¼ cup] plus 1 tablespoon butter
8 fl. oz. [1 cup] red wine
1 teaspoon sugar
1 tablespoon chopped parsley

Mix together the black pepper and Worcestershire sauce in a teacup. Using a pastry brush, coat both sides of the liver slices with the mixture. Put the 6 tablespoons of flour on a plate and dip the liver slices in it to coat both sides generously.

Melt 2 ounces [¼ cup] of the butter in a large frying-pan over moderate heat. When the foam subsides, add the liver slices and fry them for 2 minutes on each side. Transfer them to a heated serving dish. Cover and keep warm.

Add the remaining butter to the frying-pan and melt it over moderate heat. Add the remaining 1 teaspoon of flour. Mix well. Gradually stir in the wine and sugar. Increase the heat to high and bring the mixture to the boil. Taste and add salt and pepper if necessary.

Pour the sauce over the liver. Sprinkle with parsley. Serve at once.

Callos Vizcainos

TRIPE IN WINE SAUCE

Tripe cooked in wine and stock with tomatoes and onions and flavoured with herbs, Callos Vizcainos (khy-yohs vith-khy-nohs) *is an appetizing Spanish dish.*

4 SERVINGS

2 lb. tripe, blanched
10 fl. oz. [1¼ cups] chicken stock
10 fl. oz. [1¼ cups] dry white wine
½ teaspoon dried thyme
1 bay leaf
3 medium-sized onions, 1 left whole and 2 finely chopped
4 tomatoes, blanched, peeled, seeded and coarsely chopped
2 teaspoons tomato purée
1 celery stalk, finely chopped
½ teaspoon salt
¼ teaspoon black pepper

Low Cal

Cut the tripe into strips about 2-inches long.

Place the stock, wine, thyme, bay leaf, 1 whole onion and the tripe strips in a large saucepan over moderate heat. Bring the liquid to the boil. Reduce the heat and cook the tripe slowly for about 1 hour, or until it is tender.

Remove the tripe from the saucepan with a slotted spoon and keep it warm.

Add the tomatoes, tomato purée, celery and the chopped onions to the liquid in the pan and simmer over low heat for 30 minutes.

Remove the pan from the heat and pour the mixture through a strainer, placed over a bowl, mashing the tomatoes, celery and onions with the back of a spoon to extract all their juices.

Return the tripe and the strained sauce to the pan. Add the salt and pepper and cook slowly over low heat for 20 minutes.

Turn into a warmed serving dish and serve at once.

Calories

A calorie is a unit of heat required to raise the temperature of 1 kilogram of water by 1°C. Food is measured in these units which provide energy.

Every food has a different number of calories. High protein foods (fish, meat and cheese, etc.) have a higher number of these units of heat, while fruits and vegetables have lower quantities.

The number of calories one should include in the day's meals depends on the individual—growing children and manual workers require more calories than an elderly person or someone who sits at a desk most of the day. It also depends on the weight and type of the individual. Some people burn up more energy than others from nervous tension.

Calories are in all foods, but it is important to be sure that the daily diet contains certain amounts of the three major food groups—protein, fats and carbohydrates—in order to obtain a well-balanced diet essential to good health.

In this chart the approximate calories per ounce of some of the main foods are given. Remember that raw food cooked in a lot of fat or oil, and meat which has a lot of fat will have more calories.

Calorie Chart — it is easy to count up the calories in your menus from the numbers given below.

Fruit

Fruit	*Calories per ounce*
Apples	10
Apricots	8
Avocado	25
Bananas	22
Blackcurrants	8
Blackberries	8
Cherries	13
Figs (green)	12
Gooseberries	5
Grapes	17
Grapefruit	6
Lemon juice	2
Melon	7
Orange juice	11
Peaches	11
Pears	11
Pineapple	13
Plums	11
Raspberries	7
Strawberries	7

Note: All dried fruits are higher in calories: Currants (69), Dates (70), Prunes (46), Raisins (70), Sultanas (71).

Nuts

Nuts	*Calories per ounce*
Almonds	170
Brazil nuts	183
Chestnuts	49
Cob nuts	113
Coconut (fresh)	104
Peanuts	171
Walnuts	156

Vegetables

Vegetables	*Calories per ounce*
Artichokes	4
Asparagus	5
Beans—broad	12
Beans—French	2
Beans—runner	2
Beetroot [Beets]	13
Brussels Sprouts	5
Cabbage	3
Carrots	5
Cauliflower	3
Celery	1
Leeks	7
Mushrooms (raw 2) fried	62
Onions	4
Parsnips	16
Peas	14
Potatoes	23
Spinach	7
Swedes [Rutabaga]	5
Tomatoes (raw 4) fried	20

Note: These figures, unless stated, are for boiled vegetables.

Fish

Fish	*Calories per ounce*
Bass (steamed)	36
Bream (steamed)	34
Cod (steamed 23) fried	40
Crab (boiled)	36
Flounder (steamed 27) fried	61
Haddock (steamed 28) fried	50
Hake (steamed 30) fried	58
Halibut (steamed)	37
Herring (fried in oatmeal)	67
Kippers (baked)	57
Lobster (boiled)	34
Mackerel (fried)	53
Mullet (steamed)	36
Mussels (boiled)	25
Oysters (raw)	14
Plaice (steamed 26) fried	66
Prawns or Shrimps (boiled)	30
Salmon (steamed)	57
Sardines (canned)	84
Turbot (steamed)	28

Meat, poultry and game

Meat, poultry and game	*Calories per ounce*
Bacon, lean (fried)	169
Beef (roasted)	64
Beef steak (fried)	78
Chicken (roasted)	54
Duck (roasted)	89
Goose (roasted)	92
Grouse (roasted)	49
Ham (boiled)	62
Kidney (stewed)	45
Lamb (roasted)	83
Lamb chop (fried)	97
Liver (fried)	74
Pheasant (roasted)	61
Pork (roasted)	90
Pork chops (grilled) [broiled]	92
Pork Sausages (fried)	93
Rabbit (stewed)	51
Tongue (pickled)	88
Turkey (roasted)	56
Veal (roasted)	66

Dairy foods, fats and oils

Dairy foods, fats and oils	*Calories per ounce*
Butter	226
Cheese	
Cheddar	120
Cream	232
Camembert	88
Cottage	30
Danish blue	103
Gruyère	132
Parmesan	118
Stilton	135
Cream (double) [heavy]	131
Cream (single) [light]	62
Eggs (standard size egg—2½ oz.)	46
Lard	262
Low fat spread	105
Milk	19
Margarine	226
Olive Oil	264
Suet	262
Yogurt (low fat)	15

Cereal foods

Cereal foods	*Calories per ounce*
Biscuits (plain)	123
Bread (brown)	68
Bread (white)	69
Cornflakes	104
Cornflour [cornstarch]	100
Flour	95
Macaroni (boiled)	32
Semolina	100
Spaghetti	104

Sugar and Jams

Sugar and Jams	*Calories per ounce*
Sugar	112
Golden [corn] Syrup	84
Honey	82
Jam	74

Calvados

An apple brandy distilled from cider in Normandy, France, the best Calvados matures for six years in oaken casks, which give it a golden brown colour.

Camembert

The best-known of French cheeses, Camembert bears the name of a small village in Normandy although today this cheese is produced all over France. Camembert is pale yellow, smooth and round. It is a soft, ripened cheese made from unskimmed cows' milk and inoculated with a white mould. Camembert should always be kept at room temperature and while it may be used for cooking, it is best eaten by itself or with fruit.

Camembert Croquettes

Camembert Croquettes (kroh-ket) *are bite-sized balls of Camembert cheese, deep-fried and served piping hot as an hors d'oeuvre.*

26 CROQUETTES

1 ripe Camembert, rind removed
$1\frac{1}{2}$ oz. [3 tablespoons] **butter**
2 tablespoons flour
6 fl. oz. [$\frac{3}{4}$ cup] **milk**
$\frac{1}{4}$ teaspoon salt
$\frac{1}{8}$ teaspoon white pepper
$\frac{1}{8}$ teaspoon cayenne pepper
1 egg yolk
1 egg, lightly beaten
3 oz. [1 cup] **dry white breadcrumbs**
sufficient oil for deep-frying
2 tablespoons grated Parmesan cheese

Press the cheese through a strainer with the back of a spoon.

In a medium-sized saucepan melt the butter over low heat. With a wooden spoon stir in the flour and cook the mixture, stirring constantly, for 2 minutes. Remove the pan from the heat and gradually stir in the milk.

Return the pan to the heat and continue stirring until the mixture comes to the boil. The sauce must be very thick. Add the salt, pepper and cayenne, and stir to mix.

Remove the pan from the heat and allow the mixture to cool.

Stir in the Camembert and the egg yolk and blend well. Turn the mixture on to a large plate and refrigerate for at least 1 hour.

With floured hands, and on a floured surface, shape the cheese mixture into 26 small balls. Dip each ball in the beaten egg and roll it in the breadcrumbs.

Heat the oil over moderately high heat in a large, deep frying-pan. Place the balls in a deep frying-basket and plunge into the hot oil. Fry them for 30 seconds or until the balls are golden brown.

Remove the basket from the oil. Drain the croquettes on kitchen paper towels and place them on a warmed serving dish. Sprinkle them with the Parmesan cheese and serve at once.

Camomile

A bitter-tasting herb which looks like a daisy, camomile is used for making medicinal teas.

Canadian Whisky

Canada has a long distilling tradition—there were rum distilleries in Quebec before the French Revolution. Whisky was first distilled during the early 19th century, its production being greatly encouraged by a huge grain surplus harvested in the country at that time.

Canadian whisky is light in colour and to taste. By law, it is produced only from cereal grains, corn, rye, wheat, barley and malt being those most commonly used. Distilling methods follow those employed in the United States, which are in turn loosely based upon Scottish practices. Canadian whisky must be aged in wooden casks for at least two years before it can be sold, and is now usually aged for six years before being marketed.

All Canadian whisky is blended, that is, is a mixture of pure 'straight' whisky and neutral spirits, usually made from grain.

Canapés

These are small, dainty savouries that are served hot or cold as cocktail snacks, appetizers or after a meal. The base of canapés can be small biscuits, pastry or fried bread, cut into fancy shapes.

The toppings should be colourful, tasty and can be meat, fish, eggs or vegetables. Sometimes a thin layer of aspic jelly is spooned over each canapé and this keeps the topping from drying out.

If canapés are served with drinks or before a meal, a selection of different flavours, textures and colours should be made and then arranged on a large tray.

Canapés du Crabe

CRAB CANAPES

A creamy crab mixture on elegant toast fingers, Canapés du Crabe (kah-nah-pay doo krahb) *may be served either as a cocktail savoury or as a tasty first course.*

18 CANAPES

$1\frac{1}{2}$ oz. [3 tablespoons] **butter**
1 tablespoon finely chopped onion
1 tablespoon flour
6 fl. oz. single cream [$\frac{3}{4}$ cup light cream]
$\frac{1}{2}$ lb. crabmeat, flaked
$\frac{1}{4}$ teaspoon salt
$\frac{1}{8}$ teaspoon white pepper
$\frac{1}{8}$ teaspoon Tabasco sauce
1 teaspoon fresh lemon juice
6 slices of toast, crusts removed and each slice cut into 3 fingers
1 tablespoon cream cheese
$\frac{1}{2}$ teaspoon paprika
2 teaspoons chopped capers

In a small saucepan melt 1 tablespoon of butter over moderate heat. When the foam subsides, add the onion and fry for 4 to 5 minutes, or until the onion is light brown in colour.

Remove the saucepan from the heat and stir in the flour. Pour in the cream, return the pan to the heat and bring the cream to the boil, stirring continuously with a wooden spoon. Add the crab, salt, pepper, Tabasco and lemon juice. Bring to the boil again.

Remove the pan from the heat and spread the toast fingers with the crab mixture.

Preheat the grill [broiler] to high.

In a small bowl, blend the cream cheese and remaining butter together with a fork to a smooth paste. Add the paprika. Dot a teaspoonful of the cheese paste over the crab mixture.

Place the canapés under the grill [broiler] and cook for 1 minute. Transfer the canapés to a warmed serving dish and garnish with the chopped capers.

Canapés des Crevettes

SHRIMP CANAPES

Spicy shrimps on bite-sized squares of fried bread, these decorative Canapés des Crevettes (kah-nah-pay day kreh-vet) *may be served either hot or cold. The quantities of curry powder, cayenne and chilli sauce may be increased if a hotter flavour is liked.*

12 CANAPES

2 oz. [$\frac{1}{4}$ cup] **butter**
$3\frac{1}{2}$ **oz. canned shrimps, drained**
$\frac{1}{4}$ teaspoon curry powder
$\frac{1}{8}$ teaspoon cayenne pepper
$\frac{1}{8}$ teaspoon chilli sauce
$\frac{1}{4}$ teaspoon salt
juice of $\frac{1}{4}$ lemon
4 slices fried bread, crusts removed and each slice cut into 3 ovals
chopped parsley

In a small saucepan, melt the butter over moderately low heat. As soon as the foam subsides, add the shrimps, curry powder, cayenne, chilli sauce, salt and lemon juice and simmer gently for 4 minutes.

With a slotted spoon, remove the shrimps from the pan and place them on the pieces of fried bread. Garnish each canapé with chopped parsley.

Canapés aux Ecrevisses

LOBSTER CANAPES

Canapés aux Ecrevisses (kah-nah-pay oh-zay-kreh-vees) *made of lobster marinated in oil and vinegar, mixed with a creamy mayonnaise and spread on fingers of toasted bread, are excellent to serve at a cocktail party. They look especially attractive if garnished with small crisp lettuce leaves or slices of cucumber.*

18 CANAPES

- 1 tablespoon wine vinegar
- 3 tablespoons olive oil
- $\frac{1}{4}$ teaspoon sugar
- $\frac{1}{4}$ teaspoon salt
- $\frac{1}{4}$ teaspoon black pepper
- 4 oz. canned lobster, drained and flaked
- 1 tablespoon chopped parsley
- 1 lean bacon slice, grilled until brown and crisp and crumbled
- 1 celery stalk, finely chopped
- 1 teaspoon finely chopped chives
- $\frac{1}{8}$ teaspoon cayenne pepper
- 4 to 6 tablespoons mayonnaise
- 6 slices of toast, crusts removed and each slice cut into 3 fingers

In a small bowl mix the vinegar, oil, sugar, salt and pepper together with a spoon. Place the lobster meat in the bowl, mix well and leave to marinate for at least 1 hour.

With a slotted spoon remove the lobster from the marinade and place it in a small mixing bowl. Discard the marinade. Add the parsley, bacon, celery, chives, cayenne and mayonnaise and mix well together with a fork. Taste for seasoning and add more salt and pepper if necessary.

Spread the mixture on the fingers of toast and serve.

Canapés aux Epinards

SPINACH AND CHEESE CANAPES

An unusual and tempting mixture of spinach and cheese on crisp croûtes Canapés aux Epinards (kah-nah-pay oh-zay-pee-nahr) *may be served either with cocktails or as an interesting first course for a dinner party. The canapés may be prepared well in advance and reheated by grilling* [broiling], *just before serving.*

24 CANAPES

- 1 teaspoon salt
- $1\frac{1}{2}$ lb. spinach, washed and stalks removed
- 2 oz. [$\frac{1}{4}$ cup] butter
- $\frac{1}{2}$ teaspoon black pepper
- 3 oz. [$\frac{3}{4}$ cup] grated cheese
- 1 tablespoon olive oil
- 24 triangles of white bread
- 1 oz. [$\frac{1}{3}$ cup] fine, dry white breadcrumbs
- 2 tablespoons butter, melted

Half-fill a large saucepan with cold water. Add the salt and bring the water to the boil over high heat. Put the spinach in the pan and reduce the heat to moderate. Cook the spinach for 7 to 12 minutes or until it is tender.

Drain the spinach in a colander and squeeze it dry between two plates. Chop it finely and return it to the saucepan. Add 2 tablespoons of the butter, the pepper and two-thirds of the cheese and stir to mix. Cover the pan and set it aside in a warm place.

In a large frying-pan, melt the remaining butter and the oil over moderately high heat. When the foam subsides, add the triangles of bread.

Fry for 10 minutes on each side, or until lightly browned.

Remove the croûtes from the pan with a slotted spoon and place them on kitchen paper towels to drain.

Preheat the grill [broiler] to high.

Place a tablespoon of the spinach and cheese mixture on each croûte and top with the remaining cheese, breadcrumbs and melted butter.

Place the canapés under the grill [broiler] and cook for 2 to 3 minutes or until they are hot and the cheese lightly browned. Serve at once.

Canapés Piquants

Bite-sized squares of toast spread with a spicy cream cheese mixture and quickly baked, Canapés Piquants (kah-nah-pay pee-kahn) *are quick and easy to make, and are sure to please your guests.*

24 CANAPES

- 4 oz. cream cheese
- 1 shallot, minced [ground]
- 1 egg, lightly beaten
- $\frac{1}{2}$ teaspoon Tabasco sauce
- 6 slices of toasted bread, crusts removed and each slice cut into 4 squares

Preheat the oven to fairly hot 375°F (Gas Mark 5, 190°C).

Put the cheese, shallot, egg and Tabasco into a medium-sized mixing bowl. Using a wire whisk or wooden spoon, beat the mixture until it is light and creamy.

Spread the cheese mixture on the squares of toast and place the squares on a baking sheet.

Bake the canapés in the oven for 5 to 10 minutes, or until they are just beginning to brown. Remove the canapés from the oven, transfer them to a warmed serving plate and serve at once.

Canapés aux Sardines

SARDINE CANAPES

A tasty combination of sardines, egg and anchovies on squares of white bread and butter, Canapés aux Sardines (kah-nah-payz oh sahr-deen) *may be prepared well in advance and kept, covered, in the refrigerator until you are ready to serve.*

16 CANAPES

- 4 slices white bread, crusts removed
- 2 tablespoons butter
- 1 can sardines, drained of oil
- ¼ teaspoon black pepper
- ½ teaspoon fresh lemon juice
- 2 teaspoons chopped parsley
- 3 hard-boiled eggs, thinly sliced
- 16 anchovy fillets, rolled

Butter each slice of bread. Cut each slice into 4 squares.

In a small mixing bowl, mash the sardines, pepper, lemon juice and parsley to a paste with a fork.

Spread the mixture on the squares of bread. Place a slice of hard-boiled egg on top of the sardine mixture and garnish with the rolled anchovy fillets.

A colourful and tempting selection of cocktail canapés — from left to right: Canapés du Crabe (recipe given), thin slices of salami with gherkin fans on rounds of toast, Canapés aux Sardines, Canapés de Crevettes, Canapés aux Epinards (recipes given), slices of tomato piped with a cream cheese, garlic and parsley mixture on crisp, savoury biscuits, small squares of pâté garnished with stuffed olives on brown bread and lemon butter and thin slices of smoked salmon garnished with lemon twists and parsley on brown bread.

Canard Braisé avec Choucroute

BRAISED DUCK WITH SAUERKRAUT

An unusual way to serve duck, Canard Braisé avec Choucroute (kah-nahr bray-zay ah-vek shoo-croot) *is a delicious one-dish main course. It is well complemented by one of the heavier white Alsatian wines, such as Traminer.*

4 SERVINGS

- 1 x 4 lb. duck
- 1 teaspoon salt
- 1 teaspoon black pepper
- 3 oz. [$\frac{3}{8}$ cup] butter
- 2 oz. salt pork, diced
- 4 tablespoons vegetable oil
- 2 medium-sized onions, thinly sliced
- 2 medium-sized carrots, scraped and sliced in julienne strips (about $1\frac{1}{2}$-inches long and $\frac{1}{8}$-inch wide)
- 1 small cooking apple, peeled, cored and coarsely chopped
- 2 lb. canned sauerkraut
- 8 fl. oz. [1 cup] dry white wine
- 6 fl. oz. [$\frac{3}{4}$ cup] chicken stock or stock made with a stock cube
- 1 garlic clove
- 6 peppercorns
- 4 parsley sprigs
- 1 bay leaf
- 10 juniper berries (optional)

Preheat the oven to warm 325°F (Gas Mark 3, 170°C).

Prepare the duck for braising by clipping the wing ends and neck and trussing it so that the wings and legs are close to the body. Prick the skin around the thighs, back and lower breast. Rub half of the salt and pepper into the cavity. Close the cavity with a skewer.

In a very large flameproof casserole, melt the butter over moderate heat. Place the duck in the casserole and brown it on all sides, turning it with two large spoons.

Cover the casserole and put it in the oven for 2 hours, or until the juices run clear when the thigh is pierced with a fork.

After the duck has been cooking for 1 hour, prepare the choucroute.

In a small saucepan half-full of boiling water blanch the diced salt pork over moderate heat for about 5 minutes to remove the excess salt. Drain the salt pork and dry thoroughly on kitchen paper towels.

In a large, deep frying-pan heat the vegetable oil over moderate heat. Add the diced salt pork and fry it for about 10 minutes, or until the dice resemble very small croûtons. Add the onions and carrots to the pan and cook for 5 to 6 minutes, taking care that the vegetables do not brown. Add the chopped apple and the sauerkraut and with a metal spoon stir well. Pour in the wine and the stock. Tie together in a small cheesecloth bag the garlic clove, peppercorns, parsley, bay leaf and juniper berries (if used) and add the bag to the frying-pan.

Increase the heat to high and bring the contents of the frying-pan to the boil. Cover the pan, reduce the heat to very low and simmer the choucroute for 35 to 40 minutes. Remove the cheesecloth bag at the end of the cooking period, although, if used, the juniper berries may be added to the choucroute mixture. Season the choucroute with the remaining salt and pepper.

When the duck is cooked, transfer it from its casserole to a heated serving plate. Untruss the duck. Heap the choucroute around the sides of the duck. Serve immediately.

Canard Braisé au Chou Rouge

BRAISED DUCK WITH RED CABBAGE

Another delicious braised duck dish, Canard Braisé au Chou Rouge (kah-nahr bray-zay oh shoo rooj) *is an attractive main dish for a dinner party. For an even more interesting flavour, add 1 pound of canned chestnuts (peeled and ready to serve) to the red cabbage mixture for the last hour of cooking.*

4 SERVINGS

- 4 oz. [$\frac{1}{2}$ cup] butter
- 2 medium-sized onions, finely chopped
- 1 garlic clove, finely chopped
- 1 large red cabbage, shredded
- 2 medium-sized tart cooking apples, peeled, cored and coarsely chopped
- 1 small onion, studded with 4 cloves
- 1 teaspoon ground allspice
- $1\frac{1}{2}$ teaspoons salt
- 1 teaspoon black pepper
- 10 fl. oz. [$1\frac{1}{4}$ cups] light dry red wine
- 5 fl. oz. [$\frac{5}{8}$ cup] beef stock or stock made with a stock cube
- 1 x 4 lb. duck

Preheat the oven to warm 325°F (Gas Mark 3, 170°C).

In a large flameproof casserole melt half the butter over moderate heat. Add the chopped onions and garlic and cook them for 10 minutes or until the onions are translucent but not brown. Add the cabbage, apples, clove-studded onion, allspice, 1 teaspoon salt and half the pepper and simmer for 5 minutes, stirring occasionally to make sure the cabbage is browning evenly. Pour in the wine and stock. Raise the heat to high and bring the liquid to the boil.

Cover the casserole tightly, place it in the centre of oven and braise for $3\frac{1}{2}$ hours.

After the cabbage has been cooking for $1\frac{1}{2}$ hours prepare the duck for braising.

Clip the wing ends and neck and truss the duck so that the wings and legs are close to the body. Prick the skin around the thighs, back and lower breast. Rub the remaining salt and pepper into the cavity. Close the cavity with a skewer.

In a large saucepan, melt the remaining butter over moderate heat. Place the duck in the pan and brown it slowly on all sides, turning it with two large spoons.

Transfer the duck to a roasting tin and place it in the oven. Braise for 2 hours or until the juices run clear when the thigh is pierced with a fork.

Remove the duck from the oven. Untruss it and set it aside on a heated serving platter. Remove the casserole from the oven and taste the cabbage mixture for seasoning. Add salt and pepper if desired. All the cooking liquid should have been absorbed into the cabbage, but if it is a little wet, drain the cabbage before arranging it around the duck. Serve immediately.

Canard à l'Orange

ROAST DUCK IN ORANGE SAUCE

One of the classic duck recipes of haute cuisine, Canard à l'Orange (kah-nahr ah loh-ronj) *is a rich and succulent dish. Serve it with sautéed potatoes, buttered courgettes* [zucchini] *and a really good wine—Haut Medoc, for instance, if a light red wine is preferred, or a strong white Burgundy such as Pouligny-Montrachet or Pouilly-Fuissé.*

4 SERVINGS

- 1 x 4 lb. duck
- $\frac{1}{2}$ teaspoon salt
- $\frac{1}{2}$ teaspoon black pepper
- 2 tablespoons butter, cut in small pieces

SAUCE

- 2 large oranges
- 2 tablespoons sugar
- 2 tablespoons white wine vinegar
- 8 fl. oz. [1 cup] rich brown sauce
- 2 tablespoons orange-flavoured liqueur
- $\frac{1}{2}$ teaspoon salt
- $\frac{1}{2}$ teaspoon black pepper
- 1 teaspoon redcurrant jelly (optional)
- watercress or parsley sprigs

Preheat the oven to hot 425°F (Gas Mark 7, 220°C).

Prepare the duck for roasting by clipping its wing ends and neck. Truss it with string so that the wings and legs are close to the body. Rub the cavity with salt and pepper and close the cavity with a skewer. Place the bird in a shallow roasting pan and dot with the butter.

Roast in the middle of the oven for 20 minutes, then turn the heat down to moderate 350°F (Gas Mark 4, 180°C) and cook for a further 60 minutes, or until the juices run faintly rosy to clear when the thigh is pierced with a fork. The duck should be basted occasionally with the pan juices while it cooks and should be turned to ensure even cooking.

While the duck is cooking cut the rind of one orange into fine strips. In a small saucepan over moderate heat, blanch the strips in 5 fluid ounces [$\frac{5}{8}$ cup] of boiling water for 10 minutes to remove excess bitterness. Drain the orange strips and set them aside.

Squeeze the juice from one-half of the peeled orange and set aside. Peel the pith from the remaining half orange and slice the orange. Slice the other orange leaving it unpeeled. Set all the slices aside.

About 6 or 7 minutes before the duck is ready, in a small saucepan over low heat, combine the sugar and vinegar together, stirring with a metal spoon to dissolve the sugar. Raise the heat to moderate and bring the syrup to the boil. When it turns amber in colour, remove the pan from the heat and set it aside.

When the duck is cooked, remove it from the oven and place it on a heated serving platter. Cover it with foil to keep it warm.

Skim the fat from the top of the pan juices and, over high heat, bring the juices to a boil, scraping in any brown pieces that may have accumulated on the bottom and sides of the pan. Lower the heat to moderate and add the brown sauce. Mix well with a wooden spoon. Bring the mixture to a boil and cook for 5 minutes. Skim off any fat which rises to the surface.

Add the reserved orange rind strips and orange juice, the liqueur, salt, pepper and sugar-and-vinegar syrup to the mixture. Cook for a further 3 to 4 minutes to allow the ingredients to blend and to thicken the sauce slightly. If the sauce requires further thickening or if an especially rich sauce is desired, stir in the redcurrant jelly. The sauce is now ready to serve.

Untruss the duck and garnish it with unpeeled orange slices. Arrange the peeled orange slices and the watercress or parsley sprigs around the sides of the bird. Spoon some of the sauce over the duck and serve the rest of it separately.

Roast duck with a rich orange liqueur sauce, Canard à l'Orange is a classic French dish.

Canary Island Chicken

Chicken stewed in white wine and sprinkled with chopped hard-boiled eggs and parsley, Canary Island Chicken is an unusual and colourful dish. It is excellent served with boiled new potatoes or rice and French beans.

4 SERVINGS

- **2 oz. [½ cup] seasoned flour, made with 2 oz. plain flour [½ cup all-purpose flour], 1 teaspoon salt and ½ teaspoon black pepper**
- **1 x 4 lb. chicken, cut into eight serving pieces**
- **2 fl. oz. [¼ cup] olive oil**
- **2 oz. [¼ cup] butter**
- **2 garlic cloves, crushed**
- **2 medium-sized onions, coarsely chopped**
- **10 fl. oz. [1¼ cups] dry white wine**
- **10 fl. oz. [1¼ cups] chicken stock**
- **bouquet garni, consisting of 4 parsley sprigs, 1 thyme spray and 1 bay leaf tied together**
- **1 teaspoon saffron**
- **1 tablespoon hot water**
- **2 oz. [½ cup] slivered almonds**
- **2 oz. [¼ cup] beurre manié**
- **2 hard-boiled eggs, finely chopped**
- **1 tablespoon chopped parsley**

Sprinkle the seasoned flour on to a plate. Roll the chicken pieces in it until they are well coated. Shake off any excess flour and set the chicken aside.

In a medium-sized flameproof casserole or large saucepan heat the oil and butter over moderate heat. When the foam subsides add the garlic and onions. Fry them for 8 to 10 minutes, or until the onions are soft and translucent but not brown.

Add the chicken pieces to the casserole and lightly brown them for 2 to 3 minutes on each side.

Pour in the wine and chicken stock. Add the bouquet garni. Cover the casserole, reduce the heat to low and simmer for 45 minutes, or until the chicken is almost tender.

In a cup dissolve the saffron in the hot water and add it to the casserole with the almonds. Simmer the chicken for another 15 minutes, but do not re-cover the casserole.

Take out the chicken pieces and arrange them on a warmed serving dish. Remove and discard the bouquet garni. Gradually add the *beurre manié* to the sauce in the casserole, stirring constantly. Cook for 2 to 3 minutes or until the sauce is well blended and thick.

Pour the sauce over the chicken. Sprinkle the top with the chopped egg and parsley and serve at once.

Canary Island Chicken, topped with chopped eggs and parsley, is a colourful and unusual dish.

Canary Pudding

This light, steamed sponge pudding is made from equal weights of eggs, sugar, butter and flour. It can be made as one large pudding or as four small separate puddings, and is usually served with jam sauce.

4 SERVINGS

- **4 oz. [½ cup] plus 1 tablespoon butter**
- **4 oz. [½ cup] castor sugar**
- **¼ teaspoon vanilla essence or 1 teaspoon grated lemon rind**
- **2 large eggs**
- **4 oz. [1 cup] self-raising flour**
- **1 to 2 tablespoons milk**

JAM SAUCE

- **4 oz. strawberry, raspberry or cherry jam**
- **1 teaspoon lemon juice**
- **1 to 2 tablespoons water**

In a large mixing bowl cream 4 ounces [½ cup] of the butter with a wooden spoon. Gradually beat in the castor sugar. Continue beating until the mixture is pale and fluffy.

Add the vanilla essence or lemon rind. Beating continuously, add one egg and one tablespoon of flour. When the egg and flour are well mixed with the butter mixture beat in the remaining egg with another tablespoon of flour. Fold in the remaining flour with a metal spatula. If the mixture is too thick, add a spoonful or two of the milk to give it a dropping consistency.

Grease a 1½-pint pudding basin with the remaining butter and pour the sponge mixture into the basin. The basin should be about three-quarters full.

Butter a piece of greaseproof or waxed paper and cover the basin with it. Tie securely around the rim of the bowl with a piece of string.

Place the bowl in a steamer. If you do not have a steamer, put the bowl in a large saucepan on an inverted saucer or rack so that the bottom of the bowl does not touch the saucepan. Pour boiling water into the saucepan to come halfway up the side of the bowl.

Take care during the cooking that the water does not boil dry. Cover the saucepan and steam for 1½ hours.

To make the jam sauce, melt the jam in a small saucepan over moderate heat. Stir the jam continuously and add the lemon juice. If the sauce is too thick add one or two tablespoons of water and mix thoroughly. Strain the sauce before pouring it over the pudding.

Turn the pudding carefully on to a warm serving dish and pour the jam sauce over.

Candied Fruits

This is an old-fashioned way of preserving fruit in a thick sugar syrup, and while the process takes several days the preparation itself is very simple.

One can buy candied fruits in the shops, but because they are usually imported they are expensive. Made at home when the fruit is in season it is very economical. A selection in the store cupboard means you have attractive colourful decorations for sweets and puddings, additions to cakes or a sweet meat to be served on its own after dinner.

The Fruit

Fruits used for candying should be firm and at the peak of their perfection. The firmer fruits give a more successful result than the soft fruits such as raspberries, strawberries and blackberries.

Apricots, cherries, peaches, pears, pineapple and plums are ideal and the fruits should be prepared as for cooking. Depending on the size of your bowls, it is better to prepare fruit in smaller quantities, otherwise you may find it difficult to keep topping up the syrup. Small fruits such as cherries only need stoning. Larger fruits—apricots, plums, peaches—should be peeled and then halved or quartered. It is better to candy each fruit separately, otherwise the flavour of each will be lost. Weigh the fruit and place it in a large saucepan. Cover with cold water, bring to the boil and simmer until the fruit is just soft—take care not to overcook the fruit as the end result will not be so successful. Drain the fruit into a heatproof bowl and reserve the cooking water.

Syrup

For every pound of fruit make a syrup with 10 fluid ounces [$1\frac{1}{4}$ cups] of the reserved cooking water and 6 ounces [$\frac{3}{4}$ cup] of sugar. Place the water and sugar in a heavy based saucepan, bring to the boil slowly and cook over moderate heat until a thin syrup forms.

Candying the fruit

Pour the hot syrup over the fruit (make sure it is covered with syrup) and leave for 24 hours.

Every day for *3* days, drain off the syrup into a saucepan and add 2 ounces [$\frac{1}{4}$ cup] of sugar each time. Bring to the boil and pour the syrup over the fruit.

On the *5th* day, drain off the syrup into a saucepan and add 3 ounces [$\frac{3}{8}$ cup] of sugar. Bring to the boil and when the sugar is dissolved pour over the fruit. Leave for 2 days, repeat the process and leave the fruit soaking in the syrup for 4 days.

To dry

Using a slotted spoon lift the fruit out of the syrup and spread it out on clean, dry baking sheets. Leave the fruit to dry out in a very cool oven (100°F) or in a warming cupboard. Turn the fruit occasionally so it dries on all sides. It is ready when it is really dry and not sticky.

To store

Pack the fruit in wax or cardboard cartons, each layer separated by a piece of greaseproof or waxed paper. Cover with a lid or piece of paper tied round with string. It is important that the containers are not airtight, otherwise the fruit might go mouldy.

Crystallized Fruit

This gives a sugary finish to the fruit which makes an attractive gift if packed in pretty boxes. Dip the dried candied fruit in boiling water, drain well, and coat each piece of fruit with sugar.

Candied fruits may be used as attractive decorations for desserts or eaten on their own after dinner.

Caneton aux Cerises

ROAST DUCKLING WITH CHERRIES

A colourful, festive main dish, Caneton aux Cerises (kahn-tohn oh seh-reeze) *is perfect for any special occasion. The sharpness of the cherries contrasts well with the rich meat. Serve with duchesse potatoes and broccoli.*

4 SERVINGS

1 x 4 lb. duck with giblets reserved
bouquet garni, consisting of 4 parsley sprigs, 1 thyme spray and 1 bay leaf tied together
1 onion, chopped
1 carrot, scraped and sliced
$\frac{1}{2}$ teaspoon salt
$\frac{1}{2}$ teaspoon black pepper

SAUCE

2 oz. [$\frac{1}{4}$ cup] sugar
50 ml [2 fl. oz.] vinegar
4 teaspoons arrowroot
4 tablespoons port or Madeira
1 tablespoon lemon juice
14 oz. canned, stoned cherries, drained
2 tablespoons butter, cut into small pieces

First make the stock. Place the duck giblets (excluding the liver), onion, carrot and bouquet garni in a saucepan. Pour over 1 pint [$2\frac{1}{2}$ cups] of water. Bring to the boil over moderate heat. Then reduce

the heat to low and simmer the stock for 30 minutes. Strain and reserve 16 fluid ounces [2 cups] of the stock.

Preheat the oven to hot 425°F (Gas Mark 7, 220°C).

Prepare the duckling for roasting by clipping the wing ends and neck and trussing it so that the wings and legs are close to the body. Prick the skin around the thighs, back and lower breast. Rub the cavity with salt and pepper and close the cavity with a skewer.

Place the duckling in a medium-sized shallow roasting pan. Put the pan in the middle of the oven and roast for about 15 minutes, or until the skin begins to brown.

Turn the duckling on one side. Reduce the heat to moderate 350°F (Gas Mark 4, 180°C). Roast for another 30 minutes, removing the fat with a bulb baster or large spoon as it accumulates around the bird. Turn the duckling on to its other side and roast for another 30 minutes. Remove any more fat from the pan.

While the duckling is roasting, prepare the sauce. Put the sugar and vinegar in a medium-sized saucepan over low heat. Cook the syrup, stirring, until the sugar

Duckling braised with turnips, carrots and onions, Caneton aux Navets is a superbly rich dinner party dish.

dissolves, then increase the heat to high and bring the syrup to the boil. Boil the syrup for 7 minutes, or until it becomes a dark brown colour. Stirring constantly, pour in half of the stock. Lower the heat and simmer for 1 minute, or until the caramelized syrup melts. Add the rest of the stock and stir to mix.

In a small bowl, mix the arrowroot, add a little hot sauce to it, then add this mixture to the pan of sauce, stirring constantly until the sauce thickens. Remove the pan from the heat and set aside.

Put the lemon juice and the port or Madeira into a small saucepan over moderate heat. Cook for 2 minutes. Add the cherries and stir gently with a wooden spoon until the mixture comes to the boil. Remove the pan from the heat and let it stand for about 20 minutes.

When the duckling is cooked, remove it from the roasting pan and place it on a hot serving dish. Untruss the duckling. Place the roasting pan over high heat and bring the meat juices to the boil. Boil rapidly to reduce the liquid by about half. Strain the liquid into the sauce.

Reheat the sauce over low heat, stirring constantly. Gently stir in the cherries and cook the sauce for 3 to 4 minutes, stirring occasionally.

Mix the butter, a little at a time, into the sauce and pour it over the duckling or serve separately in a sauceboat.

Caneton aux Navets

BRAISED DUCKLING WITH TURNIPS

Braised duckling with a traditional accompaniment of turnips, Caneton aux Navets (kahn-tohn oh nah-vay) *is a rich dinner party dish. It may be served with petits pois and boiled new potatoes.*

4 SERVINGS

- 1 x 4 lb. duck with the giblets reserved
- 2 onions, finely chopped
- 2 carrots, scraped and sliced
- 2 bouquets garnis, each consisting of 4 parsley sprigs, 1 thyme spray and 1 bay leaf tied together

- $1\frac{1}{2}$ teaspoons salt
- $\frac{1}{2}$ teaspoon black pepper
- 3 oz. [$\frac{3}{8}$ cup] butter
- 2 lb. small white turnips, peeled and quartered
- $\frac{1}{2}$ teaspoon fresh lemon juice
- 2 tablespoons beurre manié

First make the stock. Place the duck giblets (excluding the liver), 1 onion, 1 carrot and a bouquet garni in a saucepan. Pour over 16 fluid ounces [2 cups] of water. Bring to the boil over moderate heat. Then reduce the heat to low and simmer the stock for 30 minutes. Strain and reserve 6 fluid ounces [$\frac{3}{4}$ cup].

Preheat the oven to warm 325°F (Gas Mark 3, 170°C).

Prepare the duckling for braising by clipping the wing ends and neck and trussing it so that the wings and legs are close to the body. Prick the skin around the thighs, back and lower breast. Rub the cavity with 1 teaspoon salt and half the pepper. Close the cavity with a skewer.

In a large frying-pan melt 2 ounces [$\frac{1}{4}$ cup] of the butter over high heat. When the foam subsides, add the duckling and brown it on all sides. Remove the duckling from the pan and set aside.

In a large, flameproof casserole, melt the remaining butter over moderate heat. Add the other onion and carrot and cook, stirring occasionally, for 10 to 12 minutes, or until they are soft and lightly browned.

Place the duckling on top of the carrot and onion in the casserole and add the remaining salt, the pepper and the second bouquet garni. Cover the casserole tightly and place it in the oven. Braise for 1 hour.

Remove the duckling from the casserole and strain the cooking juices into a small bowl. Skim off any surface fat with a spoon or bulb baster.

Return the duckling to the casserole and arrange the turnips around it. Pour the strained cooking juices and brown stock over the duckling.

Place the casserole over moderate heat and bring the liquid to the boil. Remove the casserole from the heat, cover it and return it to the oven. Braise for 20 minutes, or until the turnips are cooked.

Remove the casserole from the oven. Transfer the duckling to a warmed serving dish and arrange the turnips around it.

Skim as much fat as possible off the surface of the braising juices in the casserole. Add the lemon juice to the liquid and additional salt and pepper if necessary. Add the beurre manié, a little at a time, stirring continuously until the sauce thickens.

Pour the braising juice into a sauce boat and serve with the duck.

Caneton à l'Alsacienne

ROAST DUCKLING WITH APPLE AND SAUSAGE STUFFING

Roast duckling with a richly flavoured apple and sausage stuffing, Caneton à l'Alsacienne (kahn-tohn ah lahl-sahz-yen) *is traditionally served with turnips and wafer thin potatoes.*

4 SERVINGS

- 1 x 4 lb. duck with the giblets reserved
- 1 onion, chopped
- 2 carrots, scraped and sliced
- bouquet garni, consisting of 4 parsley sprigs, 1 thyme spray and 1 bay leaf tied together
- 2 to 3 tablespoons port
- 1 tablespoon butter, softened

STUFFING

- $1\frac{1}{2}$ tablespoons butter
- 8 oz. pork sausage meat
- 1 lb. tart apples, peeled, cored and sliced
- $\frac{1}{4}$ teaspoon ground cinnamon
- $\frac{1}{4}$ teaspoon salt
- $\frac{1}{2}$ teaspoon dried sage
- 3 tablespoons brandy
- 2 fl. oz. [$\frac{1}{4}$ cup] port
- 3 oz. cooked ham, finely chopped

First make the stock. Place the duck giblets (excluding the liver), onion, carrots and bouquet garni in a saucepan. Pour over 1 pint [$2\frac{1}{2}$ cups] of water. Bring to the boil over moderate heat. Then reduce the heat to low and simmer the stock for 30 minutes. Strain and reserve 16 fluid ounces [2 cups] of the stock.

To make the stuffing, in a small frying-pan melt the butter over moderate heat. When the foam subsides, add the sausage meat. Fry for 6 to 8 minutes, stirring occasionally.

With a slotted spoon, remove the sausage meat from the pan and put it in a medium-sized mixing bowl. Sauté the apple pieces in the butter remaining in the frying-pan over moderately high heat for 4 to 6 minutes, or until they are lightly browned and tender.

With a slotted spoon, transfer the apple slices from the pan to a small bowl and sprinkle them with the cinnamon, salt, sage and brandy.

Pour the port and 2 fluid ounces [$\frac{1}{4}$ cup] of the duck stock into a saucepan. Boil the liquid over high heat until it has reduced to about 2 tablespoons. Pour the liquid over the sausage meat and set the bowl aside to allow the mixture to cool.

Preheat the oven to hot 425°F (Gas Mark 7, 220°C).

When the sausage and apple mixture has cooled, add the ham and mix it well together with a fork.

Loosely stuff the mixture into the duckling. Skewer or sew up the opening of the duckling and truss it by tying the drumsticks together and fastening the wings underneath the body. With a fork, prick the skin round the thighs, back and lower breast.

Place the duckling, breast side up in a roasting pan and put it in the oven. Roast the duckling for 15 minutes to brown it, then reduce the oven temperature to moderate 350°F (Gas Mark 4, 180°C) and turn the duckling on one side.

Using a bulb baster or large spoon, occasionally remove the fat which accumulates in the bottom of the pan.

After the duckling has been roasting for 45 minutes, turn it on to the other side. Roast for a further 15 minutes. Turn the duckling breast side up again. Continue to roast the duckling for a further 15 to 20 minutes.

To test if the duckling is cooked, prick the thigh with a skewer or the point of a sharp knife. The juices that run out should be only faintly rosy.

Remove the duckling from the oven and place it on a serving dish. Untruss the duckling and cover it with aluminium foil to keep it warm.

Remove and discard all except 1 tablespoon of the roasting juices from the pan. Add the remaining brown stock and over moderately high heat, boil the liquid, stirring constantly, until it has reduced by at least half.

Add the port to the sauce and simmer for 1 minute.

Remove the pan from the heat and stir in the butter. Strain the sauce into a warmed sauceboat. Pour a little of the sauce over the duckling and serve it at once, accompanied by the rest of the sauce.

Canja

PORTUGUESE CHICKEN SOUP WITH LEMON

A light lemon flavoured chicken soup that is traditionally Portuguese, Canja (kan-ja) *should be prepared and chilled in the refrigerator a day before serving. This makes the excess fat easier to remove. Canja is also an ideal soup to home freeze.*

6 SERVINGS

- 1 x 5 lb. boiling chicken with giblets
- 6 pints [15 cups] water
- 1 large onion, chopped
- rind of 1 lemon
- 1 teaspoon salt
- $2\frac{1}{2}$ oz. [$\frac{1}{2}$ cup] long-grain rice
- 2 tablespoons lemon juice

Low Cal

Put the chicken and giblets in a large saucepan. Pour on the water and place the pan over high heat. Bring the water to the boil. As the scum rises to the surface, skim it off with a slotted spoon. When all the scum has been removed, add the onion, lemon rind and salt. Reduce the heat to moderately low, so that the liquid is just simmering. Partially cover the saucepan, leaving enough space for the steam to escape. Leave the chicken to cook for 3 to 3½ hours.

Let the chicken cool in the liquid. Remove the chicken from the pan. Wrap it in aluminium foil and refrigerate. Strain the stock into a bowl, cover and refrigerate. When the stock is quite cold, remove the fat which has congealed on the surface.

Put the stock into a medium-sized saucepan and bring it to the boil over moderate heat. Add the rice. Cover the pan and simmer for 15 minutes or until the rice is cooked.

Take the chicken from the refrigerator. Remove the skin and discard. Remove all the white meat and chop it into small pieces. Keep the dark meat for another meal and discard the bones.

Add the chicken meat and lemon juice to the soup in the pan. Simmer for about 10 minutes, or until the chicken is heated through. Pour into a large soup tureen or individual bowls and serve.

Pasta stuffed with meat and spinach in tomato and cream sauces, Cannelloni di Manzo e Spinace is a tasty dish.

Cannelloni

ITALIAN PASTA

Cannelloni (kahn-nel-Oh-nee) *are large squares of Italian pasta made from flour and eggs and cooked in boiling salted water, then stuffed with a variety of mixtures, rolled up and browned in the oven. Sometimes they are baked with butter and sprinkled with Parmesan cheese or, as in Tuscany, they are covered with a sauce and baked until the top is golden brown.*

8 OZ. CANNELLONI

- 8 oz. [2 cups] flour
- ¼ teaspoon salt
- 3 eggs

Sift the flour and salt into a medium-sized mixing bowl. Add the eggs. Using your hands mix the flour and eggs together and form them into a ball.

Place the ball of dough on a floured board and knead it for 10 minutes until it is smooth, but stiff. If necessary, add more flour to obtain the essential stiffness.

Divide the dough into four pieces and roll out each piece into a very thin sheet. Leave the dough sheets, covered with a cloth, for at least 30 minutes.

With a sharp knife, cut the dough into 4-inch by 3-inch rectangles and use as required.

Cannelloni can also be bought ready made from most delicatessen shops.

Cannelloni con Pollo e Prosciutto

ITALIAN PASTA FILLED WITH CHICKEN AND PROSCIUTTO

This mouth-watering mixture of chicken breasts, livers and prosciutto, Cannelloni con Pollo e Prosciutto (kah-nel-oh-nee kohn poh-loh ee proh-shoo-to) *is not only a delicious dish but a very convenient one too, since the pasta and filling may be prepared well in advance.*

6 SERVINGS

- 6 oz. [¾ cup] butter
- 2 whole chicken breasts, boned
- 3 chicken livers

5 slices prosciutto
3 oz. [$\frac{3}{4}$ cup] Parmesan cheese, grated
$4\frac{1}{2}$ tablespoons flour
1 pint [$2\frac{1}{2}$ cups] milk, scalded (heated to just under boiling point.)
5 fl. oz. single cream [$\frac{5}{8}$ cup light cream]
$\frac{1}{2}$ teaspoon salt
$\frac{1}{4}$ teaspoon white pepper
8 oz. home-made or bought cannelloni

In a large, deep frying-pan, melt 4 tablespoons of the butter over moderate heat. Add the chicken breasts to the pan and fry them for 4 to 5 minutes, or until they are lightly browned on both sides.

With a slotted spoon, transfer the chicken breasts to a bowl.

Add the chicken livers to the pan and fry them for 1 to 2 minutes on each side. With the slotted spoon, transfer the chicken livers to the bowl containing the chicken breasts.

With a food mincer [grinder], mince [grind] the chicken breasts, livers and prosciutto together or chop them finely with a sharp knife. Add 1 ounce [$\frac{1}{4}$ cup] of the Parmesan to the minced [ground] meat and mix well together with a fork.

In a medium-sized saucepan, melt another 4 tablespoons of the butter over moderate heat. With a wooden spoon, stir the flour into the butter and cook, stirring, for 2 minutes. Remove the pan from the heat and gradually stir in the milk. Return the pan to the heat and cook, stirring constantly, until the sauce thickens.

Remove the pan from the heat and add the cream, salt and pepper.

Add about one-quarter of the sauce to the meat-and-cheese mixture in the bowl and mix well together. Set the rest of the sauce aside.

In a large saucepan, bring 3 to 4 pints [$2\frac{1}{2}$ quarts] of water to the boil over high heat. Drop the cannelloni into the boiling water and cook them for 6 to 15 minutes, depending on the thickness of the pasta, or until the pasta is tender. With a slotted spoon, remove the pasta from the pan and place it on a dampened cloth to drain.

Preheat the oven to fairly hot 375°F (Gas Mark 5, 190°C). Using 1 tablespoon of the butter, lightly grease a large baking dish.

Spread about 2 tablespoons of the meat-and-cheese mixture on each pasta square. Fold the pasta over the filling to make a roll.

Place the cannelloni in either one or two layers, placing the join side downwards, in the buttered baking dish. Sprinkle each layer with the remaining Parmesan cheese and cover with the reserved sauce.

Dot the top of the dish with small pieces of the remaining butter and place the dish in the oven. Bake for 30 minutes, or until the sauce-covered cannelloni is lightly browned.

Cannelloni di Manzo e Spinace

ITALIAN PASTA FILLED WITH A SAVOURY MEAT AND SPINACH MIXTURE BAKED IN TOMATO AND CREAM SAUCES

A famous Italian dish, Cannelloni di Manzo e Spinace (kahn-nel-OH-nee dee MAHN-zoh ee spin-AH-cheh) *is economical and very tasty.*

4 SERVINGS

TOMATO SAUCE
2 tablespoons olive oil
1 small onion, finely chopped
14 oz. canned, peeled Italian tomatoes, undrained
$2\frac{1}{2}$ oz. canned tomato purée
$\frac{1}{2}$ tablespoon finely chopped fresh basil or $\frac{1}{2}$ teaspoon dried basil
$\frac{1}{2}$ teaspoon dried oregano
1 teaspoon sugar
$\frac{1}{2}$ teaspoon salt
$\frac{1}{2}$ teaspoon freshly ground black pepper

FILLING
$1\frac{1}{2}$ tablespoons olive oil
1 tablespoon butter
1 small onion, finely chopped
2 garlic cloves, finely chopped
8 oz. lean minced [ground] beef
6 oz. fresh spinach, cooked, drained, squeezed and finely chopped or a small packet frozen chopped spinach (thawed)
1 oz. [4 tablespoons] Parmesan cheese, grated
$1\frac{1}{2}$ tablespoons double [heavy] cream
1 egg
$\frac{1}{2}$ teaspoon dried oregano
$\frac{1}{4}$ teaspoon salt
$\frac{1}{4}$ teaspoon black pepper

CREAM SAUCE
2 tablespoons butter
4 tablespoons flour
5 fl. oz. [$\frac{5}{8}$ cup] plus 2 tablespoons milk, warmed
3 tablespoons double [heavy] cream
$\frac{1}{4}$ teaspoon salt
$\frac{1}{8}$ teaspoon white pepper

PASTA
1 teaspoon salt
8 oz. bought or home-made cannelloni, cut into rectangles 3 inches by 4 inches
3 oz. [$\frac{3}{4}$ cup] Parmesan cheese, grated
1 tablespoon butter, cut into small pieces

To make the tomato sauce, in a medium-sized saucepan heat the oil over moderate heat. Add the onion and fry it for about 7 minutes, or until it is soft but not brown. Stir in the tomatoes, the tomato purée, basil, oregano, sugar, salt and pepper. Reduce the heat to low, cover the pan and simmer the sauce for about 40 minutes, stirring occasionally.

Remove the pan from the heat and set aside.

To make the filling, in a large frying-pan heat the oil and butter over moderate heat. Add the onion and garlic and fry, stirring occasionally, for 7 minutes, or until they are soft but not coloured. Add the meat. Cook for 10 minutes or until the meat is brown, stirring occasionally. Add the spinach, and, stirring, cook for 3 to 4 minutes or until all the moisture has evaporated.

Transfer the meat and spinach mixture to a medium-sized bowl. Add the Parmesan, cream, egg, oregano, salt and pepper. Mix well with a spoon and set aside.

Prepare the cream sauce. In a small, saucepan melt the butter over moderate heat. Remove the pan from the heat and, with a wooden spoon, stir in the flour. Gradually stir in 5 fluid ounces [$\frac{5}{8}$ cup] of the milk and cream.

Return the pan to the heat. Cook, stirring constantly, until the sauce comes to the boil. The sauce will be very thick. Remove the pan from the heat and add the salt and pepper. Pour the 2 tablespoons of milk over the top of the sauce to prevent a skin forming and set the pan aside.

Preheat the oven to fairly hot 375°F (Gas Mark 5, 190°C).

In a large saucepan, bring 3 to 4 pints [$2\frac{1}{2}$ quarts] of water to the boil over high heat. Add the teaspoon of salt with the cannelloni pieces and cook them for 6 to 15 minutes or until the cannelloni is tender. With a slotted spoon, remove the pasta from the pan and place it on a dampened cloth to drain.

When the cannelloni is cool enough to handle, place a tablespoonful of the filling in the centre of each pasta rectangle and roll them up.

Pour a thin layer of tomato sauce into the bottom of a large shallow ovenproof dish. Place the cannelloni in tne dish in a single or double layer.

Stir the milk into the cream sauce and spoon over the cannelloni. Pour the remaining tomato sauce over the top.

Sprinkle with the Parmesan cheese and dot with the tablespoon of butter.

Place the dish in the oven and bake the cannelloni for 30 minutes, or until the sauce is bubbling and the cheese has melted.

Serve immediately from the dish.

Cantaloup

This is a variety of melon which, it is believed, was first grown in Europe in the seventeenth century at Cantalupo, near Rome. A cantaloup is round with a rough, ribbed warty skin. The flesh, which can vary in colour from deep orange to pinkish-yellow to a pale green, is sweet, juicy and of excellent flavour.

Cantaloup Surprise

A simple, refreshing dessert, Cantaloup Surprise may be prepared in advance and makes a particularly exquisite end to a rich meal. It may be made with any variety of musk melon, such as cantaloup, charentais, honeydew or ogen.

A simple, refreshing dessert, Cantaloup Surprise is prepared here with a South African ogen melon.

4 SERVINGS

- 1 medium-sized cantaloup
- 10 oz. fresh or frozen and thawed strawberries
- 5 tablespoons sugar
- 4 tablespoons sherry

Low Cal

With a sharp knife, cut off the top of the cantaloup. Scoop out the seeds. Using a large spoon, carefully remove the melon flesh until only a fairly thin shell remains. Chop and reserve the flesh. Dry the shell with kitchen paper towels.

In a medium-sized mixing bowl, combine two-thirds of the strawberries with 4 tablespoons of the sugar and the sherry, mixing them well with a spoon to make sure the fruit is well coated with the sherry and sugar. Spoon the strawberry mixture into the melon shell and add enough of the melon flesh to completely fill the shell. Set aside.

Put the remaining strawberries on a plate and sprinkle with the remaining sugar. Arrange them decoratively on top of the cantaloup. Chill in the refrigerator for at least 30 minutes before serving.

Cantonese Roast Pork

This is a popular Cantonese dish of roast marinated pork glazed with honey. It is traditionally eaten with rice, mustard and a soy-chilli dip, which is made of 8 tablespoons of soy sauce mixed with 4 tablespoons chilli sauce.

4 SERVINGS

- 2 lb. pork fillet
- 2 tablespoons vegetable oil
- 2½ tablespoons clear honey

MARINADE

- 4 tablespoons soy sauce
- 1 tablespoon sugar
- 3 tablespoons dry sherry
- 4 grindings black pepper
- ½ teaspoon cinnamon
- 2 garlic cloves, crushed
- ½ teaspoon salt
- ½ teaspoon monosodium glutamate (optional)
- ¼ teaspoon dried rosemary
- ¼ teaspoon dried marjoram

With a sharp knife, cut the pork fillet along the grain into strips about 6 inches long and 1 inch wide.

In a large shallow bowl, combine the soy sauce, sugar, sherry, pepper, cinnamon, garlic, salt, monosodium glutamate (if used), rosemary and marjoram. Mix the marinade with a fork.

Place the pork in the bowl and leave it to marinate for 3 hours. Turn the pork strips every 20 minutes.

Preheat the oven to hot 425°F (Gas Mark 7, 220°C).

Put enough water in a roasting tin to make a 1-inch layer on the bottom. Place a wire rack in the tin.

With a slotted spoon, transfer the pork from the marinade to the rack in the roasting tin. Reserve the marinade.

Place the tin in the oven and roast the pork for 12 minutes.

Mix the oil into the reserved marinade.

Remove the pork from the oven and, using a pastry brush, brush the strips with the marinade-and-oil mixture.

Reduce the oven heat to moderate 350°F (Gas Mark 4, 180°C).

Return the pork to the oven and roast for a further 10 minutes.

Brush the pork strips with the honey and roast for 5 minutes longer.

Remove the pork from the oven and cut the strips crosswise into ½-inch slices.

Place the pork in a warmed serving dish and serve at once.

An exotic summer dish, Cape Cod Salad is marinated lobster stuffed with celery and pineapple.

Cape Cod Salad

Lobster with pineapple and celery, Cape Cod Salad is an exotic summer dish. It may be served as part of a cold buffet or as a starter.

4 SERVINGS

MARINADE
- 2 garlic cloves, crushed
- ½ teaspoon salt
- 6 grindings black pepper
- ½ teaspoon prepared mustard
- ¼ teaspoon sugar
- 1 tablespoon red wine vinegar
- 3 tablespoons olive oil

LOBSTER
- 1 x 2 lb. lobster, cooked
- 2 tablespoons mayonnaise
- ½ teaspoon soy sauce
- 4 grindings black pepper
- ½ teaspoon cayenne pepper
- 4 oz. [½ cup] fresh pineapple, diced
- 2 celery stalks, chopped
- 1 lettuce, washed and chilled
- ½ lemon, cut into slices

First prepare the marinade. In a medium-sized mixing bowl, combine the garlic, salt, pepper, mustard and sugar. With a wooden spoon or fork, stir in the vinegar until well blended. Gradually beat in the oil. Set aside.

Cut the soft undershell from the lobster body with scissors. Remove the meat and cut it into ¼-inch slices. Reserve the lobster body shell.

Crack the claws with a hammer or a nutcracker and remove the meat. Slice it and discard the claw shells.

If the marinade has separated, lightly beat it again with the fork. Toss the lobster slices in the marinade and refrigerate, covered, for about 45 minutes, stirring occasionally.

Remove the bowl from the refrigerator and drain the lobster meat, discarding the marinade.

In a large mixing bowl, beat together the mayonnaise, soy sauce, pepper, cayenne and pinch of salt with a wooden spoon. Add the lobster, pineapple and celery and mix well.

Pile the mixture into the reserved lobster shell.

Arrange the lettuce leaves on a large serving plate. Place the shell on the lettuce and garnish with the lemon slices.

Cape ai Ferri

GRILLED [BROILED] SCALLOPS

Scallops brushed with oil, grilled and served with hot garlic-flavoured butter sauce, Cape ai Ferri (KAHP-pee eye FAY-ree) *is a delicious Italian first course. Allow 3 to 4 scallops per person, depending on the size of the scallops and the richness of the course to follow.*

4 SERVINGS

- 12 to 16 scallops
- 2 tablespoons olive oil
- 4 oz. [½ cup] butter
- 2 garlic cloves, crushed
- ½ teaspoon salt
- 6 grindings black pepper
- 2 tablespoons chopped parsley
- 2 lemons, cut in quarters

Preheat the grill [broiler] to its highest setting.

Using a pastry brush, brush the scallops with 2 tablespoons oil. Place the scallops under the grill [broiler] and grill [broil] for 3 to 4 minutes on both sides.

Transfer the scallops to a warmed serving dish. Meanwhile prepare the sauce. In a small saucepan, melt the butter over moderate heat. Mix in the garlic, salt and pepper.

When the sauce is hot, remove the pan from the heat and pour the butter mixture over the scallops. Garnish the scallops with the parsley and lemon wedges and serve at once.

Cape Gooseberry

The cape gooseberry is a small, yellow-green tropical fruit, in size and shape similar to the common gooseberry. It is covered by a pale brown, crinkly, paper-thin husk, and contains many small seeds. It is sometimes known as the husk tomato. The fruit grows well in tropical and sub-tropical countries, and was originally native to Brazil. Its name derives from the Cape in South Africa where it is grown extensively.

It is also grown in Northern India and commercially in southern France, where it is known as physalis.

The cape gooseberry's pleasant and distinctive flavour makes it suitable for cooking in compôtes, sauces, jams, jellies and pies, or for eating raw as a dessert fruit.

Caper

This is the floral bud of the caper-bush, a shrub native to southern Europe, where it grows wild. It is also cultivated in France. Capers are pickled in vinegar, and are used to flavour a sauce which in England is a traditional accompaniment to boiled mutton. They are also used in antipasto, or added to mayonnaise and salad dressings. Good capers are olive green in colour, firm, and have a piece of stalk still attached to them. The best capers are from the French areas of Var and Bouches-des-Rhône, and are known as *nonesuch* capers.

Caper sauce

Quick and easy to prepare, this creamy sauce with a slightly piquant flavour is a traditional accompaniment to boiled mutton, but it goes equally well with boiled chicken. This sauce may also be served with boiled beef but use beef stock and leave out the cream.

15 FLUID OUNCES

- 2 tablespoons butter
- 4 tablespoons flour
- 16 fl. oz. [2 cups] chicken stock or stock made with a chicken stock cube, warmed
- 2 teaspoons vinegar
- $\frac{1}{2}$ teaspoon prepared mustard
- $\frac{1}{2}$ teaspoon salt
- $\frac{1}{4}$ teaspoon white pepper
- $1\frac{1}{2}$ tablespoons capers
- $1\frac{1}{2}$ tablespoons single [light] cream

In a medium-sized saucepan, melt the butter over moderate heat. With a wooden spoon, stir the flour into the butter and cook, stirring, for 1 minute.

Remove the pan from the heat and gradually stir in the stock. Add the vinegar, mustard, salt, pepper and capers.

Return the pan to the heat and cook, stirring constantly, until the sauce comes to the boil. Reduce the heat to low and gently simmer the sauce for 5 minutes.

Remove the pan from the heat and stir in the cream. Pour the sauce into a warmed sauceboat and serve at once.

Capercaillie

A capercaillie is a large game bird, also known as capercailzie, wood grouse, or cock-o'-the-wood, which is generally found in Scotland. The bird feeds on young shoots of pine trees, which gives the flesh a fairly strong flavour.

Capercaillie are drawn as soon as they are shot, and then hung for at least a week. If preferred, they can be hung longer as this improves their tenderness. Some connoisseurs think they are at their best when high, and even recommend that they be hung until only the breast remains edible.

A very young hen bird is best for roasting. It should be larded well with bacon and cooked in a fairly hot oven 400°F (Gas Mark 6, 200°C) for $\frac{1}{2}$ to $\frac{3}{4}$ hour, and basted frequently during cooking.

Capillaire

Capillaire is a flavouring syrup for punches and cocktails, originally made by boiling maidenhair fern in sweetened water. The name *capillaire* is derived from the French for this fern. The syrup can also be made from water, sugar, eggs, and orange-flower water, lemon essence, or bitter almonds.

Capon

A capon is a castrated cockerel, specially reared for the table and killed at 6 to 10 months old. The idea of caponizing cockerels originated in Ancient Rome, when a law was passed prohibiting the fattening and killing of hens for the table, lest they become extinct. The law did not mention cocks, and cooks took advantage of this loophole by castrating cocks and fattening these instead of hens.

There is more flesh on a capon than on any other type of bird. The fat is marbled and distributed throughout the flesh rather than in pockets, as with other fowl. The bird can be cooked and served in any way suitable for chicken and turkey. They generally weigh between 6 and 10 lb.

Hens are also caponized, and these are called *poulardes,* which is French for 'fat hen'.

If a recipe requires a boned capon, most large butcher's shops will do this, providing they are given plenty of notice.

Capon, Russian-Style

The decoration on this Russian-style capon may look very intricate, but in fact it is not difficult to do. The capon should be accompanied by home-made mayonnaise and a potato and onion salad.

4 – 6 SERVINGS

- 3 slices stale white bread, crusts removed
- 6 fl. oz. [$\frac{3}{4}$ cup] milk
- 6 oz. minced [ground] veal
- $1\frac{1}{2}$ oz. [3 tablespoons] butter, melted
- $\frac{1}{4}$ teaspoon grated nutmeg
- $1\frac{1}{2}$ teaspoons salt
- 6 grindings black pepper
- 1 egg, lightly beaten
- 3 celery stalks, chopped
- 1 x 6 to 7 lb. capon, boned and ready for stuffing (bones and giblets reserved)
- 3 carrots, scraped and chopped
- 1 onion, halved
- 2 parsley sprigs
- 1 bay leaf
- 8 peppercorns
- 1 oz. gelatine dissolved in 2 tablespoons water
- 3 tablespoons dry sherry

DECORATION

- thin strips of cucumber peel
- black olives, stoned
- cucumber pieces and slices
- tomato quarters
- watercress

In a medium-sized mixing bowl, cover the bread with the milk and leave it to soak for 2 minutes. With your hands, squeeze the excess milk out of the bread. Pour off the excess milk and return the bread to the bowl.

Add the veal, melted butter, nutmeg, $\frac{1}{2}$ teaspoon salt and the pepper to the bread and, with a fork, mix well together.

Stir the beaten egg and 1 of the chopped celery stalks into the mixture. Lay the capon with the skin side downwards on the working surface. With your hands, put the mixture into the centre of the capon. Push the legs inside out so that the shape of the capon meat is square. Tuck the wings in too. Fold the ends in first and then the sides. Sew up the join with a trussing needle and thread, or secure with a skewer.

Tie the capon neatly in a clean piece of cheesecloth. Place it in a large saucepan and pour in enough water to come more than halfway up the bird. Add the reserved bones and giblets (excluding the liver), the carrots, the remaining celery, onion, parsley, bay leaf, remaining salt and peppercorns.

Place the pan over high heat and bring the water to the boil. Reduce the heat to low, cover the pan and simmer for about 2 to $2\frac{1}{2}$ hours, or until the capon is tender.

Remove the pan from the heat. Lift the capon out of the pan and put it on a plate. Tighten and adjust the cheesecloth and put another plate and

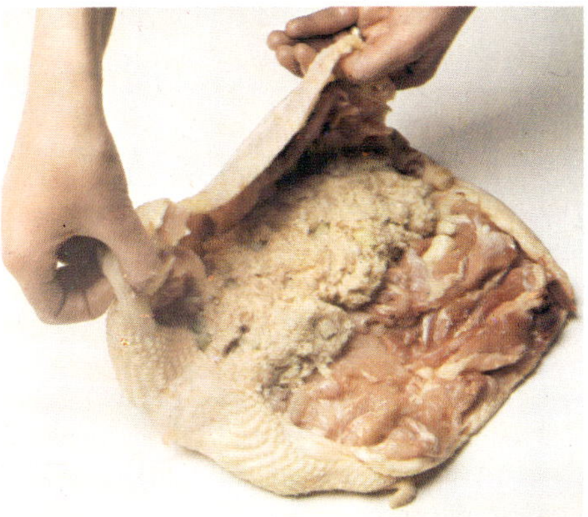

For Capon, Russian-Style, push the stuffing into the centre of the capon. Fold the ends and sides in.

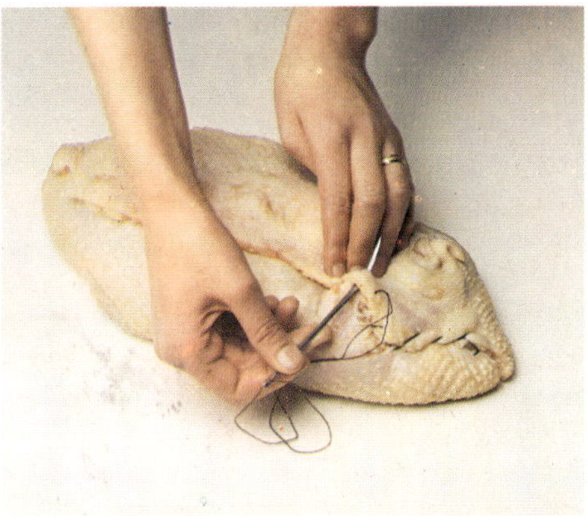

Sew up the join with a trussing needle and thread or secure it firmly with a skewer.

Neatly tie the stuffed capon in a clean piece of cheesecloth and place it in a large saucepan.

a 4-pound weight on top. Leave the capon for 12 hours or overnight in a cold place or in the refrigerator.

Strain the stock into a bowl. Cover the bowl and place it in the refrigerator until you are ready to use it.

Five hours before serving remove the stock from the refrigerator. Skim off the fat and measure the stock. There should be about 1 pint [$2\frac{1}{2}$ cups]. Put the stock in a saucepan and bring it to the boil over moderate heat. Add the dissolved gelatine to the hot stock. Stir well to mix in the gelatine and leave the stock to cool to lukewarm. Stir in the sherry.

Meanwhile remove the weighted plate from the capon and snip off the cheesecloth. Place the capon on a wire rack over a baking tray.

When the stock is on the point of setting, spoon a little over the capon. Arrange the cucumber peel, black olives and small pieces of cucumber, to resemble a flower, on the top. Place in the refrigerator to set.

Carefully re-heat the remaining stock and spoon over the decoration. Return the capon, with the tray, to the refrigerator and leave until set.

Place the capon on a serving dish. Chop the jellied stock on the tray and spoon it on to the dish with the cucumber slices, the tomato quarters and the sprigs of watercress.

Caponata

AUBERGINES [EGGPLANT] IN SWEET AND SOUR SAUCE

A tangy vegetable dish, Caponata may be served as an appetizer to a dinner or as an extra-special accompaniment to cold roasted meat. It is important that a good quality vinegar be used, otherwise the blend of flavours will not be so delicate. Caponata can be stored in the refrigerator for up to 2 weeks.

4 TO 6 SERVINGS

4 small aubergines [eggplant]
2 teaspoons salt
4 fl. oz. [$\frac{1}{2}$ cup] olive oil
4 celery stalks, finely sliced
2 large onions, thinly sliced
4 oz. canned tomato purée diluted in 2 fl. oz. [$\frac{1}{4}$ cup] water
1 tablespoon capers
2 oz. green olives, stoned and chopped
3 fl. oz. [$\frac{3}{8}$ cup] red wine vinegar
1 tablespoon sugar

Peel and dice the aubergines [eggplant]. Sprinkle them with the salt and leave them for about 45 minutes to extract as much liquid as possible. Rinse the aubergines [eggplant] with cold water, drain them in a colander and pat them dry with kitchen paper towels.

In a large frying-pan, heat 3 fluid ounces [$\frac{3}{8}$ cup] of oil over moderate heat. Add the diced aubergine [eggplant] and cook for 8 to 10 minutes, or until soft and brown. With a slotted spoon, remove them from the pan and leave them to drain in a colander. Dry them slightly on kitchen paper towels and set aside.

Pour the remaining oil into the frying-pan and add the celery and onions. Cook them for 8 minutes, or until they are lightly coloured. Pour in the tomato purée mixture and stir to coat the vegetables. Reduce the heat to low and simmer the mixture, covered, for 15 minutes.

Cappelletti in Brodo is a nourishing and filling chicken soup with small pieces of stuffed pasta.

Stir in the capers, olives, vinegar and sugar, mixing until all the ingredients are blended. Return the aubergine [eggplant] to the pan and coat thoroughly with the sauce. Cook the mixture over low heat for 20 minutes.

Remove the caponata from the heat and transfer it to a serving dish. Chill in the refrigerator for at least 2 hours, or until you are ready to serve.

Cappelletti in Brodo

STUFFED PASTA IN BROTH

This nourishing and easy-to-make Italian soup makes a satisfying first course. Cappelletti in Brodo (kahp-ell-Ett-tee in BROH-doh) *accompanied by a large mixed salad and bread also makes an excellent meal.*

10 SERVINGS

- 15 oz. [$3\frac{3}{4}$ cups] **flour**
- 3 **eggs**
- 2 **tablespoons butter**
- 8 **oz. lean pork fillet, minced** [ground]
- 4 **oz. cooked chicken breast, minced** [ground]
- 2 **oz. Mortadella sausage, minced** [ground]
- 1 **oz. Parma ham, minced** [ground]
- 5 **oz.** [$1\frac{1}{4}$ cups] **Parmesan cheese, grated**
- 1 **egg yolk, lightly beaten**
- 1 **teaspoon ground mace**
- $\frac{1}{2}$ **teaspoon salt**
- 6 **grindings black pepper**
- 4 **pints** [$2\frac{1}{2}$ quarts] **chicken stock**

Place 13 ounces [$3\frac{1}{4}$ cups] of flour on a large board or marble slab and make a well in the centre. Put the eggs one by one into the well and, using your fingers, blend the ingredients together to form a dough.

Sprinkle the dough with a little of the remaining flour and knead it for 10 minutes, or until the dough is soft, sprinkling a little more flour on the dough from time to time. Place the dough in a floured bowl, cover the bowl and leave it in a cool place for at least 20 minutes or until ready to use.

Melt the butter in a large frying-pan over moderate heat. Add the pork and, stirring continuously, cook for 25 to 30 minutes or until the pork is well cooked. Add the chicken, Mortadella sausage and Parma ham and cook for 2 minutes more.

Remove the pan from the heat and stir in 3 ounces [$\frac{3}{4}$ cup] of the grated Parmesan cheese, the egg yolk, mace, salt and pepper, blending the ingredients well. Set aside.

On a lightly floured board or marble slab, roll out the dough until it is paper thin. Cut the dough into circles, approximately 2-inches in diameter.

Place $\frac{3}{4}$ teaspoon of the meat mixture on each piece of dough, slightly to one side. Fold the dough over the meat to form a semi-circle. Seal the edges by pressing them firmly together with your fingertips. Now fold the semi-circle around your finger so that the two ends meet and overlap slightly. Press the ends firmly together.

In a very large saucepan, bring the chicken stock to the boil over moderate heat. Reduce the heat to low, add the cappelletti and simmer, uncovered, for 10 to 12 minutes. Serve immediately.

The remaining Parmesan cheese should be passed around in a separate bowl to be sprinkled on top of the cappelletti.

Capsicum is the family name for a wide range of large and small peppers.

Capsicum

Capsicum, meaning 'little case' in Latin, is the family name for a wide range of peppers, large and small. Capsicums were originally South American plants, but were introduced into Hungary in the sixteenth century, and are now closely associated with Hungarian cooking.

Bell peppers are large, varying in colour between red, yellow and green, and in strength from sweetish to hot and pungent. Other peppers can be red or green, long or round, and can differ greatly in size. Depending on their degree of strength, they can be used as vegetables, or simply for flavouring.

Carafe

A carafe is a container filled with wine for the table. Carafe wine generally means a cheap local wine, or in a restaurant the 'house' wine—usually a *vin ordinaire* that is bought in bulk and which is less expensive than a bottled wine.

Caramel

Caramel is a sugar syrup cooked over high heat until it is a light brown colour. It is used for flavouring, coating moulds for Crème Caramel and as a topping for cakes. To make Caramel Syrup, add another 2 tablespoons of water after the caramel is made. Do not let the caramel become too brown or it will be bitter.

2 FLUID OUNCES

- 4 **oz.** [$\frac{1}{2}$ cup] **granulated or lump sugar**
- 2 **fl. oz.** [$\frac{1}{4}$ cup] **water**

Put the sugar and water into a saucepan and place it over low heat. Stir the mixture with a metal spoon until the sugar dissolves. Then increase the heat to high and boil the syrup for 5 to 6 minutes or until it becomes a rich brown colour. Remove the pan from the heat and use the caramel immediately.

Alternatively, using castor sugar and omitting the water, cook the sugar in the pan, over moderately low heat. Do not stir the sugar until it begins to colour and then stir carefully. This method will take slightly longer but the result will be identical.

LINING A MOULD WITH CARAMEL

If a metal mould is used, the caramel can be made in the mould itself.

As soon as the caramel changes colour, remove the mould from the heat and tilt and rotate the mould so that the inside is evenly coated with caramel.

If a china mould is used, the caramel should be made in a saucepan. While the caramel is cooking, warm the mould in hot water. Dry the mould thoroughly and pour the caramel into it, tilting and rotating the mould so that the inside is evenly coated.

Caramel Apricots

This unusual dessert, which is so easy to prepare, may be made at any time of year, using either fresh or canned apricots. Any fruit may be substituted for apricots, particularly peaches, pears or apples, which have been lightly poached, or bananas. Be sure the apricots are very ripe and soft.

4 SERVINGS

- **1 lb. fresh or canned and drained apricots**
- **2 oz.** [$\frac{1}{3}$ cup] **almonds, blanched and toasted**
- **10 fl. oz. double cream** [$1\frac{1}{4}$ cups heavy cream]
- **4 oz.** [$\frac{5}{8}$ cup] **soft brown sugar**

If the apricots are fresh, prepare them by washing, halving and stoning [pitting]. Crack the kernels and extract the nuts. Arrange the apricots in the bottom of a flameproof serving dish. Sprinkle the top of the apricots with apricot nuts and the toasted almonds.

In a medium-sized mixing bowl, whip the cream with a wire whisk or rotary beater until it is stiff. Spoon the cream on top of the nuts and, with a knife, spread it over evenly. Place the dish in the refrigerator to chill for 2 hours.

Five minutes before serving, preheat the grill [broiler] to high. Sprinkle the top of the cream with the sugar in a thick layer. Place the dish under the grill [broiler] and cook it for 3 minutes or until the sugar melts and forms a crust. Remove the dish from the heat and serve at once.

Caramel Icing

This sweet, light brown icing may be spread on a vanilla sponge cake or buns. For a more decorative effect, the iced cake may be sprinkled with chopped almonds, walnuts or hazelnuts.

ENOUGH FOR AN 8—10-INCH CAKE

- **12 oz.** [2 cups] **brown sugar**
- **8 to 10 fl. oz. single cream** [1 to $1\frac{1}{4}$ cups light cream]
- **$1\frac{1}{2}$ oz.** [3 tablespoons] **butter**
- **1 teaspoon vanilla essence**

In a medium-sized saucepan, dissolve the sugar in 8 fluid ounces [1 cup] of cream over low heat, stirring constantly with a wooden spoon. When the sugar is completely dissolved, increase the heat to moderate, cover the pan and cook the syrup for 2 minutes.

Uncover the pan and continue cooking the syrup, without stirring, until it reaches 240°F on a sugar thermometer (the soft ball stage).

Add the butter to the syrup and stir it until it melts.

Remove the pan from the heat and blend in the vanilla essence. Beat the icing with a wooden spoon until it becomes thick and creamy.

If the icing becomes too thick to spread, add a little extra cream to thin it.

Spread the warm icing over the cake and leave it to cool and set before serving.

Caramels

Home-made sweets can be a lot of fun to make and they are, of course, much cheaper than the shop bought ones. Caramels are among the easiest of all sweets to make and they may be flavoured as you choose – with chocolates, coffee or maple syrup. For a really professional look, wrap the caramels in waxed paper.

50 CARAMELS

- **4 oz.** [$\frac{1}{2}$ cup] **plus 1 teaspoon butter**
- **8 oz.** [$1\frac{1}{4}$ cups] **soft brown sugar**
- **3 tablespoons water**
- **$\frac{1}{2}$ teaspoon vanilla essence**
- **3 tablespoons single** [light] **cream**

Using the teaspoon of butter, lightly grease a large shallow square or rectangular baking pan.

In a medium-sized saucepan, dissolve the brown sugar in the water over moderate heat, stirring constantly with a metal spoon. Add the remaining butter, the vanilla essence and the cream to the pan and boil the mixture, without stirring, until it reaches 250°F on a sugar thermometer. If you do not have a thermometer, test by removing a teaspoonful of the mixture from the pan and dropping it into a cup of cold water. If the mixture immediately forms a ball, the correct temperature has been reached.

Remove the pan from the heat and pour the caramel into the buttered pan. Set the pan aside to allow the caramel to cool.

When the caramel is cold, use a sharp knife to cut it into squares. Remove the squares from the pan and keep them in an airtight container until you are ready to eat them.

Caramel Sauce

Caramel Sauce is delicious with ice-cream. It may be kept in the refrigerator for 1 to 2 weeks, so it is useful to have as a standby to serve with cold desserts.

4 SERVINGS

- **6 oz.** [$\frac{3}{4}$ cup] **sugar**
- **3 tablespoons water**
- **4 fl. oz. double cream** [$\frac{1}{2}$ cup heavy cream]
- **$\frac{1}{2}$ teaspoon vanilla essence**

Combine the sugar with the water in a heavy-based saucepan over low heat, stirring until the sugar dissolves. Increase the heat to moderately high, and boil rapidly until the syrup is a light brown colour. Lower the heat and continue boiling until it is light brown. Remove the pan from the heat and cool.

Stir in the cream and vanilla essence, mixing well until all the ingredients are thoroughly blended. Chill.

Note: If you would prefer to serve this sauce hot, warm the blended syrup, cream and vanilla essence gently in a double saucepan or in a small bowl placed over a saucepan of boiling water. Do not let the syrup come to the boil after adding the cream.

Caraway Knots

Caraway Knots are both decorative and tasty. The caraway seeds are sprinkled over the top just before baking, which gives them a deliciously savoury flavour. They can be served warm or cold with butter or cheese, ideal for a picnic or an informal farmhouse-style lunch.

20 KNOTS

- **2 oz.** [$\frac{1}{4}$ cup] **butter**
- **18 fl. oz.** [$2\frac{1}{4}$ cups] **milk**
- **2 lb.** [8 cups] **strong flour**
- **$\frac{1}{4}$ teaspoon salt**
- **1 tablespoon sugar**
- **1 sachet easy-blend dried yeast**
- **2 tablespoons caraway seeds**
- **1 egg, beaten**
- **a little extra oil for greasing**

GLAZING AND DECORATING

- **a little lightly beaten egg**
- **$\frac{1}{2}$ oz.** [1 tablespoon] **caraway seeds**

Melt the butter, add the milk and set aside until the mixture cools to lukewarm.

Stir the flour, salt and sugar into a large mixing bowl; stir in the yeast and caraway seeds.

Make a well in the centre and pour in all the milk mixture and the egg. Using a wooden spoon, your hands or a dough hook, gradually incorporate the flour into the liquid and knead until smooth and elastic and no longer sticky – about 10 minutes by hand or 2 minutes if you are

For Caraway Knots, form the ropes of dough into a loop, with crossed ends.

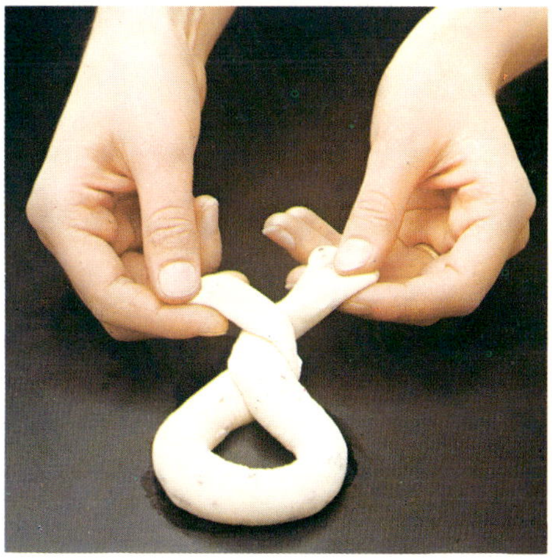

Make a twist at the base of the loop and spread the tips apart.

Bring the loop over to the tips and pinch them to the loop.

using the dough hook on a food processor.

Place the dough in a clean, oiled, large mixing bowl and cover with oiled polythene. Put in a warm place and leave to rise for 1-1½ hours or until the dough has doubled in size.

Lightly grease several baking [cookie] sheets.

Turn the dough out on to a lightly floured surface and knead with your hands for 1-2 minutes or until smooth.

Shape the dough into a 12-inch long roll and cut into 20 equal pieces. Roll each piece into a thin rope about 14 inches long. Shape each rope by forming into a loop and crossing the ends over. Make a twist at the base of the loop and spread the tips apart. Bring the loop over to the tips and pinch them firmly on to it (see Steps) and leave to rise on the baking sheets for 20-30 minutes, until doubled in size.

Preheat the oven to fairly hot 400°C (Gas Mark 6, 200°C).

Glaze the knots with the beaten egg and sprinkle them with caraway seeds. Bake for 15-20 minutes or until they are golden brown and sound hollow when tapped on the bottom.

Serve warm or cold with butter or cheese.

Caraway Seed

This spice, which has been used for thousands of years, grows wild in Europe (including Britain), Turkey, Persia and North Africa, and has become naturalized in North America. It is cultivated in Holland, Russia, the Balkans and other parts of Europe, but not in Britain.

Caraway seed is an aid to digestion, and is therefore traditionally included in dishes which tend to cause indigestion.

The root of the caraway is cooked and eaten as a vegetable in some parts of Europe, but the seed is most commonly used. Caraway seed is used in cakes and biscuits in Austrian and German cooking, and in cheese, bread and pastries. The Hungarians add it to goulashes, and it is also cooked with sauerkraut, cabbage and potato dishes. An aromatic oil can be obtained from the seeds, which is used to flavour drinks such as kummel, anisette, and schnapps, and it is also used medicinally.

Caraway Seed Biscuits

These simple, savoury biscuits are ideal for packed lunches with cheese and fruit.

ABOUT 50 SMALL BISCUITS

2 oz. [$\frac{1}{4}$ cup] plus 1 teaspoon butter
4 oz. [1 cup] plus 1 teaspoon flour
$\frac{1}{8}$ teaspoon salt
1 small egg
1 tablespoon water
4 teaspoons caraway seeds
$\frac{1}{2}$ egg yolk, lightly beaten

Preheat the oven to fairly hot 375°F (Gas Mark 5, 190°C). Lightly grease a baking sheet with the teaspoon of butter. Sprinkle over the teaspoon of flour and tip and rotate the sheet to distribute the flour evenly. Shake off any excess flour.

Sift the remaining flour and salt into a medium-sized mixing bowl. Add the remaining butter and, with a table knife, cut it into the flour until the butter is in small pieces. With your fingertips, rub the butter into the flour until the mixture resembles fine breadcrumbs. Add the egg, water and 3 teaspoons of the caraway seeds. Mix with your fingers to a stiff dough. Wrap the dough in greaseproof or waxed paper and place it in the refrigerator to chill for 1 hour.

On a lightly floured surface, roll out the dough to a rectangle about $\frac{1}{4}$-inch thick. With a pastry cutter or a sharp knife, cut it into small squares, strips, rounds or decorative shapes. Place them on the baking sheet. With a pastry brush, coat them with the beaten egg yolk and sprinkle them with the remaining caraway seeds.

Bake the biscuits in the oven for 20 minutes or until they are firm and golden. Remove the baking sheet from the oven and transfer the biscuits to a wire rack to cool. When they are completely cold, store them in an airtight tin.

Caraway Seed Sponge Cake

The caraway seeds in this popular, traditional British cake give it a distinctive flavour.

ONE 7-INCH CAKE

2 oz. [$\frac{1}{4}$ cup] butter, softened
$\frac{1}{2}$ teaspoon lemon flavouring
2 tablespoons water
3 egg yolks, lightly beaten
3 egg whites
5 oz. [$\frac{5}{8}$ cup] sugar
1 teaspoon baking powder
$\frac{1}{2}$ teaspoon salt
1 teaspoon ground mace
2 teaspoons caraway seeds
6 oz. [$1\frac{1}{2}$ cups] flour

Preheat the oven to fairly hot 400°F (Gas Mark 6, 200°C). Grease a 7-inch cake tin with 1 teaspoon of the softened butter and set aside.

In a large mixing bowl, combine the remaining butter, the lemon flavouring, water and the egg yolks. With a wooden spoon, beat well until the ingredients are blended.

In a medium-sized mixing bowl, beat the egg whites with a wire whisk or rotary beater until they form stiff peaks. Add the sugar and continue whisking for 1 minute. With a metal spoon, carefully fold the egg whites into the mixture.

In a medium-sized mixing bowl, combine the baking powder, salt, mace, caraway seeds and flour together. Gradually fold the flour mixture into the butter-and-egg mixture.

Pour the mixture into the greased cake tin and place the tin in the oven. Bake for about 35 minutes, in the centre of the oven, or until a skewer inserted into the centre of the cake comes out clean.

Remove the cake from the oven and turn it out on to a wire rack to cool.

Carbohydrates

Carbohydrates, composed of carbon, hydrogen and oxygen, are one of the major nutrients which we obtain from our food. Some types of carbohydrate cannot be digested by the body but play a useful role as roughage or dietary fibre. The carbohydrates which are digested are boken down to produce glucose which the body uses for energy.

Sugars are one group of carbohydrates, such as *lactose* which is found in milk, *fructose* as sugar in fruits, *glucose* and *sucrose* which are normally called 'sugar'. Sucrose and foods containing it, such as sweets [candies], preserves, soft drinks and instant puddings, tend to be eaten in over-indulgent amounts in our society. This often results in tooth decay and probably contributes to problems of overweight. Sugar is also a source of 'empty calories' and may displace other more nutritious foods. Nutritionists are generally agreed that we should strictly limit the amount of sugar (sucrose) we and our children consume.

The other major class of carbohydrates are the starches, which are present in flour (plus bread and pasta), rice, potatoes, corn and other cereals. Starches are broken down more slowly than simple sugars and so tend to be more sustaining.

Starch-containing foods, particularly if they are unrefined like wholemeal flour and wholegrain rice, are also good sources of protein, minerals, vitamins and fibre. These nutritious foods are usually relatively inexpensive and should be included in generous quantities in the daily diet. Contrary to popular opinion, these foods are unlikely to cause obesity unless combined with fats and sugars, such as in chips [French fries], pastries and cakes.

	Grams per Ounce
FLOUR PRODUCTS AND CEREALS	
Biscuits (plain)	21.4
Bread (brown)	14.2
Bread (White)	14.9
Cornflakes	25.2
Cornflour [cornstarch]	26.2
Flour	20.8
Macaroni (boiled)	7.2
Rice	24.6
Semolina	22.0
Spaghetti	23.9
FRUIT	
Apricots (dried)	12.3
Apricots (canned)	7.9
Bananas (fresh)	5.5
Currants (dried)	18.0
Dates (dried)	18.1
Fruit salad (canned)	7.1
Mandarins (canned)	4.7
Peaches (dried)	15.0
Peaches (canned)	6.5
Pears (canned)	5.7
Pineapple (canned)	5.7
Prunes	11.4
Raisins	18.3
Sultanas	18.4
VEGETABLES	
Beans (canned)	4.9
Beans - haricot (dried)	12.9
Lentils (boiled)	5.2
Peas (canned, processed)	5.4
Potatoes (boiled)	5.6
SUGARS, SWEETS AND JAMS	
Sugar	29.7
Golden Syrup	22.4
Treacle [molasses]	19.1
Jam	19.6
Honey	21.7
Chocolate - plain	14.9
Chocolate - milk	15.5

Carbon Dioxide

A gas formed by the union of one atom of carbon with two atoms of oxygen, carbon dioxide is released in large quantities during alcoholic fermentation, caused by the reaction of yeast with sugar. Carbon dioxide is the gas which forms the froth on beer, cider and sparkling wines. In the making of bread, the fermentation involved in the rising of the dough causes carbon dioxide to be given off, and it is this that puffs up the bread and makes it light.

Carbon dioxide is soluble in water, when it forms carbonic acid, which is found in many mineral waters. When the gas is introduced under pressure into ordinary water, it forms soda water.

Carbonnade

A French culinary term originally used to describe meat grilled [broiled] over hot coals, carbonnade today describes a dish of stewed or braised meat with beer and is one of the best known Flemish dishes.

Carbonnade à la Flamande

FLEMISH BEEF STEW WITH BEER

A beef stew made with beer, Carbonnade à la Flamande (kahr-bon-nahd ah lah flah-mond) *is one of Belgium's classic dishes. It is best served with buttered noodles and plenty of ice cold beer.*

4 SERVINGS

2 oz. [½ cup] flour
1 teaspoon salt
¼ teaspoon freshly ground black pepper
2 lb. chuck steak, cut into 1-inch cubes
4 tablespoons vegetable oil
6 medium-sized onions, thinly sliced
2 garlic cloves, chopped
18 fl. oz. [2¼ cups] canned or bottled beer
1 tablespoon brown sugar
bouquet garni, consisting of 4 parsley sprigs, 1 thyme spray and 1 bay leaf tied together

A classic beef stew with beer, Carbonnade à la Flamande is delicious served with noodles and ice-cold beer.

Sift the flour, salt and pepper into a small mixing bowl. Roll the cubes of meat in the seasoned flour until they are well coated.

In a flameproof casserole heat the oil over moderate heat. Add the meat cubes to the casserole a few at a time and brown them on all sides. As the meat cubes brown remove them with a slotted spoon and set them aside on a plate.

When all the meat cubes have been browned, add the onions and garlic to the pan and fry them for 8 to 10 minutes or until the onions are soft and translucent but not brown. Add more oil if necessary. Return the meat to the casserole and add the beer, sugar and bouquet garni.

Cover the casserole, reduce the heat to low and simmer the stew gently for about 2 hours, or until the meat is tender when pierced with a skewer. After $1\frac{1}{2}$ hours cooking, remove the lid and simmer the stew uncovered for the remaining 30 minutes. This will reduce the liquid slightly. Remove the casserole from the heat, remove and discard the bouquet garni and serve.

Carbonnade de Boeuf à la Provençale

CASSEROLE OF BEEF WITH GARLIC

Spicier and more highly seasoned than Carbonnades à la Flamande, the Carbonnade de Boeuf à la Provençale (kahr-bon-nahd de berf ah lah proh-von-sahl) *is an equally delicious dish. The basis of the carbonnade is its marinade, and the longer the meat is left in it the spicier it will become. If you prefer, the meat can be left to marinate overnight in the refrigerator.*

6 SERVINGS

3 lb. chuck steak, cut into $\frac{1}{2}$-inch cubes
2 fl. oz. [$\frac{1}{4}$ cup] olive oil
2 medium-sized onions, sliced
2 garlic cloves, chopped
3 tomatoes, blanched, peeled, seeded and chopped
1 lb. potatoes, peeled and sliced
8 fl. oz. [1 cup] beef stock
$\frac{1}{2}$ teaspoon salt
6 grindings black pepper
2 oz. [$\frac{1}{2}$ cup] Parmesan cheese, grated

MARINADE

4 fl. oz. [$\frac{1}{2}$ cup] red wine vinegar
3 garlic cloves, finely chopped
1 medium-sized onion, coarsely chopped
1 bay leaf
1 teaspoon thyme
1 tablespoon chopped parsley
1 teaspoon salt
6 grindings black pepper

To make the marinade, in a large, fairly shallow dish, combine the vinegar, chopped garlic, chopped onion, bay leaf, thyme, parsley, salt and pepper. Add the beef cubes to the marinade and, with a large serving spoon, turn the meat over in the marinade to coat it well. Set the dish aside and leave the meat to marinate for at least 8 hours at room temperature, basting the meat from time to time.

In a frying-pan, heat the olive oil over moderate heat. When the oil is hot, reduce the heat to low and add the sliced onions and garlic. Cover the pan (with aluminium foil if the pan does not have a closely fitting lid), and simmer the onions and garlic gently for 10 minutes, stirring occasionally to prevent the onions from sticking to the bottom of the pan.

Preheat the oven to moderate 350°F (Gas Mark 4, 180°C).

Using a slotted spoon, remove the meat from the marinade. Discard the marinade.

In a large, deep, flameproof casserole, lay the meat, cooked onion-and-garlic mixture, chopped tomatoes and potatoes alternately in layers, starting with the meat and ending with a layer of potatoes. Pour in enough beef stock so that the top layer is just covered. Season with the salt and pepper. Put the casserole over high heat and bring the liquid to the boil. When the mixture is bubbling, cover the pot and transfer it to the centre of the oven. Bake for 2 hours.

Raise the oven temperature to fairly hot 400°F (Gas Mark 6, 200°C). Baste the meat and potato mixture with 1 to 2 spoonfuls of the cooking liquid and sprinkle the grated Parmesan cheese over the potato slices.

Continue baking, uncovered, for 45 minutes. Remove the casserole from the oven and serve immediately.

Carcass

A carcass is the bone structure of an animal. In France the term is used particularly to describe that of a fowl. Butchers speaking of a sheep's carcass mean the drawn and trimmed body of the slaughtered animal.

Cardamom

The cardamom plant, a member of the ginger family, originated in India. The aromatic seeds are called 'Seeds of Paradise' in the Orient, and have a cool but pungent flavour. They are used in flavouring pullaos and biryanis, in curry powder blends and in other forms of Indian cooking. In Scandinavia, Germany and Russia, cardamom seeds are incorporated in liqueurs, cakes, biscuits [cookies] and pastries.

Cardamom seeds are very hard and have to be crushed before being used - this can be done with a wooden spoon. A teaspoonful may be added to a pastry mixture before the liquid is added. Cardamom may be used in gingerbread, coffee cake, fruit dishes or in rice pudding. A few crushed seeds may be handed with sugar for black coffee.

The seeds lose their flavour quickly once they have been crushed. They should, therefore, be bought in the pod and crushed only just before they are to be used. Jars of ground cardamom can also be bought.

Cardamom Biscuits [Cookies]

Cardamom Biscuits [Cookies] *are Scandinavian in origin and are traditionally made during the Christmas season. They can be stored for several weeks in an airtight container and, in fact, their flavour improves with keeping.*

48 BISCUITS [COOKIES]

6 oz. [$\frac{3}{4}$ cup] butter
8 oz. [$1\frac{1}{4}$ cups] light brown sugar
1 egg, lightly beaten
2 fl. oz. single cream [$\frac{1}{4}$ cup light cream]
$\frac{1}{2}$ teaspoon almond essence
1 lb. [4 cups] flour
1 teaspoon baking powder
2 teaspoons freshly ground cardamom
1 tablespoon margarine

In a large mixing bowl, cream the butter and sugar together with a wooden spoon until the mixture is light and fluffy. Add the egg, cream and almond essence and beat until the ingredients are well blended.

In a separate bowl, sift together the flour, baking powder and ground cardamom. Add the flour mixture, a little at a time, to the butter mixture, beating vigorously with a wooden spoon until a stiff dough is formed. Using your hands, knead the dough until it is smooth.

Roll the dough into two sausage shapes about 2-inches in diameter.

Wrap the dough in greaseproof or waxed paper and place it in the refrigerator. Chill the dough for at least 5 to 6 hours or, if possible, overnight. The dough should be well chilled before it is baked.

Preheat the oven to fairly hot 400°F (Gas Mark 6, 200°C). Lightly grease a baking sheet with the margarine.

Take the dough out of the refrigerator and unwrap it. Cut and shape the dough into $\frac{1}{4}$-inch thick circles. Place the circles on the sheet, leaving about a $\frac{1}{4}$-inch space between each circle.

Bake the biscuits [cookies] in the middle of the oven for about 12 minutes, or until they start to brown.

Cool the biscuits [cookies] on a wire rack and store in an airtight container.

Cardamom Cake

A fragrant cake from Sweden, Cardamom Cake makes winter's days seem brighter, especially when accompanied by a drink of hot glogg. If possible, grind the cardamom seeds yourself.

ONE 7-INCH CAKE

1 teaspoon butter or margarine
2 teaspoons flour
7 oz. [1¾ cups] self-raising flour
1 teaspoon freshly ground cardamom
4 oz. [½ cup] sugar
4 oz. [1 cup] mixed candied peel, finely chopped
2 eggs
4 oz. [½ cup] butter or margarine melted
2 tablespoons icing [confectioners'] sugar [optional]

Preheat the oven to moderate 350°F (Gas Mark 4, 180°C). Grease a 7-inch cake tin with the 1 teaspoon of butter or margarine and dust it with the 2 teaspoons of flour, shaking out the excess. Set the greased cake tin aside.

Sift the self-raising flour, cardamom and sugar into a large mixing bowl. Add the candied peel and set the bowl aside.

In a medium-sized bowl, beat the eggs until they are frothy. Add the melted butter or margarine, and mix well together. Pour this mixture into the flour mixture a little at a time, stirring constantly until all the ingredients are blended, and the batter is of a dropping consistency. If the batter is too thick, add a little milk.

Pour the cake batter into the prepared tin and bake in the middle of the oven for 45 minutes, or until the cake is cooked. Test by inserting a skewer into the centre of the cake. If the skewer comes out clean and dry, the cake is cooked.

Remove the tin from the oven and turn the cake out on to a wire rack. Cool the cake completely. If you like, sprinkle the top of the cake with icing [confectioners'] sugar.

These Scandinavian Cardamom Biscuits [Cookies] and Cake are delicious served with tea or coffee.

Cardamom Honey Dressing

This nourishing and unusual dressing may be served with fresh fruit salad and melon or with waffles or pancakes. Use a blender or beat by hand with a wire whisk or rotary beater.

11 FLUID OUNCES

½ teaspoon cardamom seeds
10 fl. oz. [1¼ cups] clear honey
2 tablespoons lemon juice
¼ teaspoon orange-flower water

Place the cardamom on a sheet of greaseproof or waxed paper and fold the paper over the cardamom, so that it is completely enclosed. With the back of a wooden spoon, coarsely crush the cardamom seeds.

In a blender, blend the honey at high speed until it is light in colour. Gradually add the lemon juice and orange-flower water to the honey, and then stir in the crushed cardamom. Pour the dressing into a screw-top jar and use it as required.

Cardoon

A plant of the same family as the artichoke or thistle, the cardoon is a flavourful vegetable. The leaves are cooked in the same way as spinach, the leaf-ribs (called 'beet-chard') like asparagus, and the main root is boiled and served cold, often in salads. The cardoon root is prepared by first being cooked in a white vegetable stock and then simmered in a sauce. In the United States, the cardoon is sometimes known as chard.

Carmine

A bright red colouring, carmine is derived from cochineal and is used to colour various kinds of foods, particularly confectionery. Carmine is a bright red whereas cochineal is a bluish-red.

Carob

Also known as the Locust Bean, Locust Seed or St. John's Bread, carob is the fruit of a Mediterranean shrub. It is much used in the Near East and in Chinese cooking. The whole pod, which is rather sweet and insipid in flavour, is used in dishes or made into a syrup. It is rich in protein and in sugar.

The 'locusts' which St. John the Baptist is said to have eaten were these fruits, and not the insects, as is generally believed. It is through this misunderstanding that the plant's alternative names arose.

Carp in White Wine

Carp in White Wine is a simple, quickly made way to serve this delicious fish. For a special occasion, a glass of Chablis or Pouilly Fumé goes with it extremely well.

6 SERVINGS

2 celery stalks, chopped
1 cucumber, peeled and chopped
1 tablespoon chopped parsley
10 peppercorns
½ teaspoon dried dill
1 garlic clove, crushed
2 bay leaves
⅛ teaspoon ground mace
2 teaspoons salt
3 lb. carp, filleted and cut into 6 steaks
16 fl. oz. [2 cups] dry white wine
12 fl. oz. [1½ cups] water
3 oz. [⅜ cup] butter
3 tablespoons flour

In a large saucepan or flameproof casserole put the celery, cucumber, parsley, peppercorns, dill, garlic, bay leaves, mace and salt and place the carp steaks on top. Pour over the wine and water. The fish should be just covered with liquid, so add more wine or water if necessary.

Place the pan over moderate heat. Bring the liquid to simmering point and reduce the heat to low. Cover the pan and simmer the fish for 20 minutes or until it is tender.

Carefully transfer the carp to a warmed serving dish and cover it with aluminium foil. Strain the liquid from the fish and reserve it. Discard the vegetables and flavourings.

In a medium-sized saucepan, melt the butter over low heat. Remove the pan from the heat and, with a wooden spoon, stir in the flour, mixing to a smooth paste (roux).

A superb dinner party dish, Carpe Mâtelote is carp braised with vegetables and a red wine sauce.

Gradually add the strained cooking liquid to the roux, stirring constantly with a wooden spoon. Return the pan to moderate heat. Continue cooking and stirring the sauce for about 5 minutes, or until it becomes thick and smooth.

Pour the sauce over the carp and serve immediately.

Carpe Matelote

CARP WITH A RED WINE SAUCE

Braised carp served with a red wine sauce makes this fish dish a special treat. Glazed onions and pastry crescents are traditional accompaniments to Carpe Matelote (kahrp maht-loht).

4 SERVINGS

2 oz. [¼ cup] butter
2 onions, sliced
2 carrots, scraped and sliced
2 celery stalks, sliced
bouquet garni, consisting of 4 parsley sprigs, 1 thyme spray and 1 bay leaf tied together

2 garlic cloves, crushed
6 peppercorns
$2\frac{1}{2}$ to 3 lb. carp, cleaned
4 fl. oz. [$\frac{1}{2}$ cup] dry red wine
3 tablespoons red wine vinegar
4 tablespoons Beurre Noir, hot

SAUCE

2 tablespoons butter
1 large onion, finely chopped
3 oz. mushrooms, wiped and chopped
12 fl. oz. [$1\frac{1}{2}$ cups] dry red wine
bouquet garni, consisting of 4 parsley sprigs, 1 thyme spray and 1 bay leaf tied together
2 tablespoons beurre manié
$\frac{1}{4}$ teaspoon salt
4 grindings black pepper

Preheat the oven to cool 300°F (Gas Mark 2, 150°C).

In a fish kettle melt the butter over low heat. Add the onions, carrots and celery. Cover the kettle and cook the vegetables for 5 minutes.

Add the bouquet garni, garlic and peppercorns to the vegetables. Place the carp on top. Pour the wine and vinegar over the fish and cover it with a sheet of well-buttered greaseproof paper or aluminium foil. Bring the liquid to a simmer over moderate heat.

Cover the kettle and place it in the oven to bake for 1 hour. Using a bulb baster or large spoon, occasionally baste the carp.

Meanwhile prepare the sauce. In a medium-sized saucepan melt the butter over moderately high heat. Add the onion and fry it for 5 to 6 minutes, or until it is lightly browned. Add the mushrooms to the pan and cook for 2 to 3 minutes. Shake the pan to coat the mushrooms thoroughly with the butter. Pour in the wine and add the bouquet garni. Bring the liquid to the boil and cook the sauce until it has reduced by half.

Remove and discard the bouquet garni. Slowly add the beurre manié to the sauce, stirring constantly. Stir in the salt and pepper. Remove the pan from the heat and pour the sauce into a warmed sauceboat.

Transfer the carp from the fish kettle to a warmed serving dish. Discard the cooking liquid and vegetables. Pour the beurre noir over the carp and serve it with the sauce.

Carotene

A chemical substance which is converted to Vitamin A in the body, carotene is a yellow or orange pigment which takes its name from carrots, as they contain considerable amounts of it. Carotene is also in other vegetables, as well as fruit, butter, eggs, fish and meat.

Carottes à L'Algérienne

CARROTS ALGERIAN-STYLE

A spicy and unusual way to serve carrots, Carottes à l'Algérienne (kah-roht ah laht jayr-yen) *is equally delicious hot or cold. Serve it with boiled beef, or roasted pork or lamb.*

4 SERVINGS

2 lb. carrots, scraped and cut into $\frac{1}{2}$-inch slices
5 tablespoons olive oil
1 teaspoon salt
$\frac{1}{2}$ teaspoon white pepper
$\frac{1}{2}$ teaspoon ground cinnamon
$\frac{1}{2}$ teaspoon cumin seeds
3 garlic cloves, finely chopped
$\frac{1}{2}$ teaspoon dried thyme
1 bay leaf
1 teaspoon lemon juice

Low Cal

Put the carrot slices into a medium-sized saucepan. Add enough water just to cover the carrots and bring it to the boil over moderate heat. Cover the pan and cook the carrots for 15 minutes, or until they are firm but tender when pierced with a skewer. Using a slotted spoon, remove the carrots from the pan and transfer them to a bowl. Reserve 5 fluid ounces [$\frac{5}{8}$ cup] of the cooking liquid.

In a medium-sized saucepan, mix together the oil, salt, pepper, cinnamon, cumin seeds, garlic and thyme over very low heat. Simmer for 10 minutes. Add the reserved cooking liquid and the bay leaf, cover the pan and simmer for a further 15 to 20 minutes.

Add the carrots to the saucepan. Toss them in the sauce and cook for 2 to 3 minutes to heat the carrots thoroughly. Sprinkle over the lemon juice, remove the bay leaf and serve immediately if the dish is to be eaten hot.

Carrots with cumin, cinnamon, thyme and garlic, Carottes à l'Algérienne is a spicy and unusual vegetable dish.

Carottes aux Champignons

CARROTS WITH MUSHROOMS

An unusual and delicious way of serving carrots, Carottes aux Champignons (kah-roht oh shom-peen-yon) *is a combination of carrots and mushrooms tossed together in a buttery sauce.*

4 SERVINGS

1 lb. carrots, scraped and sliced
½ teaspoon salt
10 fl. oz. [1¼ cups] water
1 tablespoon sugar
2 oz. [¼ cup] butter
4 oz. mushrooms, wiped and quartered
1 tablespoon finely chopped onion

In a medium-sized saucepan place the carrots, salt, water, sugar and 2 tablespoons of the butter over moderate heat. Bring the water to the boil and cover the pan. Reduce the heat to low and simmer the carrots for about 30 minutes, or until they are tender and most of the liquid has been absorbed.

While the carrots are cooking, prepare the mushrooms.

In a small frying-pan melt the remaining butter over moderate heat. Add the mushrooms and fry them gently for about 5 minutes, or until they are softened. Mix in the onions with a wooden spoon and cook gently for another 3 to 4 minutes.

Add the mushroom mixture to the carrots. Taste and add more salt and pepper if necessary. Turn into a hot serving dish and serve immediately.

Carottes à la Crème

BRAISED CARROTS IN BUTTER AND CREAM SAUCE

A simple yet elegantly rich dish, Carottes à la Crème (Kah-rot a lah krem) *makes a wonderful accompaniment to steaks.*

4 SERVINGS

1 lb. carrots, scraped and sliced
½ teaspoon salt
10 fl. oz. [1¼ cups] water
1 tablespoon sugar
1 tablespoon butter
10 fl. oz. single cream [1¼ cups light cream]
1 tablespoon chopped parsley

Put the carrots and salt in a medium-sized saucepan. Pour over the water and add the sugar and butter. Cover and cook slowly over low heat for 15 minutes.

Remove the pan from the heat and slowly add the cream stirring constantly. Return the pan to the heat and simmer for a further 15 minutes or until the carrots are tender.

Turn into a hot serving dish and sprinkle with the chopped parsley.

Carottes Glacées

GLAZED CARROTS

Carottes Glacées (kah-roht glah-say) *are cooked slowly in water and sugar. As the water reduces, the carrots become glazed and syrupy.*

4 SERVINGS

1 lb. carrots, scraped and cut into ½ inch slices
8 fl. oz. [1 cup] water
1 tablespoon sugar
1 tablespoon butter
1 teaspoon salt
1 tablespoon chopped parsley

Put the carrots in a medium-sized saucepan with the water, sugar, butter and salt. Cover the pan and cook over low heat for about 30 minutes, or until the carrots are tender and a small amount of thick rich syrup remains.

Turn into a hot serving dish. Sprinkle with the parsley and serve.

Carottes à la Neige

BAKED PUREED CARROTS

A smooth, light vegetable dish, Carottes à la Neige (kah-roht a lah nehj) *is ideal for a formal dinner party. It goes well with fish or chicken.*

4 SERVINGS

1 teaspoon butter
1 pint [2½ cups] chicken stock
1 lb. carrots, scraped and quartered
½ teaspoon salt
¼ teaspoon white pepper
1 teaspoon marjoram
1 teaspoon flour
3 egg yolks, lightly beaten
3 egg whites

Lightly grease a shallow baking dish with the butter. Set aside.

In a large saucepan, bring the stock to the boil over high heat. Add the carrots to the pan and reduce the heat to moderate. Cook the carrots for 10 to 15 minutes, or until they are tender.

Preheat the oven to moderate 350°F (Gas Mark 4, 180°C).

Remove the pan from the heat. With a slotted spoon, transfer the carrots to a strainer, food mill or blender. Purée the carrots and transfer them to a medium-sized mixing bowl. Alternatively, mash the carrots with a potato masher in the mixing bowl.

Season the carrot purée with the salt and pepper and stir in the marjoram and flour. Add 1 to 2 tablespoons of the stock in which the carrots were cooked and blend well. Stir the egg yolks into the purée.

In another mixing bowl, beat the egg whites with a wire whisk until they form stiff peaks. With a rubber spatula or metal spoon carefully fold the egg whites into the carrot mixture.

Turn the mixture into the buttered baking dish and place it in the oven. Bake for 15 minutes.

Remove the dish from the oven and serve at once.

Carottes aux Raisins

CARROTS AND ONIONS WITH RAISINS IN WINE SAUCE

A fascinating and exotic-tasting blend of vegetables and herbs, Carottes aux Raisins (kah-roht oh ray-zan) *makes a most impressive accompaniment to a meat entrée at a dinner party.*

4 SERVINGS

2 oz. [¼ cup] butter
1 lb. carrots, scraped and cut into 1-inch slices
8 oz. small white onions, peeled and left whole
4 oz. [¾ cup] large seedless raisins
1 teaspoon salt
1 teaspoon freshly ground black pepper
½ teaspoon cayenne pepper
1 teaspoon dried thyme
1 bay leaf
4 fl. oz. [½ cup] medium-dry white wine
2 fl. oz. double cream [¼ cup heavy cream]

In a large saucepan melt the butter over moderate heat. Add the carrots, onions and raisins. Stirring constantly, cook them for 3 to 4 minutes to brown them slightly. Add the salt, pepper, cayenne, thyme and bay leaf to the pan. Pour in the wine, mixing well to blend. Cover the pan, reduce the heat to very low and simmer for 45 to 50 minutes, or until the carrots and onions are tender but still firm.

Remove the pan from the heat and take out the bay leaf. Stir in the cream. Return the pan to very low heat for 1 to 2 minutes to warm the sauce slightly. Turn into a warmed vegetable dish and serve immediately.

Carottes aux Raisins is an aromatic dish of vegetables and herbs in white wine and cream.

Carottes Vichy

This method of preparing carrots preserves their full flavour and colour. Carottes Vichy (kah-roht vee shee) *is a simple but delicious accompaniment to any meat dish.*

4 SERVINGS

- **2 oz. [$\frac{1}{4}$ cup] butter**
- **2 lb. young carrots, scraped and thinly sliced**
- **1 teaspoon sugar**
- **1 teaspoon salt**
- **4 grindings black pepper**
- **1 tablespoon chopped parsley**

In a large frying-pan melt the butter over moderate heat. Add the carrots, sugar, salt and pepper. Cook gently for 10 to 12 minutes, or until the carrots are tender but still crisp. Stir occasionally but take care not to break the carrots. Shake the pan gently to coat the carrots with the cooking liquid.

When the carrots are ready, turn them into a warmed serving dish and sprinkle the parsley on top.

Carp

A freshwater fish, carp is thought to have originated in China. It was introduced to Europe in the seventeenth century and to North America in the nineteenth. The best season for eating carp is from November to the end of March.

All carp must be carefully cleaned, and the spleen, which lies behind the head, should be removed. The fish should be washed in several changes of clean water, and finally in water and lemon juice – these repeated washings are necessary to remove a muddy taste which the fish often has. If the fish is to be poached it is unnecessary to scale it, as the whole skin is easily removed after cooking. Otherwise, the fish must be scaled.

The roe of the carp is a delicacy and can be cooked in butter and served separately.

Both the North Germans and the Poles traditionally eat carp on Christmas Eve. In Germany it is the custom not to scale the fish, however it is cooked, so that each person can take a scale from his portion to keep for good luck in the next year!

Carp with Black Sauce

Carp served with a mouth-watering prune, walnut and raisin sauce, this Czech dinner party dish is impressive, yet surprisingly easy to prepare. Boiled new potatoes and a cucumber salad will complement the carp beautifully.

6 SERVINGS

- **8 fl. oz. [1 cup] white wine vinegar**
- **$1\frac{1}{2}$ pints [$3\frac{3}{4}$ cups] water**
- **4 fl. oz. [$\frac{1}{2}$ cup] beer**
- **2 medium-sized onions, sliced**
- **2 celery stalks, finely chopped**
- **2 small carrots, scraped and finely chopped**
- **1 garlic clove, crushed**
- **2 bay leaves**
- **6 cloves**
- **1 teaspoon ground allspice**
- **6 peppercorns**
- **1 teaspoon ground cumin**
- **1 x 4 lb. carp, cut into 6 cutlets and soaked for 1 hour in cold water**

BLACK SAUCE

- **1 tablespoon butter**
- **6 oz. [1 cup] cooked prunes, stoned and coarsely chopped**
- **juice and grated rind of 1 lemon**
- **2 oz. [$\frac{1}{3}$ cup] seedless raisins**
- **2 oz. [$\frac{1}{2}$ cup] walnuts, finely chopped**
- **1 tablespoon brown sugar**

Place the vinegar, water, beer, onions, celery, carrots, garlic, bay leaves, cloves, allspice, peppercorns and cumin in a large deep saucepan over moderate heat. Bring the liquid to the boil, reduce the heat to low and simmer the liquid and vegetables for 30 minutes.

Add the carp to the pan, cover it and simmer over low heat for 30 minutes, or until the fish flakes easily when pierced with a fork.

While the fish is cooking, make the sauce. In a medium-sized saucepan, melt the butter over moderate heat. Add the prunes, lemon juice and grated rind, raisins, walnuts and sugar to the pan. With a wooden spoon, stir to mix the ingredients well.

With a slotted spoon remove the fish, and place it on a warmed serving dish. Strain the cooking liquid, pressing down hard on the vegetables with the back of a wooden spoon. Reserve about 16 fluid ounces [2 cups] of the liquid and discard the vegetables.

Add the drained fish liquid to the prune mixture and simmer it over low heat for 5 minutes. Remove the pan from the heat and pour the sauce over the fish.

Carpetbag Steak

Steak stuffed with oysters, Carpetbag Steak is a famous and delicious Australian recipe. It may be served with a green salad.

4 SERVINGS

1½ to 2 lb. rump or fillet steak, in one piece, cut about 2-inches thick
12 fresh oysters or 8 oz. canned oysters, drained
¼ teaspoon salt
⅛ teaspoon freshly ground black pepper
¼ teaspoon cayenne pepper
1 tablespoon melted butter
1 bunch watercress, washed

Preheat the grill [broiler] to high.

With a small, sharp knife slit the steak lengthways to form a pocket. Fill the pocket with the oysters. Sprinkle the

salt, pepper and cayenne on to the oysters.

Using a trussing needle and strong thread or fine string, tightly sew up the opening.

Place the steak under the grill [broiler] and brush the top with melted butter. Grill [broil] for 5 to 6 minutes on each side brushing the underside with melted butter when it is turned. Reduce the heat to moderate and continue cooking for 8 to 10 minutes on each side, depending on whether you like your steak rare, medium or well done.

Remove the string or thread and place the steak on a warmed serving dish. Garnish with watercress and serve at once.

Carrageen Moss

Also known as carragheen or Irish moss, carrageen moss is a dark purple or green edible seaweed, used in most parts of Ireland and gathered on the rocks at low tide. It is also common on coasts in Northern Europe and North America.

When bleached and dried, carrageen will keep for years, and is used as a substitute for gelatine, being sold commercially as a thickening agent. In Northern Ireland, carrageen is mixed with hot milk to serve as a nightcap or made into a pudding, and it has also been claimed that carrageen will cure indigestion, coughs and colds.

Carré d'Agneau au Cidre

LAMB IN CIDER SAUCE

Carré d'Agneau au Cidre (kah-ray d'ahn-yoh oh see-dr') *is a tasty, easy to prepare family supper dish. Good vegetable accompaniments are croquette potatoes and green beans.*

4 SERVINGS

1 best end neck of lamb, in one piece consisting of 8 chops (carré)
$\frac{3}{4}$ teaspoon salt
6 grindings black pepper
1 garlic clove, halved
2 tablespoons olive oil
2 carrots, scraped and chopped
2 small turnips, peeled and quartered
2 leeks, white part only, washed and chopped
2 small onions, chopped
2 streaky bacon slices, chopped
1 teaspoon dried marjoram
10 fl. oz. [$1\frac{1}{4}$ cups] chicken stock
10 fl. oz. [$1\frac{1}{4}$ cups] cider
4 tablespoons fresh white breadcrumbs
2 oz. [$\frac{1}{4}$ cup] beurre manié
$\frac{1}{8}$ teaspoon white pepper

Preheat the oven to moderate 350°F (Gas Mark 4, 180°C).

Rub the lamb with $\frac{1}{2}$ teaspoon of the salt, the pepper and cut side of garlic.

In a large flameproof casserole, heat the oil over moderate heat. Place the meat in the pan and brown it for 3 minutes on each side.

Remove the meat from the casserole and set it aside.

Place the carrots, turnips, leeks, onions and bacon in the casserole and fry them for 10 minutes, stirring frequently.

Return the meat to the casserole and add the marjoram.

Pour in the stock and cider and bring the liquid to the boil. Cover the casserole and place it in the oven to cook for 1 hour.

Preheat the grill [broiler] to its highest setting.

Remove the casserole from the oven. Transfer the meat to the grill [broiler] pan. Generously coat the fat side of the meat with the breadcrumbs and place it under the grill [broiler] for 5 minutes, or until the crumbs are evenly browned.

Remove the meat from under the grill [broiler] and place it on a warmed serving dish.

Strain the cooking liquid from the casserole into a medium-sized saucepan. Discard the vegetables. Place the pan over moderate heat and stir in the beurre manié, in small pieces. Continue cooking and stirring for 5 minutes until the sauce thickens and is smooth. Add the remaining salt and the white pepper.

Pour the sauce into a warmed sauceboat to serve separately with the carré d' agneau.

A sensational dish for a dinner party, Carpetbag Steak is a famous Australian recipe of rump or fillet steak stuffed with oysters.

Carrot

The carrot is an herbaceous plant with a large, edible root. Native to the Afghanistan area, it is cultivated throughout the world as a vegetable. Carrot roots range from long and tapering to short and bulbous. Although white, yellow and purple carrots exist, the orange variety is the most popular. Carrots grow in cool to moderate temperatures and are thus available all year round. They are a rich source of Vitamin A and contain a good amount of sugar.

Though carrots are available all the year round, it is best to buy them when they are new. The older carrots sold during the winter months have coarser skins and, sometimes, woody cores which have to be removed. But no matter whether the carrots are old or new, they should not be peeled, as the flavour and vitamins are close to the skin. To remove the skin, scrape the carrots with a table knife or stiff scrubbing brush. If after cooking, the remaining skin looks unsightly, rub it off with your fingers. Old carrots are always used for flavouring stocks used in making soups and sauces. To cook carrots: wash and trim them and scrape well. Steam them whole, quartered or sliced. Whole young carrots will take about 30 minutes to steam and old carrots up to $1\frac{1}{2}$ hours. Boiling carrots in a small quantity of salted water will take half that time.

Carrot Cake

This unusual American Jewish cake is made with eggs, carrots and ground almonds. The finished cake has a moist consistency rather like cheesecake.

ONE 9-INCH CAKE

1 teaspoon butter
6 eggs, separated
8 oz. [1 cup] sugar
12 oz. carrots, cooked and puréed
1 tablespoon grated orange rind
1 tablespoon brandy
12 oz. [$1\frac{3}{4}$ cups] ground almonds

Preheat the oven to warm 325°F (Gas Mark 3, 170°C). With the butter, grease a 9-inch loose-bottomed cake tin.

Made with carrots, ground almonds and eggs, this unusual American Carrot Cake has a very moist consistency.

In a medium-sized bowl, beat the egg yolks with a wire whisk until they begin to thicken. Gradually add the sugar and continue beating until the mixture is thick and creamy. Add the carrot purée, orange rind, brandy and almonds and stir to mix thoroughly.

In a large bowl, beat the egg whites with a wire whisk or a rotary beater until they form stiff peaks. With a metal spoon or rubber spatula fold the egg whites into the carrot mixture.

Pour the mixture into the cake tin and bake in the centre of the oven for about 50 minutes, or until a skewer inserted into the centre of the cake comes out clean.

Remove the cake from the oven and leave it to cool in the tin for 15 minutes. Turn the cake out on to a wire rack.

Carrots with Onions

A subtle and delicious vegetable dish, Carrots with Onions is simple to make and is an excellent accompaniment to steak or liver.

6 SERVINGS

1 lb. carrots, scraped and sliced
1 lb. small white onions, peeled and left whole

1 bay leaf
1 pint [$2\frac{1}{2}$ cups] chicken stock
2 tablespoons butter
$\frac{1}{2}$ teaspoon salt
$\frac{1}{4}$ teaspoon black pepper
2 tablespoons chopped fresh parsley

In a medium-sized saucepan, cook the carrots, onions and bay leaf together in the chicken stock over moderate heat for 15 minutes, or until they are tender. Remove and discard the bay leaf. Drain the vegetables in a colander and discard the cooking liquid.

Return the carrots and onions to the saucepan. Add the butter, salt and pepper. Place the pan over low heat and toss the vegetables in the butter until they are well coated. Turn the vegetables into a serving dish.

Sprinkle with the chopped parsley and serve immediately.

Carrot and Radish salad

This is a Japanese salad, ideally made with Japanese radish, or daikon, *which is available at shops specializing in Eastern food. Serve it with any cold meat.*

4 SERVINGS

5 oz. carrots, scraped
10 oz. radishes, peeled
1 teaspoon salt
5 fl. oz. [$\frac{5}{8}$ cup] cider vinegar
2 tablespoons sugar
1 tablespoon soy sauce
$\frac{1}{2}$-inch piece of fresh root ginger, peeled and chopped
$\frac{1}{2}$ teaspoon monosodium glutamate (optional)

With a sharp knife, cut the carrots and radishes into long, thin strips and place them in a bowl. Sprinkle the strips with the salt and set them aside for 45 minutes.

Drain off the water that appears and dry the strips with kitchen paper towels. Transfer the carrots and radish strips to a salad bowl.

Put the vinegar, sugar, soy sauce, ginger and monosodium glutamate (if used) in a screw-top jar. Shake the jar to mix the ingredients well and pour the dressing over the vegetables. Toss gently and serve.

Carrot Soufflé

This superbly light Carrot Soufflé may be served with any roast meat or poached fish dish. Alternatively, it may be served sprinkled with Parmesan cheese, as an unusual slimmers' lunch dish, accompanied by a green salad.

4 SERVINGS

$\frac{3}{4}$ lb. carrots, diced into small pieces
1 oz. [2 tablespoons] butter, plus extra for greasing
$1\frac{1}{2}$ oz. [3 tablespoons] flour
10 fl. oz. [$1\frac{1}{4}$ cups] milk
2 oz. [$\frac{1}{2}$ cup] finely grated Cheddar cheese
4 egg yolks, lightly beaten
1 tableepoon freshly chopped parsley
$\frac{1}{4}$ teaspoon salt
$\frac{1}{4}$ teaspoon pepper
5 egg whites

Preheat the oven to fairly hot 400°F (Gas Mark 6, 200°C) and grease a $2\frac{1}{2}$-pint deep-sided soufflé dish or 4 individual dishes.

Boil the carrots until tender and then mash to a purée.

Melt the butter in a large saucepan, add the flour and cook gently for 2-3 minutes, stirring constantly.

Gradually add the milk and, when the sauce is smooth, add the carrot purée and then the cheese.

Remove the pan from the heat and beat in the egg yolks, add the parsley and the seasoning.

Whisk the egg whites until soft peaks form, then carefully fold into the sauce mixture with a large metal spoon or spatula.

Turn into the prepared dish and bake for 25 minutes or until the soufflé is puffed up and golden brown. Serve immediately.

Carrot Soup

Good quality, young carrots are necessary to provide a clear fresh colour and flavour for this soup. Carrot soup may be served plain, or with croûtons of bread, fried diced potatoes, or a spoonful of boiled rice.

4 SERVINGS

$1\frac{1}{2}$ oz. [3 tablespoons] butter
1 lb. carrots, scraped and coarsely grated
8 oz. potatoes, peeled and diced
1 small onion, finely chopped
$1\frac{1}{2}$ pints [$3\frac{3}{4}$ cups] chicken stock or water
$\frac{1}{2}$ teaspoon salt
$\frac{1}{2}$ teaspoon white pepper
2 tablespoons double [heavy] cream

In a medium-sized saucepan, melt the butter over moderate heat. Reduce the heat to low and add the carrots, potatoes and onion. Cook for 15 minutes, stirring occasionally with a wooden spoon to prevent the vegetables from sticking to the pan. Add the stock or water, salt and pepper and simmer for another 20 minutes, or until the vegetables are quite soft.

Remove the pan from the heat. Pour the contents of the pan through a strainer placed over a medium-sized mixing bowl. With a wooden spoon press the vegetables through the strainer, or put them through a blender.

Return the soup to the saucepan and reheat it. If the soup is too thin, simmer, uncovered, until the soup thickens. Stir in the cream, taste and add more salt and pepper if necessary. Serve in hot bowls.

Carte, à la

A French phrase, à la carte (ah lah kahrt) is used on restaurant menus to indicate dishes which may be ordered individually, as distinct from the *table d'hôte* set meal. It means literally, 'by the bill of fare'.

Casein

This is a substance in milk which has a high value as a protein. The main protein in milk is caseinogen, which is turned to casein by rennin, a substance found in rennet, and by acids. The casein is found in clots produced by the action of the rennin.

In most methods of cheese-making the milk is clotted with rennet and the casein formed in the clots traps the milk fats. The cheese, therefore, contains the protein and the fat of the milk.

Casein produced by milk in the stomach reduces the acidity of the stomach, and it is probably this that makes milk such a valuable food to people with gastric ulcers.

Cashew

The cashew is native to Brazil but is widely distributed throughout the tropics, having been carried by early explorers, particularly the Portuguese. The name cashew is derived from the Portuguese *caju*, which the Portuguese themselves adopted from the original Indian *acaju*.

The plant produces both a nut and a fruit which is sometimes known as a cashew pear. The nut is white, sweet, and kidney-shaped, and can be roasted or salted and served with drinks. The fruit can be eaten with or without preparation, as it has a pleasant, although tart, taste. In Goa, on the west coast of India, the fruit is used to make a strong liqueur.

Cassata

The name cassata (kass-AH-tah) is applied both to a Sicilian cake with cream cheese and chocolate, and, more commonly, to a type of Neapolitan ice cream consisting of a mousse mixture coated with ice. An ice cream made in coloured layers mixed with candied fruits and almonds is also known as cassata.

Cassata alla Siciliana

SICILIAN CAKE WITH CHOCOLATE ICING

At one time Cassata alla Siciliana (kass-AH-tah AHL-lah see-chil-YAH-nah) *was served only at Christmas and Easter feasts, but in Sicily today it is also presented as a wedding cake. A sponge cake spread with ricotta cheese and candied fruit and covered with a delicious chocolate-and-coffee icing, the Cassata should be prepared a day in advance.*

ONE 9-INCH CAKE

- **1 fresh Madeira [pound] cake, 9-inches long and 3-inches wide**
- **1 lb. ricotta cheese**
- **2 tablespoons double [heavy] cream**
- **2 oz. [¼ cup] sugar**
- **2½ tablespoons orange-flavoured liqueur**
- **2 tablespoons coarsely chopped mixed candied fruit**
- **1 tablespoon chopped pistachio nuts**
- **2 oz. dark cooking chocolate, coarsely grated**

CHOCOLATE ICING

- **12 oz. dark cooking chocolate, cut into small pieces**
- **6 fl. oz. [¾ cup] black coffee**
- **8 oz. unsalted butter [1 cup sweet butter], cut into small pieces and chilled**

Using a sharp knife, cut the cake lengthways into ½-inch slices.

With the back of a wooden spoon, press the ricotta through a strainer into a medium-sized mixing bowl. Using a rotary beater or wooden spoon, beat the ricotta until it is smooth. Add the cream, sugar and liqueur, beating until creamy. Using a metal spoon, fold in the candied fruit, pistachios and grated chocolate.

Place the bottom slice of the cake in the centre of a flat serving plate and spread it evenly with a fairly thick layer of the ricotta mixture. Place another slice of the cake on top and spread it with the ricotta mixture. Repeat this until all the slices of cake and ricotta mixture are used up, ending with a slice of cake on top. Gently press the loaf together.

Wrap the cake in aluminium foil and place it in the refrigerator to chill for 3 hours, or until the ricotta filling is set.

In a small, heavy saucepan, melt the chocolate with the coffee over low heat. Stir continuously until the chocolate is melted. Remove the pan from the heat and beat in the butter, a piece at a time. Continue beating until the mixture is smooth. Transfer the icing to a bowl. Allow it to cool until it is thick enough to spread.

Reserve a little of the icing for decoration, then cover the top and sides of the cake with the chocolate icing by swirling it on with a table knife. Fill a piping bag with the reserved icing and decorate the top and sides of the cake.

Cover the cake loosely with aluminium foil and refrigerate for at least 12 hours before serving.

Cassava

This plant is known as cassava in the West Indies, *manioc* in some parts of South America and Africa, and *yucca* in other regions. It is native to South America, and Brazil is the largest producer.

Cassava produces a food which is a staple of the diet of millions of people in many parts of the tropics. It is, however, of little value as a protein food and protein deficiency is a danger if the cassava is not accompanied by other protein foods.

Casserole

A cooking vessel in which meat, fish, poultry, game and vegetables are cooked gently, and usually, for a long time. Casseroles come in all shapes and sizes. They all have a tightly fitting lid and two handles. They can be made of pottery, glass, enamelled cast iron, terracotta, china, copper and enamel, and are either flameproof (to be used on top of the stove and in the oven) or ovenproof (for oven use only). The dish cooked in a casserole is often called after it.

Cassia

Cassia is a spice, closely related to cinnamon, with which it is often confused. Cassia differs from cinnamon in that the flavour extends into the leaves of the plant, which does not occur in the true cinnamon. In India cassia leaves, which look like bay leaves, are often used in curries. Cassia buds, which somewhat resemble cloves, are useful when a strong, instant flavour of cinnamon is required.

Cassis

A blackcurrant syrup or liqueur of 15 to 20 per cent alcohol, Cassis is very popular in France. It is drunk by itself, or mixed with water or vermouth. *Crème de Cassis* is a sweeter version, drunk only as a liqueur.

Cassis is also a name given to red, white and rosé wines originating in vineyards just southeast of Marseilles.

Cassoulet du Languedoc

CASSEROLE OF PORK AND LAMB WITH BEANS AND SAUSAGE

One of the most famous of French country dishes, Cassoulet du Languedoc (kah-soo-lay dolan-gay-dock) *takes almost a day to prepare. It may be prepared in stages and refrigerated for a day or two before finally being assembled and baked. Cassoulet is ideal for a buffet luncheon, served with a green or mixed salad.*

10 SERVINGS

6 pints [$3\frac{3}{4}$ quarts] water
2 lb. dried white haricot or black-eye beans
1 lb. piece unsmoked streaky bacon or lean salt pork
4 large onions, 2 sliced and 2 chopped
large bouquet garni, consisting of 8 parsley sprigs, 2 thyme sprays and 2 bay leaves tied together
6 garlic cloves, 3 left whole and 3 crushed
9 tablespoons vegetable oil
2 lb. boned loin of pork
2 lb. boned shoulder of lamb, cut into 2-inch square pieces
6 tablespoons tomato purée
1 pint [$2\frac{1}{2}$ cups] dry white wine
$1\frac{1}{2}$ pints [$3\frac{3}{4}$ cups] beef stock
$\frac{1}{2}$ teaspoon dried thyme
1 teaspoon salt
1 tablespoon freshly ground black pepper
1 lb. uncooked Spanish, French or Italian sausage, cut into 1-inch pieces
6 oz. [2 cups] dry white breadcrumbs
4 oz. [1 cup] chopped parsley

In a very large saucepan, bring the water to the boil over high heat. Add the beans and boil rapidly for 2 minutes. Remove the pan from the heat and leave the beans to soak for 1 hour.

Add the bacon or salt pork, sliced onions, bouquet garni and whole garlic cloves to the beans. Bring the liquid to the boil over high heat. With a slotted spoon, skim off any scum that rises to the surface. Continue boiling and skimming until the liquid is clear of all scum. Reduce the heat to low and simmer for 1 hour or until the beans are tender.

Carefully remove the bacon or salt pork and set it aside. Remove and discard the garlic cloves and bouquet garni. Drain the beans, reserving the cooking liquid.

Cassata alla Siciliana is a mouth-watering sponge cake spread with ricotta cheese and candied fruit and covered with chocolate-coffee icing.

When the bacon or salt pork is cool enough to handle, cut it into 2-inch thick pieces.

Preheat the oven to warm 325°F (Gas Mark 3, 170°C).

Heat 2 tablespoons of the oil in a flameproof casserole over moderate heat. When the oil is hot, add the loin of pork and, turning it carefully, brown the pork on all sides. Remove the meat from the casserole. Pour off the oil and replace it with another 2 tablespoons of oil. Put the meat back in the pot, cover and cook over high heat until the oil is very hot. Place the casserole in the oven and roast for $1\frac{3}{4}$-2 hours, basting the pork occasionally.

While the pork is roasting, cook the lamb. In a large frying-pan, heat 3 tablespoons of the oil over moderate heat. Add the lamb, a few pieces at a time, and brown them on all sides. As they brown, put the pieces of lamb to one side on a plate. When they are all browned, add the chopped onions to the pan. Cook for about 5 minutes or until the onions are beginning to brown. Add the tomato purée, the wine, stock, crushed garlic cloves, thyme, salt and pepper. Return the lamb to the frying-pan. Reduce the heat to moderately low, cover the pan and simmer for 4 to 5 minutes. Remove the pan from the heat and with a metal spoon skim off any fat that has accumulated on the surface. Remove the lamb pieces from the pan and set them aside on a plate. Reserve the cooking liquid.

When the pork is cooked, remove it from the casserole and set it aside to cool. Then cut it into $1\frac{1}{2}$ to 2-inch pieces.

Add the juices from roasting the pork to the frying-pan in which the lamb was cooked. Stir in the drained beans. If necessary, add some of the liquid reserved from cooking the beans so that the beans are completely covered. Bring the liquid to simmering point over moderate heat and cook for 5 minutes. Then remove the pan from the heat and leave it for 10 minutes so that the beans absorb the flavours of the cooking juices. Drain the beans in a colander, reserving the cooking juices.

Put a layer of the beans in the bottom of the casserole and cover them with alternating layers of pork, lamb and sausage. Then add another layer of beans and continue until all the ingredients have been added, ending with a layer of beans. Pour on enough of the reserved cooking juices so that the top layer of beans is almost covered.

Sprinkle the top layer of beans with a layer of breadcrumbs and then a layer of parsley. Add the remaining oil.

Increase the oven temperature to fairly hot 375°F (Gas Mark 5, 190°C).

Bring the liquid in the casserole to simmering point over moderate heat. Then transfer the casserole to the oven and bake for 25 minutes or until the top starts to become crisp. With the back of a wooden spoon, press the crust back into the liquid. Bake for another 35 minutes, during which time another crust will have formed.

Ten minutes before the cassoulet is ready, warm the remaining cooking juices and half of the liquid reserved from cooking the beans in a small saucepan over low heat. Pour this gravy into a sauce-boat to be served separately with the cassoulet.

Remove the casserole from the oven and serve the cassoulet straight on to warmed plates.

Cassoulet Gascogne is a warming, filling casserole of sausage and beans with garlic and parsley butter.

Cassoulet Gascogne

CASSEROLE OF SAUSAGE AND BEANS WITH GARLIC AND PARSLEY BUTTER.

This is a simple version of the famous French cassoulet. A filling dish on a cold day, Cassoulet Gascogne (kah-soo-lay gahs-kone) *may be prepared after breakfast and left to cook so that it will be ready at lunchtime. It is delicious served with hot, crusty French bread.*

4 SERVINGS

1 lb. salt pork, trimmed of excess fat and cut into 1-inch pieces
1 lb. dried white haricot beans, soaked overnight in water to cover, and drained
bouquet garni, consisting of 4 parsley sprigs, 1 thyme spray and 1 bay leaf tied together
$\frac{1}{2}$ teaspoon salt
8 grindings black pepper
1 lb. smoked pork sausages (Polish or Italian), cut into 1-inch pieces

BEURRE DE GASCOGNE

$\frac{1}{2}$ teaspoon salt
8 garlic cloves, peeled
3 oz. [$\frac{3}{8}$ cup] butter
1 teaspoon prepared mustard
2 tablespoons chopped parsley

Preheat the oven to moderate 350°F (Gas Mark 4, 180°C).

Place the salt pork and beans in a medium-sized ovenproof casserole. Pour enough boiling water into the casserole just to cover the pork and beans. Add the bouquet garni and put on the lid.

Place the casserole in the oven and cook for 3 hours, or until the beans are tender.

Remove the casserole from the oven. Taste and add the salt, if necessary, with the pepper. Stir the sausage pieces into the bean and pork mixture.

Return the casserole to the oven to cook for a further 30 minutes.

Meanwhile, prepare the Beurre de Gascogne. Half fill a small saucepan with water. Add the salt and place the pan over high heat. Bring the water to the boil. Add the garlic cloves and boil them for 10 minutes.

With a slotted spoon, transfer the garlic to a mortar or small bowl. Using a pestle or fork, mash the garlic cloves with the butter to a smooth paste. Stir in the mustard and parsley.

Remove the casserole from the oven. Strain off most of the liquid and remove and discard the bouquet garni. Stir in the Beurre de Gascogne and serve.

Cassolette

Cassolette (kah-soh-let) is the French name for small dishes made of glass, porcelain or metal, which vary in shape and size. Cassolettes are used for presenting hors d'oeuvre, small entrées, after-dinner savouries or individual sweet desserts.

Cassolettes de Carottes au Jambon

BRAISED CARROTS AND HAM

A rich vegetable accompaniment with a difference, Cassolettes de Carottes au Jambon (kah-soh-let d' kah-roht oh jahm-bohn) *is not difficult or expensive to make. It goes well with omelets or grilled* [broiled] *meats.*

4 SERVINGS

1 lb. carrots, scraped and cut into 1-inch slices
1 tablespoon butter
8 oz. lean ham, coarsely chopped
2 fl. oz. double cream [¼ cup heavy cream]
1 teaspoon ground nutmeg
½ teaspoon salt
½ teaspoon black pepper
2 oz. [½ cup] Gruyère cheese, grated
4 parsley sprigs (to garnish)

Place the carrot slices in a medium-sized saucepan. Add enough salted water to cover, and bring to the boil over moderate heat. Cook the carrots for 10 minutes. Remove the pan from the heat and drain the carrots thoroughly in a colander. Set them aside.

Melt the butter in a medium-sized frying-pan over moderate heat. When the butter foam subsides, add the bacon. Reduce the heat to low. Add the carrots to the pan and cook the ham and carrots together for about 5 to 8 minutes, turning both the carrots and the ham constantly with a slotted spoon. Stir in the cream, nutmeg, salt and pepper. Continue cooking for a further 2 to 3 minutes. Remove the pan from the heat.

Preheat the grill [broiler] to hot.

Arrange the carrot and bacon mixture in a medium-sized shallow, flameproof casserole or, if you prefer, in small individual ramekins. Sprinkle the cheese over the top of the mixture and place the casserole or ramekins under the grill [broiler] for 2 to 3 minutes or until the cheese melts and turns a very light golden colour. Remove from the heat, garnish with the parsley sprigs and serve immediately.

Catalan Fish Soup

A spicy and interesting dish, Catalan Fish Soup is a meal in itself and need only be accompanied by hot, crusty bread.

Braised carrots and bacon with a topping of cheese, Cassolettes de Carottes au Jambon is a rich vegetable dish.

4 SERVINGS

1½ oz. [3 tablespoons] butter
1¼ pints [3 cups] water
2 teaspoons salt
3½ lb. sea bream, gutted, trimmed and with bones and trimmings reserved
2 fl. oz. [¼ cup] olive oil
3 small onions, finely chopped
3 medium-sized tomatoes, blanched, peeled, seeded and chopped
16 fl. oz. [2 cups] dry white wine
2 tablespoons chopped fresh parsley
1 bay leaf
¼ teaspoon dried thyme
6 grindings black pepper
2 oz. [⅓ cup] blanched, toasted and ground almonds
3 garlic cloves, crushed

Using 1 tablespoon of the butter, grease a large ovenproof casserole and set it aside.

In a large saucepan, bring the water and 1 teaspoon of salt to the boil over high heat.

Add the bones and trimmings of the bream to the pan and reduce the heat to moderate. Cook for 30 minutes.

Remove the pan from the heat. Strain

the fish stock into a measuring jug and reserve 16 fluid ounces [2 cups]. Discard the bones and trimmings.

In another large saucepan, heat the oil and remaining butter over moderate heat. Add the onions and cook them for 5 to 6 minutes, or until they are soft but not brown.

Add the tomatoes to the pan and continue cooking for 5 minutes.

Add the reserved fish stock, wine, parsley, bay leaf, thyme, the remaining salt and the pepper to the pan and bring the sauce to the boil. Reduce the heat to low and simmer the sauce for 20 minutes.

Preheat the oven to fairly hot 400°F (Gas Mark 6, 200°C).

Add the almonds and garlic to the sauce and stir well to blend. Remove the pan from the heat.

Cut the bream flesh into 2-inch slices and place them in the buttered casserole. Pour the sauce over the fish.

Cover the casserole and place it in the oven. Cook for 30 minutes.

Remove the casserole from the oven. Take out and discard the bay leaf. Serve at once.

Catfish

The catfish is one of the most popular food-fishes in North America, where it is commercially farmed. There are several varieties of catfish, ranging in size up to 150 pounds or more - the best size for eating is from 1 to 2 pounds. It derives its name from the long whisker-like barbels on either side of its mouth. In the southern United States catfish and hush puppies (fried cornmeal puffs) is a traditional dish in the same way that fish and chips is in Britain.

Catmint [Catnip]

The leaves of this variety of mint are very strong for use in cooking in the usual way; very young shoots can, however, be used chopped in salads and stews.

Catsup

Catsup is also known as ketchup or, in the United States, catchup. The name probably originates from the Chinese *ke-tsiap,* meaning a fish brine. It is a table sauce, originally British, in which one flavour predominates - tomato, mushroom, and so on. It is made by extracting the juice of the main ingredient, boiling it to a high concentration, and seasoning it strongly. Catsup may be used by itself as a condiment, as an ingredient to flavour soups and stews, or to form the basis of other sauces.

An economical dish, Castilian Omelet is a filling and tasty mixture of eggs, onions and potatoes.

Castilian Omelet

☆ ① ⌛

An interesting variation on the basic omelet, Castilian Omelet is a tempting, filling mixture of potatoes, onion and eggs. Unlike the traditional French omelet, this is not folded over but is served flat and cut into wedge-shaped pieces. It may be served with a courgette [zucchini] *salad.*

4 SERVINGS

5 tablespoons olive oil
3 medium-sized potatoes, peeled, thinly sliced and dried on kitchen paper towels
1 large onion, finely chopped
½ garlic clove, crushed
¼ teaspoon salt
4 eggs

In a large frying-pan, heat 4 tablespoons of the oil over moderately low heat. When the oil is hot, put in the potatoes, onion, garlic and salt. Fry them slowly for 20 minutes, or until the potato slices are cooked and lightly browned on both sides. Remove the pan from the heat. With a slotted spoon, remove the potatoes and onions from the pan. Set aside on a warmed plate.

Pour off the oil from the pan. Wash and dry the pan.

In a medium-sized mixing bowl, lightly beat the eggs with a fork. Add the potato and onion mixture to the eggs and stir gently so that the ingredients are well mixed, taking care not to break the potato slices.

Preheat the grill [broiler] to moderate.

Pour the remaining oil into the cleaned frying-pan and place it over moderate heat. When the oil is hot, pour in the egg-and-potato mixture. Tip and rotate the pan so that the mixture covers the bottom of the pan completely.

Cook the omelet for about 5 minutes, or until the underside is golden brown. Shake the pan occasionally so that the omelet does not stick.

Remove the pan from the heat and place it under the grill [broiler]. Cook for 2 to 3 minutes, or until the top is firm and evenly browned.

Slide the omelet on to a warmed serving dish and serve hot.

Castilian Soup

Castilian Soup - thick tomato soup with rice and green pepper - makes a sustaining first course for a cold day's main meal.

4 TO 6 SERVINGS

10 fl. oz. [1¼ cups] water
2 small green peppers, white pith removed, cored, seeded and cut into strips
2 oz. [¼ cup] butter
2 lb. tomatoes, blanched, peeled, seeded and coarsely chopped
1 large onion, finely chopped
4 tablespoons flour
1½ pints [3¾ cups] chicken stock
½ teaspoon dried basil
1 small bay leaf
1 tablespoon lemon juice
2 teaspoons brown sugar
1 teaspoon salt
½ teaspoon black pepper
4 oz. [¾ cup] cold cooked rice

Low Cal

In a medium-sized saucepan, bring the water to the boil over high heat. Add the green pepper. Reduce the heat to moderate and simmer for 10 minutes. Drain the green pepper and dry with kitchen paper towels. Discard the water.

In the same saucepan, melt 2 tablespoons of the butter over moderate heat. Add the tomatoes and half the onion to the pan. Cook them for 8 to 10 minutes or until the onion is soft and translucent. Remove the pan from the heat and push the tomato-and-onion mixture through a strainer into a bowl.

Melt the rest of the butter in the pan and cook the remaining onion in it for 8 to 10 minutes or until it is soft and golden. Remove the pan from the heat. With a wooden spoon, stir in the flour. Return the pan to the heat and cook the mixture for 5 minutes.

Mix in the strained tomato mixture and the stock. Cook the soup for 25 to 30 minutes or until it is thick and smooth, stirring constantly. Add the basil, bay leaf, lemon juice, sugar, salt, pepper, rice and green pepper. Reduce the heat to low and simmer the soup for 15 minutes, stirring occasionally. Remove the bay leaf and ladle the soup into a warmed tureen or individual bowls.

Caul

A caul is a thin membrane, resembling a thick veil ribbed with fat, which covers the lower portion of an animal's intestines. It was at one time used commercially as a skin for sausages and similar preparations, and is still used for this purpose domestically. The best type is the pork caul. It is used more in French and Italian cooking than in British or American.

Cauliflower

Cauliflower is a variety of cabbage and its name is derived from an old English word for flowering cabbage. It is cultivated for its flowers, which form a compact, round, hard white head surrounded by leaves. It is available in summer and autumn, and is a good source of vitamin C, providing half a day's requirement in an average helping. Cauliflowers range in size from small, about 1 pound, to very large, 4 or 5 pounds. A 2 to 3 pound cauliflower is enough for 4 helpings. Choose a cauliflower which has a firm white head and fresh green leaves. Cut off the leaves, leaving only the very tender small leaves closest to the stalk, and trim the stalk. Either leave the head whole or separate into flowerets. Soak the cauliflower in salted water for 20 minutes to draw out any insects. Cook the cauliflower in salted boiling water in a covered pan. An averaged sized cauliflower will take about 15 minutes to cook and the flowerets should take half that time. After cooking, the cauliflower should be tender but firm and never mushy.

Cauliflower Cheese

This dish is tasty, nourishing and economical. It can be an entire course in itself, or could be accompanied by crisply fried bacon for a contrast in texture and flavours.

4 SERVINGS

1 cauliflower, trimmed and washed
2 tablespoons butter
2 tablespoons flour
10 fl. oz. [1¼ cups] milk
1 egg yolk (optional)
6 oz. [1½ cups] Cheddar or similar hard cheese, grated
½ teaspoon salt
¼ teaspoon freshly ground black pepper

Put the cauliflower into a large saucepan, cover it with cold water and bring to the boil over high heat. Cover the pan and simmer the cauliflower for 15 minutes or until the cauliflower is tender when pierced with a knife. Alternatively, when boiling point is reached turn off the heat and leave the cauliflower to cook in the hot water. This should take 15 minutes. When the cauliflower is tender, drain it. It may then be left whole or broken into smaller flowerets as preferred. Place the cauliflower on a flameproof dish, and keep warm.

Preheat the grill [broiler] to high.

Make a white sauce by melting the butter in a small saucepan over moderate heat. When the butter is melted, remove the pan from the heat and beat in the flour, using a wooden spoon. When the mixture is smooth, add the milk, stirring continuously, and then return the pan to the heat. Bring the sauce to the boil, still stirring, and cook for 1 to 2 minutes or until it thickens.

An egg yolk can be added to the sauce for a richer result. The yolk should be beaten in a small bowl, and 3 or 4 tablespoons of the hot sauce added to it and beaten in well. This mixture is then whisked into the white sauce.

Remove the sauce from the heat and add most of the grated cheese, the salt and pepper. Stir until the cheese is melted and taste the mixture. Add more salt and pepper if necessary. Pour the sauce over the cauliflower in the flameproof dish, and sprinkle the remaining grated cheese on top. Brown the dish under the hot grill [broiler] for 1 to 2 minutes and serve at once.

Cauliflower with Italian Sauce

An exceptionally tasty wine-flavoured sauce is the basis for this delicious dish that makes an interesting accompaniment to roast meat, or can even be served as a light meal by itself.

4 SERVINGS

2 tablespoons butter
1 medium-sized onion, chopped
3 large mushrooms, wiped and sliced
2 tablespoons cooked shredded ham
1 tablespoon flour
2 teaspoons tomato purée
½ teaspoon salt
4 grindings black pepper
3 fl. oz. [⅜ cup] white wine
6 fl. oz. [¾ cup] beef stock
1 cauliflower, washed and in flowerets

In a medium-sized saucepan melt the butter over moderate heat. When the foam subsides, reduce the heat to low and add the onion, mushrooms and ham. Cook the mixture for 10 minutes, stirring frequently. Remove the pan from the heat. Mix in the flour. Replace the pan on the heat and cook, stirring, for 2 minutes. Add the tomato purée, salt, pepper, wine and stock. Increase the heat to high and bring the liquid to the boil. Reduce the heat to low again and simmer gently, uncovered, for 20 minutes.

While the sauce is cooking, in a large saucepan, cook the cauliflower flowerets in boiling salted water over moderate heat for 9 to 12 minutes, or until they are tender. Drain the flowerets and arrange them in a warmed, deep-sided serving dish.

When the sauce is ready, pour it over the cauliflower pieces and serve at once.

Cauliflower Mexicana

This is a spicy version of cauliflower cheese, which will delight those who like really piquant dishes.

2 SERVINGS

1 medium-sized cauliflower, in flowerets
1 tablespoon butter
1 medium-sized onion, finely sliced
5 oz. canned tomato purée mixed with 5 fl. oz. [$\frac{5}{8}$ cup] water
1 teaspoon mild chilli powder
1 tablespoon capers
2 tablespoons chopped parsley
3 tablespoons breadcrumbs
3 tablespoons grated Parmesan cheese
1 tablespoon olive oil

Preheat the oven to hot 425°F (Gas Mark 7, 220°C).

Prepare, boil and drain the cauliflower flowerets.

Melt the butter in a small frying-pan over low heat, add the sliced onion and cook for 5 minutes, or until it is transparent but not brown.

Put the onion in a flameproof casserole with the tomato purée and water, chilli powder, capers and parsley. Stir with a metal spoon and bring the mixture to a boil over moderate heat on top of the stove. Add the cauliflower and stir to coat the flowerets well. Sprinkle the top with the breadcrumbs, cheese and olive oil and bake, in the middle of the oven, for 10 to 15 minutes, or until the cheese and crumb mixture is a golden brown.

Serve at once.

Cauliflower Mexicana is a spicy vegetable dish, with chilli powder, capers and Parmesan cheese.

Cauliflower with Mustard Sauce

A piquant mustard sauce makes this cauliflower dish a delicious accompaniment to grilled [broiled] *meat or fish.*

4 SERVINGS

1 cauliflower
2 teaspoons butter
2 teaspoons flour
6 fl. oz. [$\frac{3}{4}$ cup] milk
4 teaspoons prepared mayonnaise
3 teaspoons dry English mustard
$1\frac{1}{2}$ teaspoons lemon juice
$\frac{1}{4}$ teaspoon cayenne pepper

Prepare and boil the cauliflower. Drain it well and place it on a serving dish. Set aside and keep hot.

Melt the butter in a medium-sized saucepan over low heat. Remove the pan from the heat and add the flour, stirring with a wooden spoon until it forms a roux, or paste. Add the milk, a little at a time, stirring continuously until the mixture is smooth and thick. Return the pan to the heat.

Add the mayonnaise, mustard, lemon juice and cayenne pepper, stirring constantly. Continue to cook, and stir, for 1 to 2 minutes. Pour the mustard sauce over the cauliflower.

Cauliflower Polonaise

A classic way of serving cauliflower, Cauliflower Polonaise goes well with roast beef or with other roast meat.

4 SERVINGS

1 medium-sized cauliflower, in flowerets
2 oz. [$\frac{1}{4}$ cup] butter
3 oz. [$1\frac{1}{2}$ cups] fresh breadcrumbs
1 hard-boiled egg, finely chopped
2 tablespoons chopped fresh parsley

Prepare, boil and drain the cauliflower.

Heap the flowerets in a heated serving platter and set aside.

Melt the butter in a small frying-pan over moderate heat and add the breadcrumbs, mixing the ingredients together with a wooden spoon until they are well blended and the breadcrumbs begin to brown.

Pour the butter-breadcrumb mixture over the flowerets and sprinkle them with chopped egg and parsley. Serve hot.

Cauliflower Salad

This colourful salad gets its unique taste from the blending of the sharp blue-veined Roquefort cheese with a tangy vinaigrette dressing. It makes an excellent summer luncheon by itself (needing only some French bread and a light white wine to complete the meal). It also makes a good accompaniment to roast meat or game.

4 SERVINGS

1 medium-sized cauliflower
2 oz. [$\frac{1}{2}$ cup] walnuts, chopped
9 tablespoons olive oil
$4\frac{1}{2}$ tablespoons white wine vinegar
1 teaspoon lemon juice
$\frac{1}{2}$ teaspoon French mustard
1 teaspoon sugar
1 teaspoon salt
1 teaspoon freshly ground black pepper
1 tablespoon chopped fresh parsley

2 tablespoons finely crumbled Roquefort cheese

Clean and prepare the cauliflower for the salad by breaking it into flowerets and soaking in cold salted water. Then chop it into bite-sized pieces, discarding the base and the hard ends of the stems. Put the cauliflower pieces into a large salad bowl, add the chopped walnuts and set aside.

Make a vinaigrette dressing by combining the olive oil, vinegar, lemon juice, mustard, sugar, salt and pepper in a screw top jar. Shake the jar vigorously so that all the ingredients blend into one another. Add the parsley and crumbled Roquefort to the dressing and shake again.

Pour the dressing over the cauliflower and walnut mixture in the salad bowl and toss with a fork to mix thoroughly. Allow the salad to chill for 30 minutes in the refrigerator before serving.

This attractive Cauliflower Salad may be served either on its own or as a vegetable accompaniment to meat or fish.

Cauliflower Vinaigrette

This dish can be served as an hors d'oeuvre or as a salad – with cold meat. It is best served cold and can therefore be made slightly ahead of time and stored in the refrigerator until it is to be used. If fresh chervil is not available, fresh chopped parsley or fresh chopped watercress can be substituted.

4 SERVINGS

Low Cal

- 1 cauliflower, in flowerets
- 3 tablespoons olive oil
- 1 tablespoon wine vinegar
- 1 teaspoon salt
- ½ teaspoon black pepper
- 1 tablespoon fresh chopped chervil

Prepare and cook the cauliflower flowerets. Drain well and put in a salad bowl to cool.

In a small mixing bowl, combine the olive oil, white wine vinegar, salt and pepper and, using a fork, beat thoroughly. Pour the sauce over the flowerets and toss well to coat.

Sprinkle chopped fresh chervil over the cauliflower and serve.

A luxurious delicacy, Caviar should be served very cold with bread or toast and lemon slices.

Caviar

Caviar is the prepared roe (eggs) of the female fish of the sturgeon family, which includes the sturgeon, beluga, ship, sevruga and sterlet. These fish are caught in the winter months in the estuaries of the rivers which flow into the Baltic Sea and the Danube.

Caviar is prepared by first straining the roe to remove membranes, fibres and fatty matter, and then salting it. The best caviar does not keep well and because of this and the difficult preparation, it is considered a delicacy in the West. In Russia and Eastern Europe, a coarser quality caviar is a staple food, traditionally accompanied by vodka.

The consistency of caviar varies from fine to coarse and in colour from grey to black. (Red caviar, which comes from salmon, is inferior in quality but has a pleasant flavour.)

There is a difference of opinion about which caviar is the best. Caviar from the sturgeon is fine and grey to black in colour, and it keeps well. The roe of the beluga is large-grained and grey. Ship caviar is light-coloured and fine, while sevruga is finer still. The fine roe of the sterlet is quite dark in colour and in Russian Tsarist times was much prized and reserved for the Imperial family.

Caviar should be served very cold with plain bread or crisp toast and no other accompaniments except, perhaps, lemon juice, depending on the saltiness of the caviar. Caviar is a popular hors d'oeuvre and is used in canapés.

Cavolo in Agrodolce

SOUR-SWEET CABBAGE

A piquant Italian method of cooking cabbage, Cavolo in Agrodolce (ka-voh-loh in ah-groh-DOLL-cheh) *can be served as a vegetable accompaniment to meat or fish, or as an appetizer.*

4 SERVINGS

- 4 tablespoons vegetable oil
- 1 medium-sized onion, finely chopped
- 1 small green cabbage, coarse outer leaves removed, washed and finely shredded
- 4 tomatoes, blanched, peeled, seeded and chopped
- 2 tablespoons wine vinegar
- 1 teaspoon salt
- $\frac{1}{2}$ teaspoon black pepper
- 1 tablespoon sugar

Low Cal

In a large deep frying-pan heat the oil over moderate heat. Add the chopped onion and cook for 5-6 minutes, stirring occasionally.

Add the shredded cabbage, a handful at a time, stir well and, as the cabbage cooks down, add the next handful. Add the chopped tomatoes, vinegar, salt and pepper and stir to mix. Simmer for 15-20 minutes, or until the cabbage is cooked.

Add the sugar to the mixture in the frying-pan, stirring to blend well, and cook for 1 to 2 minutes longer. Taste and adjust the seasoning, if necessary, by adding more salt, vinegar or sugar.

Cayenne

Cayenne is a bright red, finely ground, pungent powder made from the seeds and dried pods of various capsicums. It is supposed to have originated in the district of Cayenne in French Guiana but is now also grown in other tropical countries. It is used to flavour oysters, meat stews, cheese dishes, fish and game.

Celeriac

A plant closely related to celery, celeriac, or *céleri-rave* as it is called in France, is often called the 'turnip-rooted celery' because of its shape. Only the large swollen base of the stem, brown on the outside, white on the inside, is considered edible.

Celeriac can be used raw in salads and hors d'oeuvre or cooked as a flavouring for soups and stews.

To cook celeriac, first wash and peel them. Divide into quarters, then slice. Place the slices in a large saucepan, cover with boiling salted water and cook over high heat for 10 minutes, or until the celeriac is tender. Remove from the heat and drain.

Céleri-rave Braisé

BRAISED CELERIAC

This tasty way of cooking celeriac makes an unusual accompaniment to roast meats such as pork, chicken or turkey. Céleri-rave Braisé (sayl-ree-rahve bray-zay) *is cooked on top of the stove and then finished in the oven.*

6 SERVINGS

- 4 oz. streaky bacon, cut into small dice
- 1 large celeriac, peeled and sliced
- 1 tablespoon butter
- 1 small onion, chopped
- 10 fl. oz. [$1\frac{1}{4}$ cups] home-made beef stock or stock made with a stock cube
- 6 fl. oz. [$\frac{3}{4}$ cup] dry white wine, or additional stock
- $\frac{1}{2}$ teaspoon salt
- $\frac{1}{2}$ teaspoon freshly ground black pepper
- 1 tablespoon finely chopped parsley

Preheat the oven to moderate 350°F (Gas Mark 4, 180°C).

In a large saucepan, bring $1\frac{1}{2}$ pints [$3\frac{3}{4}$ cups] of water to the boil over high heat. Add the diced bacon. Reduce the heat to moderate and simmer the bacon for 10 minutes.

Meanwhile, blanch the celeriac by dropping it into another large saucepan three-quarters full of boiling salted water. Boil the celeriac for 5 minutes, then drain it in a colander.

In a flameproof casserole, melt the butter over moderate heat.

Using a slotted spoon, transfer the diced bacon to the casserole and add the chopped onion. Fry the bacon and onion for about 10 minutes, or until the onion is transparent but not brown. With a slotted spoon, remove the bacon and onion from the casserole and put them to one side.

Put the celeriac in the casserole and spoon the bacon and onion on top. Pour over the beef stock and wine or additional stock and add the salt and pepper.

Bring the liquid to simmering point and cover the casserole. Place the casserole in the oven and bake for 1 hour, basting the celeriac occasionally.

When the celeriac is nicely browned and tender and most of the liquid has been absorbed, remove the casserole from the oven. Sprinkle the celeriac with parsley and serve it from the casserole.

Céleri-rave à la Paysanne

STUFFED CELERIAC

A rather different way of serving this vegetable is to stuff slices with a mixture of other vegetables. Céleri-rave à la Paysanne (sayl-ree-rahve ah lah pay-zahn) *can be used as a garnish or as a vegetable to serve with roast meats.*

4 SERVINGS

- 3 oz. [⅜ cup] butter
- ½ lb. carrots, scraped and finely chopped
- 1 large onion, finely chopped
- ½ teaspoon salt
- ½ teaspoon black pepper
- ½ teaspoon sugar
- 4 tablespoons vegetable stock, or stock made with a chicken stock cube
- 1 large or 2 small celeriacs
- 4 oz. [1 cup] cheese, grated

In a small saucepan melt 2 ounces [¼ cup] of the butter over moderate heat. Add the carrots, onion, salt, pepper, sugar and stock. Cook for 5 minutes, stirring so that the mixture does not stick to the pan. Cover tightly, reduce the heat to low and simmer for about 15 minutes or until the mixture is soft and all the liquid has been absorbed.

Preheat the oven to warm 325°F (Gas Mark 3, 170°C).

Peel the celeriac and cut it into slices 1-1½ inches thick. Trim the slices into neat round shapes.

Half-fill a medium-sized saucepan with water. Bring the water to the boil over high heat. Drop the slices of celeriac into the water and boil them for 10 minutes. Drain the celeriac in a colander and rinse with cold water. Scoop out the centre of each slice to about half its depth. Fill the hollows with the carrot and onion mixture.

Place the stuffed celeriac slices in a shallow ovenproof dish and cover with the grated cheese. Dot the remaining butter over the cheese and place the dish in the centre of the oven. Bake for about 20 minutes, or until the celeriac is soft and the cheese is golden brown.

Serve immediately.

Céleri-rave Vinaigrette

CELERIAC SALAD

An unusual and tasty salad, Céleri-rave Vinaigrette (sayl-ree-rahv vee-nay-gret) *is ideal for the winter months when most green salad ingredients are unobtainable.*

Céleri-rave à la Paysanne is an interesting vegetable dish of celeriac stuffed with carrots and onion.

4 SERVINGS

Low Cal

- 1 large celeriac
- 2 pints [5 cups] water
- 3 tablespoons olive oil
- 1 tablespoon wine vinegar
- ½ teaspoon salt
- ½ teaspoon freshly ground black pepper
- 1 teaspoon prepared mustard
- 1 tablespoon chopped parsley

With a small, sharp kitchen knife, cut the celeriac into julienne strips (about 1½ inches long and ⅛ inch wide).

In a medium-sized saucepan, bring the water to the boil over high heat. Drop in the julienne strips of celeriac. Bring the water back to the boil and cook for 1 minute. Drain the celeriac in a strainer, cover with cold water and drain again. Put the celeriac in a salad bowl.

In a small bowl, mix together the oil, vinegar, salt, pepper and mustard. Pour this dressing over the celeriac and toss it with a fork. Chill the celeriac salad in the refrigerator for 30 minutes. Sprinkle the salad with parsley just before serving.

Céleris Amandines

CELERY WITH ALMONDS

The almonds in this celery dish give it a crisp and unusual texture. Céleris Amandines (sayl-ree ah-mahn-dean) *makes an excellent accompaniment to roast pork.*

4 SERVINGS

- 2 medium-sized heads of celery, washed and the stalks cut in pieces
- 2 oz. [$\frac{1}{4}$ cup] butter
- 1 small onion, chopped
- $\frac{1}{2}$ teaspoon salt
- $\frac{1}{4}$ teaspoon freshly ground black pepper
- 1 tablespoon flour
- 8 fl. oz. single cream [1 cup light cream]
- 5 fl. oz. [$\frac{5}{8}$ cup] chicken stock
- 6 oz. [$1\frac{1}{2}$ cups] almonds, toasted and shredded

Prepare, parboil and drain the celery. In a medium-sized saucepan melt the butter over moderate heat. Add the celery, onion, salt and pepper. Tightly cover the pan and reduce the heat to low. Cook for 15 minutes. Stir occasionally, and, if the celery shows signs of sticking to the pan, add a little water.

Remove the pan from the heat. Sprinkle the flour into the pan and mix well. Gradually add the cream and stock, stirring continuously. Replace over moderate heat and cook, stirring constantly, until the sauce boils and thickens. Remove from heat, stir in almonds, and serve.

Céleris Braisés au Lard

BRAISED CELERY AND BACON

A refreshingly different vegetable combination, Céleris Braisés au Lard (sayl-ree bray-zay oh lahr) *goes well with roast ham or with an omelet for a light supper dish.*

4-6 SERVINGS

- 2 medium-sized heads of celery, cleaned and cut into 4-inch pieces
- 6 oz. small onions, peeled and left whole
- bouquet garni, consisting of 4 parsley sprigs, 1 thyme spray and 1 bay leaf tied together
- 1 teaspoon salt
- $\frac{1}{2}$ teaspoon freshly ground black pepper
- 8 oz. streaky bacon, coarsely chopped
- 1 tablespoon butter

Put the celery and onions in a large saucepan with enough water to cover. Add the bouquet garni, salt and pepper. Cover the saucepan and place it over high heat. Bring the water to the boil and reduce the heat to moderate. Cook the vegetables for 15 minutes, or until they are firm but tender when pierced with a fork. Drain the celery and onions in a colander, discarding the cooking liquid, and set them aside.

In a large frying-pan, fry the bacon pieces over moderate heat – there should be enough fat in the bacon to do this, but if a little extra fat is needed, take some butter from the 1 tablespoon. When the bacon is crisp, add the remaining butter to the pan and allow it to melt. Add the celery and onions and cook the mixture over moderate heat for about 5 minutes, or until the vegetables become lightly browned. Add more salt and pepper if necessary and serve immediately.

Céleris à la Grecque

CELERY, GREEK-STYLE

A delicious and refreshing hors d'oeuvre, Céleris à la Grecque (sayl-ree ah lah grek) *can be prepared several days before serving.*

4 SERVINGS

- 2 medium-sized heads of celery (or about 12 celery stalks), prepared, parboiled and drained
- 1 tablespoon chopped fresh parsley

MARINADE

- 12 fl. oz. [$1\frac{1}{2}$ cups] chicken stock
- 4 fl. oz. [$\frac{1}{2}$ cup] dry white wine
- 4 fl. oz. [$\frac{1}{2}$ cup] olive oil
- juice from 1 lemon
- 1 piece lemon rind
- 1 garlic clove, finely chopped
- bouquet garni, consisting of 4 parsley sprigs, 1 thyme spray and 1 bay leaf tied together
- 6 peppercorns
- 6 coriander seeds
- $\frac{1}{2}$ teaspoon salt
- $\frac{1}{2}$ teaspoon white pepper

In a medium-sized saucepan mix together the chicken stock, white wine, olive oil, lemon juice, lemon rind, garlic clove, bouquet garni, peppercorns, coriander seeds, salt and pepper. Bring the marinade to the boil over moderate heat. Cover the pan, reduce the heat to low and simmer the marinade for 15 minutes. Set aside.

On a chopping board, trim and quarter the celery stalks and set aside.

Bring the marinade back to boiling point over low heat and add the celery to the pan. Simmer, covered, for 25 minutes, or until the celery is thoroughly cooked. With a slotted spoon, drain the celery and place it in a shallow bowl.

Increase the heat to high and boil the marinade until it is reduced by half. Pour it over the celery. Cover the bowl and put it in the refrigerator. Leave it for at least 5-6 hours, basting the celery quarters occasionally with the marinade.

Remove the celery from the marinade and arrange on a serving dish. Pour some of the marinade over them and sprinkle the parsley over the top to garnish.

Celery

Celery is a vegetable which grows in its wild state in most temperate regions of the world. But as a cultivated vegetable it was only introduced into Britain in the 17th century from Italy.

Celery has long white stalks or ribs rising from a base and ending in curly yellow-green leaves. The stalks are the part most often eaten, either raw or cooked. The leaves should never be thrown away as they can be used as flavouring for sauces, soups and minced [ground] or stewed meat. In Britain the season for celery is from September to February, but it is after the first frosts that the best celery is available. Imported celery can be bought throughout the year.

The best celery is young celery, especially if it is to be eaten raw. Remove the outer stalks. These can be scrubbed and added to stocks or sauces. Cut off the green tops and trim the base. Cut the head into quarters lengthways or separate the stalks. Wash thoroughly under cold running water. Keep the prepared celery in iced water in the refrigerator until you are ready to use it.

The stalks of raw celery may be filled with cream cheese, a mixture of cream cheese, herbs and white wine or puréed avocado and seafood mixtures.

Whatever way you intend to cook the celery, the first step is blanching or boiling. The prepared celery is dropped into boiling water and boiled for 10 minutes after boiling point has been regained. Then it is drained and dried (if you want to serve whole or half heads, tie the tops loosely with string before the next step in cooking). For boiled celery, continue the boiling for another 8 minutes or until the celery is tender. It is then ready to be covered with a sauce or butter.

Celery Braised

A delicious way to cook celery is to braise it, as the fat and seasonings used in cooking keep the celery moist and flavoursome. The following is a basic recipe for braising celery.

4 SERVINGS

2 small heads of celery
4 oz. streaky bacon
1 small carrot, scraped and sliced
1 onion, sliced
bouquet garni consisting of 4 parsley sprigs, 1 thyme spray and 1 bay leaf tied together
½ teaspoon salt
¼ teaspoon freshly ground black pepper
1½ pints [3¾ cups] chicken stock

Prepare, trim, wash, boil and drain the celery. Lay the bacon on the bottom of a large flameproof casserole. Put in the sliced carrot and onion and place the celery heads on top. Add the bouquet garni, salt, pepper and stock, which should just cover the celery. Put the casserole over moderate heat and bring to the boil. Cover the pan, lower the heat and simmer gently for 1½ hours or preferably bake in a moderate oven, 350°F (Gas Mark 4, 180°C) for 2 hours.

If the celery is to be served with a sauce, remove the celery from the baking dish, drain well and cut in half. Place it in a serving dish, cover with the sauce and serve.

If the celery is to be served plain, remove the cover of the baking dish for the last 30 minutes of cooking and raise the heat to fairly hot 400°F (Gas Mark 6, 200°C). Remove the celery heads, cut them in half lengthways and arrange them on a serving dish. Strain the liquid in which they were cooked. Put the strained liquid in a saucepan over moderate heat and bring it to the boil. Taste the liquid and add seasoning if necessary. Make a beurre manié with 2 tablespoons flour and 1 tablespoon butter. Add it a little at a time to the simmering sauce. When the sauce is thick and smooth, pour it over the celery and serve.

A simple way to braise celery is to parboil it and then cook it in stock leaving out the other ingredients.

Céleris Braisés au Lard with bacon and onions is a simple and tasty dish to serve with roast meat.

Celery with Red Caviar, cream cheese, chives and parsley is an elegant and economical appetizer that takes only a few minutes to prepare.

Celery Creamed

Creamed celery makes a delicious vegetable dish and can be served with meat or game. It is especially good with steak or chops.

4 TO 6 SERVINGS

- 2 medium-sized heads of celery (or about 12 stalks)
- $1\frac{1}{2}$ oz. [3 tablespoons] butter
- $\frac{1}{2}$ teaspoon salt
- $\frac{1}{4}$ teaspoon black pepper
- 2 tablespoons chopped onion
- 4 fl. oz. single cream [$\frac{1}{2}$ cup light cream] mixed with 1 tablespoon flour
- 4 fl. oz. [$\frac{1}{2}$ cup] chicken stock

Prepare and parboil the celery. Drain well and cut the celery stalks into $\frac{1}{2}$-inch pieces.

In a medium-sized saucepan melt the butter over low heat. Add the celery, salt and pepper. Cover the pan tightly and simmer the mixture for 15 minutes, shaking the pan from time to time. Add the chopped onion to the celery and simmer for a further 5 minutes. The mixture should be almost dry at this point.

Add the cream and flour mixture and the chicken stock to the pan. Stirring continuously with a wooden spoon, bring to the boil over moderate heat. Cook for 1 to 2 minutes or until the sauce thickens and becomes smooth. Serve immediately.

Celery Fritters

Celery pieces, parboiled, dipped in batter and fried, make an excellent crisp vegetable and they are particularly good served with a piquant sauce.

4 SERVINGS

- 1 or 2 heads of celery

BATTER

- 5 oz. [$1\frac{1}{4}$ cups] flour
- 1 teaspoon salt
- 2 tablespoons brown ale
- 4 fl. oz. [$\frac{1}{2}$ cup] water.
- oil for deep frying

Prepare and parboil the celery for 10 minutes.

Sift the flour and salt into a small mixing bowl. Make a well in the centre and pour in the ale and water. Using a wooden spoon or a wire whisk, mix in the liquid. Beat well until the mixture is smooth and creamy. Cover the batter and leave it at room temperature for 30 minutes.

Heat the oil in a deep-frying pan. Drain the celery and cut it into small pieces. Dip the celery pieces in the batter. Drop into the hot oil and fry until golden. Drain the fritters on a plate lined with kitchen paper towels. Serve hot.

Celery with Red Caviar

An elegant and simple appetizer, Celery with Red Caviar takes only minutes to prepare and can be made an hour or so before serving. It can be accompanied, in a separate dish, by black olives.

4-6 SERVINGS

- 2 small heads of celery (or about 10 stalks)
- 8 oz. full-fat cream cheese
- 2 tablespoons chopped chives
- 2 tablespoons chopped fresh parsley
- $3\frac{1}{2}$ oz. jar red caviar
- $\frac{1}{2}$ teaspoon white pepper

Clean the celery and, on a chopping board, cut each stalk in three, crosswise. Set aside in a serving dish.

In a medium-sized mixing bowl, combine the cream cheese, chives, parsley, red caviar and pepper, beating to blend well.

Spread a little of the cream cheese mixture on to each celery piece and refrigerate for 30 minutes before serving.

Celery salt

This is salt flavoured with dried and powdered celery. It is used in soups, stews and sauces.

Celery seed

Celery seed, the dried fruit of celery, is small and brownish, with a strong flavour. It is used in tomato juice, seafood and fish dishes, pickles and chutneys, on breads and rolls, in soups, stews, white sauces and mayonnaises, in nearly all vegetable dishes and in cheese and herb-butter mixtures.

Celery with Tarragon

The tarragon and wine added to the celery give it a subtle and delicate flavour which goes particularly well with roast chicken.

4 SERVINGS

Low Cal

- 2 heads of celery (or 12 celery stalks)
- 6 fl. oz. [$\frac{3}{4}$ cup] chicken stock
- $1\frac{1}{2}$ teaspoons dried tarragon
- 3 fl. oz. [$\frac{3}{8}$ cup] dry white wine
- 2 tablespoons beurre manié
- $\frac{1}{2}$ teaspoon salt
- $\frac{1}{4}$ teaspoon black pepper

Prepare and parboil the celery, drain well and split the celery stalks in half lengthways. Then chop them into strips approximately 3-inches long.

Put the chicken stock in a medium-sized saucepan. Add the tarragon and celery strips and place the pan over moderate heat. Cover the pan and cook the celery for 12 to 15 minutes, stirring occasionally. Transfer the celery to a dish and keep warm.

Add the white wine to the cooking liquid in the saucepan and bring to the boil. Remove the pan from the heat.

Divide the beurre manié into small

pieces and add them to the liquid in the pan, one at a time, stirring with a wooden spoon until the sauce becomes smooth and thick.

Return the pan to low heat. Season the sauce with salt and pepper. Add the cooked celery and, stirring, cook the mixture for 2 to 3 minutes to reheat the celery. Serve immediately.

Celery Vinaigrette

Celery Vinaigrette (vee-nay-gret) *is a fresh cool, crisp salad to serve with cold meat or smoked fish.*

4 SERVINGS

- 6 tablespoons olive oil
- 3 tablespoons wine vinegar
- ½ teaspoon salt
- ¼ teaspoon black pepper
- 1 large head of celery, washed and dried and divided into stalks, with the leaves removed and cut into slices

In a small mixing bowl, combine the oil, vinegar, salt and pepper with a fork until the ingredients are well mixed.

Place the celery in a serving dish and pour the dressing over them. Alternatively, the dressing may be served separately in a sauce boat.

Cenci

DEEP-FRIED SWEET CRISP PASTRIES

These sweet pastries, Cenci [chen-chee] *or lovers' knots are particularly popular for coffee or tea parties. They also make a good accompaniment to ice-cream and cold desserts. Care must be taken that the dough is paper thin, however, or the crispness of the final pastry will be lost.*

4 DOZEN

- 10 oz. [2½ cups] flour
- 1½ tablespoons icing [confectioners'] sugar
- ½ teaspoon salt
- 2 eggs
- 2 egg yolks
- 2 tablespoons rum
- sufficient vegetable or nut oil for deep-frying

Sift 8 ounces [2 cups] of the flour with ½ tablespoon of sugar and the salt into a large mixing bowl. Make a well in the centre of the mixture and into it pour the eggs, egg yolks and rum.

With a wooden spoon gradually draw the flour into the liquids in the centre, stirring gently until all the ingredients are blended to a smooth dough. Shape the dough into a ball.

Spread 1 ounce [¼ cup] of flour over a baking board, place the ball of dough on it and knead for about 10 minutes or until the dough has absorbed the flour on the board and is shiny in texture. Wrap the ball in greaseproof or waxed paper and place it in the refrigerator to chill for at least 1 hour.

Sprinkle the remaining flour on to the baking board. Cut the dough into quarters and, with a rolling pin, roll out each piece until it is paper thin. With a sharp knife or a pastry cutter, divide the pastry into strips ½-inch wide and 5-inches long, shaping these lengths into loose knots. Set them aside.

Fill a deep heavy saucepan one-third full of oil and heat it until it reaches 350°F on a deep-frying thermometer, or until a small piece of dry bread dropped into the oil turns golden in 50 seconds.

Drop the pastry knots into the fat, two or three at a time, and deep-fry them until they are light brown and puffed up. Remove them from the fat with a slotted spoon and drain them on kitchen paper towels.

When the knots are ready to be served, arrange them on a serving dish and sprinkle the remaining tablespoon of sugar over them. Serve warm or cold.

Deep-fried sweet crisp pastries, Cenci, or lovers' knots, are especially good with ice-cream and cold desserts.

Cerdo a la Aragonesa is a colourful Spanish pork and tomato casserole.

Cèpe

A variety of edible fungus, the cèpe (sep) is a large fleshy mushroom which grows mostly in France, being found in forests chiefly from the end of April until the autumn. It is most easily obtained outside France canned, bottled or dried.

Cerdo a la Aragonesa

SPANISH PORK CASSEROLE

A flavourful Spanish pork casserole, Cerdo a la Aragonesa (ther-doh ah lah ar-ah-go-nay-sah) *is ideal for an informal dinner party, since it may be prepared at least an hour before your guests arrive. Serve it with saffron-flavoured rice for a really Spanish touch!*

6 SERVINGS

- 6 tablespoons seasoned flour, made with 6 tablespoons plain [all-purpose] flour, ½ teaspoon salt and ¼ teaspoon black pepper
- 3 lb. boned fillet of pork, cut into ¼-inch thick slices
- 4 tablespoons vegetable oil
- 2 onions, sliced
- 2 garlic cloves, finely chopped
- 6 tomatoes, blanched, peeled, seeded and chopped
- 12 fl. oz. [1½ cups] dry white wine
- 1 teaspoon dried sweet basil
- 1 tablespoon chopped parsley

Sprinkle the seasoned flour on to a plate. Coat the pork slices on both sides with the seasoned flour.

In a large frying-pan, heat the oil over moderate heat. Add the pork slices and brown them for 3 to 4 minutes on each side. With tongs, transfer the pork slices from the pan to a flameproof casserole or saucepan.

Add the onions and garlic to the frying-pan and fry them for 12 to 15 minutes, or until they are golden brown.

Add the tomatoes, wine and sweet basil to the frying-pan and continue cooking for 2 to 3 minutes.

Pour the sauce over the meat. Cover the casserole or saucepan and place it over low heat. Simmer for 1 hour.

Remove the casserole from the heat and sprinkle the meat with parsley. Serve at once from the casserole.

Cereal

Named after Ceres, the Roman goddess of corn, cereals are grasses cultivated for food. They grow throughout the world and usually form the staple food of the population. Wheat and rice are the most widespread varieties, but the kind of cereal grown depends on the soil and climate. Cereals provide a cheap source of calories, protein, some vitamins and minerals. Wheat and rice are the major cereals for human consumption, and barley and oats for livestock.

Cevap

YUGOSLAVIAN LAMB CHOPS WITH PAPRIKA

Lamb chops in a colourful tomato and paprika sauce, Cevap (ch'vahp) *is an inexpensive, yet very tasty, supper dish. It may be served with rice or with boiled new potatoes and Brussels sprouts.*

4 SERVINGS

- 2 oz. [¼ cup] butter
- 4 lamb chops
- 1 large leek, thoroughly washed and finely chopped
- ½ teaspoon salt
- ¼ teaspoon black pepper
- 1 tablespoon paprika
- 1 tablespoon tomato purée
- 1 bay leaf
- 10 fl. oz. [1¼ cups] brown stock

In a large frying-pan, melt the butter over moderate heat. When the foam subsides, add the chops to the pan and brown them for 2 to 3 minutes on each side.

Using tongs, remove the chops from the pan and set them aside on a plate.

Add the chopped leek to the pan and fry it for 6 to 8 minutes. Add the salt, pepper, paprika, tomato purée, bay leaf and stock to the pan and stir well to mix the ingredients together.

Return the chops to the pan, cover and simmer gently over low heat for 15 to 20 minutes, or until the chops are tender.

Remove the chops from the pan and place them in a warmed serving dish. Pour the sauce over the chops and serve at once.

Cevapcici

SKEWERED LAMB AND BEEF BALLS

A Yugoslavian favourite, Cevapcici (ch'-vahp-chee-chee) *may either be served on skewers or removed from the skewers just before serving. Small hot peppers, plain boiled rice and chutneys are ideal accompaniments.*

6 SERVINGS

- 1 tablespoon butter
- 2 onions, finely chopped
- 2 garlic cloves, finely chopped
- 1 lb. minced [ground] lamb
- 1 lb. minced [ground] beef
- 2 thick, large slices of white bread, grated into breadcrumbs

Lamb chops in a tomato and paprika sauce, Cevap is an inexpensive, yet very tasty, Yugoslavian dish.

1 egg white, lightly beaten
½ teaspoon dried sweet basil
1 teaspoon salt
1 tablespoon paprika
⅛ teaspoon cayenne

Low Cal

In a small frying-pan, melt the butter over moderate heat. When the foam subsides, add half the chopped onions and the garlic and fry them for 10 to 12 minutes, stirring occasionally.

Remove the pan from the heat and turn the onions and garlic into a large mixing bowl. Add the lamb, beef, breadcrumbs, egg white, basil, salt, paprika and cayenne to the bowl. With a fork, combine the ingredients well.

Using your hands, shape the mixture into small walnut-sized balls.

Place the meat balls on a plate and cover them with greaseproof or waxed paper. Put the plate in the refrigerator and leave it for at least 1 hour, or until the mixture is firm.

Preheat the grill [broiler] to high.

Remove the plate from the refrigerator and put the meat balls on skewers.

Place the skewers under the grill [broiler] and cook them for about 4 minutes on each side, or until the meat is dark brown on the outside.

Remove the skewers from the heat, sprinkle each skewer with the remaining chopped onion and serve at once.

Cervelles Braisées

BRAISED CALF'S BRAINS

Calf's brains cooked in butter with vegetables, herbs, wine and stock, Cervelles Braisées (sair-vell bray-zay) *may be served with rice or boiled new potatoes.*

6 SERVINGS

2 oz. [¼ cup] butter
1 carrot, scraped and finely chopped
1 onion, finely chopped
1 celery stalk, chopped
3 tablespoons chopped cooked ham
bouquet garni, consisting of 4 parsley sprigs, 1 thyme spray and 1 bay leaf tied together
¾ teaspoon salt
½ teaspoon black pepper
3 sets of prepared calf's brains
6 fl. oz. [¾ cup] dry white wine
12 fl. oz. [1½ cups] beef stock

Low Cal

In a large frying-pan, melt the butter over moderate heat. When the foam subsides, add the carrot, onion, celery, ham and bouquet garni. Sprinkle the mixture with ¼ teaspoon of salt and ¼ teaspoon of black pepper. Cook, stirring occasionally, for 10 to 15 minutes, or until the vegetables are tender but not brown.

Sprinkle the remaining salt and pepper over the brains and place them in the frying-pan with the vegetables. Spoon the butter and vegetable mixture over the brains. Cover the pan and cook over low heat for 5 minutes. Turn over the brains, baste them again and cook for a further 5 minutes.

With tongs, transfer the brains from the frying-pan to a medium-sized flameproof casserole.

Preheat the oven to warm 325°F (Gas Mark 3, 170°C).

Pour the wine into the frying-pan with the vegetables and bring it to the boil over high heat. Boil until the liquid has reduced to about half.

Remove the pan from the heat and pour the contents of the pan over the brains. Add enough stock to just cover the brains.

Place the casserole over moderate heat and bring the liquid to the boil. Cover the casserole and place it in the oven. Bake for 30 minutes. Remove the casserole from the oven and serve immediately.

Ceviche

MACKEREL FILLETS MARINATED IN LEMON JUICE

This is a traditional Mexican dish, although it is also made in most South American countries with slight variations. The original recipe uses fresh limes but, if these are difficult to obtain, Ceviche (s'veh cheh) *may be made with fresh lemon juice. If you do use limes, use 8 fluid ounces* [1 cup] *of lime juice and 8 fluid ounces* [1 cup] *of lemon juice. Ceviche makes an unusual hors d'oeuvre, accompanied by crusty bread.*

6 SERVINGS

16 fl. oz. [2 cups] fresh lemon juice
1 teaspoon dried, seeded, hot red chilli pepper, pounded in a mortar
2 large onions, thinly sliced and pushed out into rings
½ garlic clove, chopped
1 teaspoon salt
½ teaspoon black pepper
3 large mackerels, filleted and cut into 1-inch pieces
3 large sweet potatoes, unpeeled
2 crisp lettuces, washed, separated and chilled
4 ears fresh sweet corn, with outer husks and threads removed and cut across into 2-inch rounds
1 fresh red chilli, washed, split, seeded and cut into thin pieces

Low Cal

Combine the lemon juice, pounded dried chilli pepper, onion rings, garlic, salt and pepper in a pitcher.

Place the fish pieces in a shallow porcelain dish and pour the lemon juice mixture over them. If the liquid does not cover the fish, add more lemon juice.

Cover the dish and place it in the refrigerator. Leave the fish for at least 3 hours, or until it is opaque and white.

Thirty minutes before you are ready to serve the dish, bring 3 pints of water to the boil in a large saucepan over high heat. Place the sweet potatoes in the boiling water and cover the pan. Reduce the heat to moderate and cook for about 25 minutes, or until the potatoes are tender when pierced with the point of a sharp knife.

While the potatoes are cooking, arrange a bed of lettuce leaves on 6 individual plates. Set the plates aside.

Remove the pan from the heat and drain the potatoes in a colander. Peel the potatoes and cut each one into 3 slices. Keep the potato slices warm while you cook the corn.

Bring 2 pints of water to the boil over high heat. Drop the corn rounds into the boiling water and boil them for 4 to 5 minutes, or until the corn turns bright yellow.

Remove the pan from the heat and drain the corn in a colander

Remove the marinated fish from the refrigerator. Using a slotted spoon, divide the fish between the six plates. Garnish the fish with the onion rings and strips of fresh chilli pepper.

Arrange the sweet potato slices and corn rounds round the fish and serve at once.

Mackerel fillets marinated in a spicy lemon and chilli mixture, Ceviche is a traditional Mexican dish.

Chablis

Chablis (shah-blee) is a dry, rich, white BURGUNDY, pale in colour. Under the French appellation contrôlée (controlled place name) laws there are four different categories of Chablis which are, in ascending order of quality, petit Chablis, Chablis, premier cru Chablis and grand cru Chablis. Chablis goes particularly well with fish, shellfish and oysters. It may also be served with chicken.

Chafing dish

This is a vessel which is used at the table for cooking food and for keeping it warm. A true chafing dish consists of two pans, an upper one or 'blazer' which holds the food, and a lower one which holds boiling water. It is also used for cooking foods which are usually cooked in a double boiler or require special care to prevent curdling.

Chamonix

Chamonix (shah-moh-nee) *is very rich and makes an unusual finish to a dinner party menu. While some care is required in its preparation, the result is definitely worthwhile.*

6 SERVINGS

MERINGUE
4 egg whites
8 oz. [1 cup] castor sugar

FILLING
8 fl. oz. double cream [1 cup heavy cream]
2 tablespoons castor sugar
¼ teaspoon vanilla essence
2 tablespoons granulated sugar
2 tablespoons brandy (optional)
8 oz. canned unsweetened chestnut purée

Preheat the oven to very cool 275°F (Gas Mark 1, 140°C). Line a baking sheet with nonstick silicone paper and set it aside.

In a large mixing bowl, prepare the meringue by beating the egg whites with a wire whisk or rotary beater until they are stiff and firm. Add 4 teaspoons of the sugar and beat vigorously for 1 minute. Then, using the side of a metal spoon as a cutting edge, carefully fold the rest of the sugar into the egg whites.

Put the meringue mixture into a pastry bag and make nestlike shells by piping the mixture on to the baking sheet. Each shell should have a thin base of meringue, and be 2 to 3 inches in diameter and 2½ inches high with a hollow centre.

Bake the meringue shells in the oven for approximately 1 hour, or until they are very pale brown. Remove them from the oven and set them aside to cool.

Meringues filled with a delectable brandy-flavoured chestnut purée, Chamonix are an impressive dessert.

In a medium-sized mixing bowl, prepare the filling by beating the double cream with a whisk or fork until it is almost stiff. Fold in the sugar and vanilla essence and continue beating to blend well and until the cream is very thick. Beat the sugar and brandy (if you are using it) into the chestnut purée.

Assemble the chamonix by spooning the chestnut purée into a pastry bag and piping a round or two of purée around the top of each meringue shell. Spoon a portion of whipped cream into the hollow centre of each meringue.

Champ

A traditional Irish potato dish, Champ is a tasty variation on plain mashed potatoes. Champ may be accompanied by sausages to make a delicious light supper.

4 TO 6 SERVINGS

- **5 fl. oz.** [$\frac{5}{8}$ cup] **milk**
- **10 spring onions** [scallions] **with their green stalks, finely chopped**
- **$1\frac{1}{2}$ lb. hot boiled potatoes, peeled and mashed**
- **1 teaspoon salt**
- **$\frac{1}{2}$ teaspoon white pepper**
- **2 oz.** [$\frac{1}{4}$ cup] **butter, melted**
- **1 tablespoon chopped parsley**

In a medium-sized saucepan, scald the milk (bring to just under boiling point) over moderate heat. Add the onions [scallions]. Cover the saucepan, reduce the heat to low and simmer for 8 to 10 minutes, or until the onions [scallions] are tender. Drain and set aside, reserving the cooking liquid.

Put the mashed potatoes in a large, deep serving bowl, add the chopped onions [scallions] and, with a wooden spoon, beat the two together until they are well blended. Add a little of the reserved cooking milk and stir until the mixture resembles a very light creamy purée.

Season the mixture with salt and pepper and stir in the melted butter. Garnish the potatoes with parsley and serve immediately.

1966
1966
ULTRA

Champagne

Champagne is, strictly speaking, a sparkling white wine made from grapes grown in the vineyards of the Champagne area in northern France. The soil of the Champagne region, rich in chalk and limestone, is responsible for the unique quality of the wines. Almost all champagne is made from both black and white grapes. Champagne is an expensive wine because of the time, care and difficulty involved in its preparation.

Champagne ranges in sweetness from *brut*, the driest, through extra-dry, dry and *demi-sec* to *doux*, the sweetest. Because part of the fermentation process of champagne occurs in the wine bottle itself, carbon dioxide gas bubbles are released upon uncorking. These bubbles give champagne its sparkling quality.

Champagne is sold under the name or trademark of its shipper instead of the name of the vineyard. Non-vintage champagne accounts for the bulk of the trade. It is blended from the juices of grapes from vineyards of varying quality. Wines of previous years may also be mixed in with the current crop to maintain a consistency of taste in each year's production. Non-vintage wines should be drunk young.

Due to the blending process, there is not the same emphasis on a vintage year with champagne as there is with BORDEAUX and BURGUNDY. In an exceptionally good year, however, champagne is made from that year's crop alone and a date is put on the label. Vintage champagne is a fuller and more expensive wine than non-vintage champagne.

Light and effervescent Champagne is traditionally associated with luxury and special occasions and is served at weddings and other festivities. It is an ideal apéritif and also goes well with the more delicate white meats and desserts.

Champagne should not be served in a saucer-shaped glass, which disperses the bubbles, the essence of Champagne, too rapidly. A tulip or flute-shaped wine glass is appropriate for this wine.

Champagne Chicken

A dish for that extra special occasion, Champagne Chicken is rich, yet subtle, light, yet filling. If preferred, a dry white wine can be used instead of the Champagne. Serve Champagne Chicken with rice and a salade de tomates.

Champagne Chicken is a magnificent dish for a special occasion.

4 SERVINGS

1 x 4 lb. chicken, cut into serving pieces, or 8 small chicken pieces
$\frac{1}{2}$ teaspoon salt
$\frac{1}{2}$ teaspoon black pepper
2 tablespoons butter
2 onions, finely sliced
2 tablespoons brandy
8 fl. oz. [1 cup] chicken stock
5 fl. oz. [$\frac{5}{8}$ cup] Champagne
$\frac{1}{2}$ teaspoon dried thyme
$\frac{1}{4}$ teaspoon dried mace
1 bay leaf
3 tablespoons flour
6 fl. oz. double cream [$\frac{3}{4}$ cup heavy cream]
6 oz. mushrooms, cleaned and sliced
1 teaspoon cornflour [cornstarch] **dissolved in 1 teaspoon water**

Preheat the oven to hot 425°F (Gas Mark 7, 220°C).

On a wooden board, rub the chicken pieces with the salt and pepper and set them aside.

In a large, heavy flameproof casserole melt the butter over moderate heat. Add the onions and cook for about 5 minutes. Add the chicken pieces and cook them for 2 or 3 minutes, turning them with spoons or tongs until the pieces are well coated with butter but not brown.

Place the casserole in the centre of the oven and bake for 35 minutes. Remove the casserole from the oven.

Add the brandy, chicken stock, Champagne, thyme, mace and bay leaf to the casserole. Sprinkle the flour on top of the mixture and stir vigorously to mix all the ingredients together.

Put the double [heavy] cream in a frying-pan over very low heat, add the mushrooms and mix together. Do not let the cream become too hot. When the mushrooms are well coated, add them to the casserole (together with the cream) and bring the liquids in the casserole to the boil over moderate heat.

Cover the casserole and put it in the oven for a further 40 minutes.

When the chicken is cooked, remove the pieces from the casserole with tongs or a slotted spoon and arrange them in a deep serving dish. Cover and keep warm.

Boil the sauce in the casserole over high heat until it is reduced to about two-thirds of the original amount. Adjust the sauce for seasoning, adding salt and pepper as required, and simmer, stirring occasionally, for 10 minutes. If the sauce needs thickening at this point, add the cornflour [cornstarch] to the mixture and stir well until it is thoroughly dissolved.

Pour the sauce over the chicken and serve immediately.

Champignons au Beurre

MUSHROOMS SAUTEED IN BUTTER

Champignons au Beurre (shom-peen-yon oh bur) *are used as a garnish for steak, chicken or roasts, or combined with other vegetables such as carrots or onions. If you have a lot of mushrooms, cook them in several batches so that you only have one layer in the pan, otherwise they will steam rather than brown.*

4 SERVINGS

$1\frac{1}{2}$ oz. [3 tablespoons] butter
1 garlic clove, crushed
8 oz. mushrooms, washed and thinly sliced
$\frac{1}{2}$ teaspoon salt
$\frac{1}{4}$ teaspoon black pepper
1 tablespoon chopped parsley

In a large frying-pan, melt the butter over high heat. When the foam subsides, add the garlic and cook for 1 minute, stirring constantly. Add the mushrooms to the pan and sauté them for 4 to 5 minutes, or until they are lightly browned. Shake the pan so that the mushrooms become coated with the butter and brown evenly.

Season the mushrooms with salt and pepper. Remove the pan from the heat and sprinkle with the parsley.

Champignons à Blanc

STEWED MUSHROOMS

Champignons à Blanc (shom-peen-yon ah blon) *are used in sauces, fricassées or in recipes where the cooked mushrooms should remain white. For these, buy the small white mushrooms rather than the large, darker flat ones. When making the dish, add the mushrooms together with the cooking liquid to the ingredients.*

APPROXIMATELY 4 SERVINGS

Low Cal

3 fl. oz. [$\frac{3}{8}$ cup] water
$\frac{1}{8}$ teaspoon salt
2 teaspoons lemon juice
1 tablespoon butter
4 oz. mushrooms, washed, dried and cut as the recipe specifies

In a medium-sized saucepan, bring the water, salt, lemon juice and butter to the boil over moderate heat.

Add the mushrooms to the liquid in the pan and stir once or twice to completely cover the mushrooms with the liquid. Cover the pan and simmer, stirring occasionally, for 5 minutes.

Remove the pan from the heat and set it aside until you are ready to use the mushrooms.

Champignons Farcis are mushrooms filled with a cream and parsley mixture and topped with grated cheese.

Champignons Farcis

STUFFED MUSHROOMS

Mushrooms filled with a cream and parsley mixture and topped with cheese, Champignons Farcis (shom-peen-yon fahr-see) *are delicious and easy to prepare. They may be served either as an appetizing hors d'oeuvre or as an attractive garnish to a roast.*

4 SERVINGS

12 large mushrooms, wiped
1 teaspoon salt
$\frac{1}{2}$ teaspoon freshly ground black pepper
1 tablespoon melted butter
2 tablespoons butter
2 shallots or spring onions [scallions], finely chopped
1 tablespoon flour
4 fl. oz. single cream [$\frac{1}{2}$ cup light cream]
3 tablespoons chopped fresh parsley
$1\frac{1}{2}$ tablespoons grated Parmesan cheese

Preheat the oven to fairly hot 375°F (Gas Mark 5, 190°C).

Remove the stems from the mushrooms and set them aside. Season the mushroom caps with $\frac{1}{2}$ teaspoon of salt and $\frac{1}{4}$ teaspoon black pepper, and, using a pastry brush coat them with the melted butter. Arrange them, hollow side up, in a shallow baking dish.

With a sharp knife chop the mushroom stems finely. Wrap them in kitchen paper towels and twist to extract as much juice from them as possible.

In a medium-sized frying-pan melt the 2 tablespoons of butter over moderate heat.

When the foam subsides, add the chopped mushroom stems and shallots or spring onions [scallions]. Sauté them together for 4 to 5 minutes. Reduce the heat to low and, stirring constantly, add the flour. Cook for 1 minute.

Remove the pan from the heat and stir in the cream, a little at a time. When the sauce is smooth and all the ingredients are blended, return the pan to the heat and simmer the sauce for 2 to 3 minutes, or until it has thickened.

Stir in the parsley and the remaining salt and pepper and mix well.

Remove the pan from the heat and spoon a little of the mixture into each of the prepared mushroom caps.

Top each mushroom with a little grated cheese. Place the dish in the oven and bake the mushrooms for 15 minutes or until they are tender and the stuffing is lightly browned on top.

Remove from the oven and serve.

Champignons Grillés

GRILLED [BROILED] MUSHROOM CAPS

Fresh button mushrooms stuffed with garlic butter and quickly grilled [broiled], *Champignons Grillés* (shom-peen-yon gree-yay) *may be served as a vegetable accompaniment or on toast as a hot snack.*

4 SERVINGS

1 teaspoon butter
1 lb. large button mushrooms, washed and dried and stems removed
2 oz. [$\frac{1}{4}$ cup] butter, melted
$\frac{1}{2}$ teaspoon salt
$\frac{1}{4}$ teaspoon black pepper
2 to 4 oz. [$\frac{1}{4}$ to $\frac{1}{2}$ cup] Beurre d'Ail, depending on size of mushrooms

Preheat the grill [broiler] to moderate.

Lightly grease a large flameproof baking dish with the 1 teaspoon of butter.

Arrange the mushroom caps, hollow side up, in the buttered baking dish. Using a pastry brush, brush the mushroom caps with the melted butter. Sprinkle the caps with the salt and pepper.

Place the dish under the grill [broiler] and cook for 5 minutes. Turn the mushroom caps over, brush again with melted butter and cook for 5 minutes, or until the mushrooms are tender and lightly browned.

Remove the dish from the heat and place about a teaspoon of beurre d'ail in each cap, filling the caps about one-third full.

Place the dish back under the grill [broiler] and heat for 1 to 2 minutes, or until the butter is bubbling. Serve the mushrooms at once.

Champignons au Madère

MUSHROOMS IN MADEIRA SAUCE

A rich and exotic way of preparing mushrooms, Champignons au Madere (shom-peen-yon oh mah-dair) *is especially good poured over a juicy fillet steak. The sauce may be prepared in advance, then reheated and the final 1 tablespoon of butter added just before serving.*

8 FLUID OUNCES SAUCE

2 oz. [$\frac{1}{4}$ cup] butter
8 oz. mushrooms, washed, dried and sliced, quartered or chopped
3 fl. oz. [$\frac{3}{8}$ cup] Madeira
5 fl. oz. [$\frac{5}{8}$ cup] rich brown sauce
$\frac{1}{4}$ teaspoon salt
$\frac{1}{8}$ teaspoon black pepper

In a deep frying-pan, melt 3 tablespoons of the butter over moderate heat. When the foam subsides, add the mushrooms and cook them for 4 to 5 minutes.

With a slotted spoon, transfer the mushrooms to a dish and keep warm.

Pour the Madeira and the brown sauce into the pan. Increase the heat to high and bring the liquid to the boil. Boil until the liquid has reduced by half. Remove the pan from the heat and strain the sauce into a bowl. Wipe out the frying-pan and return the mushrooms and sauce to it. Place the pan over low heat. Simmer for a further 2 to 3 minutes. Season the mixture with the salt and pepper.

Remove the pan from the heat and swirl in the remaining 1 tablespoon of butter if you are serving the sauce immediately. Otherwise, set the pan aside.

Mushrooms, sherry and cream combine to make a delectable and unusual dinner party hors d'oeuvre.

Add the butter when you reheat the sauce just before serving.

Champignons Pyramide

MUSHROOMS BAKED WITH CREAM AND SHERRY

An unusual dinner party hors d'oeuvre, Champignons Pyramide (shom-peen-yohn peer-ah-meed) *is a luscious concoction of mushrooms flavoured with cream and sherry.*

4 SERVINGS

- **2 tablespoons butter**
- **1 teaspoon lemon juice**
- **1 teaspoon salt**
- **3 slices of buttered toast, cut about ½ inch thick and with crusts removed**
- **1 lb. mushrooms, wiped and with the stems removed**
- **½ teaspoon black pepper**
- **4 fl. oz. double cream [½ cup heavy cream]**
- **1 tablespoon sherry**

Preheat the oven to moderate 350°F (Gas Mark 4, 180°C).

In a small mixing bowl, combine the butter with ½ teaspoon lemon juice and ½ teaspoon salt, beating with a wooden spoon until the mixture becomes light and creamy.

Coat the bottom and sides of a deep ovenproof dish with the mixture and arrange the toast slices on the bottom. Pile the mushroom caps, pyramid-style, on the toast. Season the pyramid with the remaining salt, pepper and lemon juice and cover it with 3 fluid ounces [⅜ cup] of cream.

Cover the dish and bake in the oven for 25 to 30 minutes. Fifteen minutes before the end of the cooking period, add the remaining cream to the mixture.

Remove the dish from the oven and sprinkle the mushrooms with the sherry.

Champignons Sautés à la Crème

CREAMED MUSHROOMS

Mushrooms cooked in cream and white wine, Champignons Sautés à la Crème (shom-peen-yon soh-tay ah lah krem) *makes a delicious filling for vol-au-vents or flans.*

4 SERVINGS IF USED AS A FILLING

- **2 oz. [¼ cup] butter**
- **1 tablespoon vegetable oil**
- **8 oz. button mushrooms, washed and dried**
- **2 shallots, finely chopped**
- **1 teaspoon flour**
- **8 fl. oz. single cream [1 cup light cream]**
- **¼ teaspoon salt**
- **⅛ teaspoon white pepper**
- **3 tablespoons dry white wine**

In a deep frying-pan, melt 2 tablespoons of butter and the oil over moderate heat. When the foam subsides, add the mushrooms and sauté them for 4 to 5 minutes. Add the shallots to the pan and cook, stirring, for 2 minutes.

With a wooden spoon, stir the flour into the pan and cook for 2 to 3 minutes, stirring constantly.

Remove the pan from the heat and stir in the cream, salt and pepper. When well blended, return the pan to moderately high heat and boil the liquid until it has reduced a little and is thickened. Add the wine and boil for 1 minute.

Remove the pan from the heat and stir in the remaining butter.

Channa Dhal

CURRIED CHICK-PEAS

Simple and inexpensive to make, Channa Dhal (chun-nah dahl) *is often served as part of an Indian meal. It also makes a delicious – and exotic – accompaniment to spiced leg of lamb or roast pork. Remember to begin the preparation the day before as the chick-peas should soak in water overnight.*

6 SERVINGS

- 12 oz. [1½ cups] chick-peas, washed thoroughly, soaked in cold water overnight and drained
- 1 teaspoon salt
- 3 tablespoons clarified butter
- 1 teaspoon cumin seeds
- 1 medium-sized onion, finely chopped
- 1-inch piece root ginger, peeled and finely chopped
- 1 teaspoon turmeric
- ½ teaspoon ground cumin
- 1 teaspoon ground coriander
- 1 teaspoon garam masala
- ¼ to ½ teaspoon chilli powder
- 1 tablespoon chopped coriander leaves

Low Cal

Put the chick-peas in a medium-sized saucepan and cover with 2½ pints of water and the salt. Bring the liquid to the boil over high heat. Reduce the heat to low, half-cover the pan and cook gently for 1 hour.

In a large saucepan heat the clarified or melted butter over moderate heat. Add the cumin seeds and cook for 1 minute. Add the onion and cook for 5 minutes, stirring frequently to prevent the onion from sticking to the bottom of the pan. Stir in the ginger and continue cooking for 4 minutes, or until the onion becomes golden brown.

In a small bowl combine the turmeric, ground cumin, coriander, garam masala and chilli powder with 2 tablespoons of water to make a paste. Add the paste to the onion mixture in the pan and fry for 3 or 4 minutes, stirring constantly. Add the chick-peas and the cooking liquid to the pan. Increase the heat to high and, stirring continuously, bring the mixture to the boil. Cover the pan, reduce the heat to low and simmer for 30 minutes, or until the chick-peas are tender but still whole.

Taste the chick-peas and add more salt if necessary. Pour the mixture into a serving dish, sprinkle the top with the chopped coriander leaves and serve.

Channa Dhal, an inexpensive chick-pea curry, is excellent served with Chappattis, hot Indian bread.

Chantilly

This name originally came from a thick cream produced at a model dairy in Chantilly (shon-tee-yee), in France. It is applied to several preparations – but primarily in confectionery to fresh cream beaten to the consistency of a mousse, sweetened and flavoured with vanilla. Secondly, as a sauce it refers to a cold hollandaise or mayonnaise to which whipped cream has been added. A hot *sauce chantilly* refers to a béchamel which is mixed with whipped cream. The two cold sauces are also known as *mousseline*.

Chapatti

UNLEAVENED INDIAN BREAD

The Chapatti, made of wholewheat flour, is the staple cereal food of Northern India and, like most other Indian breads is unleavened. The traditional fat used is ghee (clarified butter) or the less expensive hydrogenated vegetable oil. Butter or vegetable fat may be used instead.

8 CHAPATTIS

8 oz. [2 cups] **wholewheat flour**
$\frac{1}{2}$ teaspoon salt
2 oz. [$\frac{1}{4}$ cup] **butter or vegetable fat**
5 fl. oz. [$\frac{5}{8}$ cup] **water**
1 tablespoon clarified or melted butter

Sift the flour and salt into a large mixing bowl. Add the butter or vegetable fat and rub it into the flour with your fingertips. Make a well in the centre and pour in 3 fluid ounces [$\frac{3}{8}$ cup] of water. Mix with your fingers, adding the rest of the water gradually.

Form the dough into a ball and place it on a floured board. Knead the dough for 10 minutes or until it becomes smooth and elastic.

Put the dough into a bowl, cover with a cloth and leave to stand for 30 minutes at room temperature.

Divide the dough into 8 portions. On the floured board, roll out the dough into a thin round shape, the size of a small plate.

Meanwhile, heat a heavy iron frying-pan over moderate heat. When it is hot, place one portion of dough in the pan. When small blisters appear on the surface, press the chapatti to flatten it. Then turn it over and cook it until it is a pale golden colour.

Remove the chapatti from the pan and brush it with a little clarified or melted butter. Place the chapatti on a plate and cover with another plate to keep it warm until all the chapattis are cooked. Serve warm.

Chapon

A Chapon (shah-pon) or *chapon à l'ail* is a crust or slice of bread rubbed with garlic and seasoned with oil and vinegar. Tossed into a salad, particularly of chicory, the chapon gives it a garlic flavour. This is especially used in Southern French cookery.

Char

A member of the salmon family, this fish is recognizable by its red belly. Char are found in fresh water, in Iceland, some English lakes and Scottish lochs. They are identical to or closely related to the *omble chevalier* found in Swiss and Savoy lakes. In the United States the name 'char' is given to some species of trout.

Char can be cooked by any method suitable for trout.

Charcoal

Charcoal is made by a special process of burning wood which produces a smoke-less fuel. Used for barbecue cooking or on special grills [broilers], the fuel imparts a special flavour to the food. As the fumes are dangerous, proper air extraction is needed if charcoal is used indoors.

Chard

This vegetable is also known as Swiss chard. It is a beetroot with dark green, yellow or bright red leaves, but without the large root of the familiar beetroot. The leaves and stalks are cooked in the same way as spinach, or can be eaten raw.

Charlotte

A Charlotte is a pudding encased in a circle of bread, cake or biscuits [cookies], enclosing a sweet filling. There are two main types of charlotte: Charlotte Russe, a cold sweet which consists of a rich custard and whipped cream mixture set with gelatine and enclosed in sponge fingers, and Fruit Charlotte, served hot, which consists of a fruit filling and thin buttered slices of bread. A savoury type of charlotte – usually cheese-flavoured – is also sometimes made.

Charlotte au Chocolat

CHOCOLATE CUSTARD IN A SPONGE FINGER MOULD

A delectable chocolate custard set in a mould lined with sponge fingers, Charlotte au Chocolat (shahr-lot oh shoh-koh-lah) *is a dessert that makes a perfect ending for a dinner party menu. Charlotte au Chocolat may be decorated with whipped cream and grated chocolate before serving.*

8 TO 10 SERVINGS

CREME ANGLAISE

6 oz. [$\frac{3}{4}$ cup] **castor sugar**
8 large egg yolks
$1\frac{1}{2}$ teaspoons cornflour [cornstarch]
6 oz. plain [semi-sweet] **cooking chocolate melted in $1\frac{1}{2}$ pints** [$3\frac{3}{4}$ cups] **scalded milk**
1 teaspoon vanilla essence
8 oz. unsalted butter [1 cup sweet butter]
6 oz. [1 cup] **ground almonds**
$\frac{1}{2}$ teaspoon almond essence
3 fl. oz. [$\frac{3}{8}$ cup] **plus 1 tablespoon rum**
3 fl. oz. [$\frac{3}{8}$ cup] **water**
36 sponge finger biscuits [cookies]

First prepare the crème anglaise. In a large mixing bowl, beat the sugar into the egg yolks with a wire whisk. Beat for 2 to 3 minutes, or until the mixture is pale yellow and forms a ribbon trail on itself when the whisk is lifted.

Beat the cornflour [cornstarch] into the mixture. Slowly pour the chocolate-flavoured milk on to the egg yolks mixture, beating constantly.

Pour the mixture into a large saucepan and place it over very low heat. With a wooden spoon, stir the mixture slowly and continuously until it is just thick enough to coat the back of the spoon. Do not let the custard reach simmering point or it will curdle.

Remove the pan from the heat. Leave the custard for 1 to 2 minutes and then pour it through a strainer into a large mixing bowl. Beat in the vanilla essence.

Place the bowl in a pan of cold water and stir the custard until it is cool. Cover the bowl and place it in the refrigerator to chill.

In a medium-sized mixing bowl, cream the butter and ground almonds together with a wooden spoon.

Remove the chilled custard from the refrigerator and slowly beat it into the almonds and butter mixture. Beat the almond essence and 1 tablespoon of rum into the mixture.

Pour the remaining rum and the water into a shallow bowl. Dip the sponge fingers into the liquid, one at a time, and place them on a rack to drain.

Line a 3-pint [$7\frac{1}{2}$-cup] mould with greaseproof or waxed paper. Cut some of the sponge fingers into a design of wedges to fit the bottom of the mould. Lay the fingers in the mould, curved sides down to cover the bottom. Arrange some more sponge fingers upright round the mould, their curved sides against the mould.

Pour the mixture into the lined mould, alternating with layers of the remaining sponge fingers. With a sharp knife, trim the sponge fingers round the top of the mould and press the trimmed-off pieces into the top of the mixture. Cover the mould with greaseproof or waxed paper and place a plate or saucer over the paper, with a weight on top.

Place the mould in the refrigerator to chill and leave it for at least 6 hours, or overnight.

Remove the mould from the refrigerator and remove the weight, plate and paper from the top of the mould. Place a serving plate upside down over the mould. Holding the plate and mould firmly together, reverse them, shaking the mould slightly. The Charlotte will then slide out on to the plate. Refrigerate the Charlotte until you are ready to serve it.

A rich and impressive dessert for a dinner party, Charlotte aux Framboises is surprisingly easy to prepare.

Charlotte aux Framboises

RASPBERRY MOULD

An impressive dessert, Charlotte aux Framboises (shahr-lot oh fram-bwahz) *takes a surprisingly short time to prepare. If raspberries are not in season the frozen ones are equally good. If using frozen fruit allow it to thaw before puréeing.*

8 TO 10 SERVINGS

28-30 sponge finger biscuits [cookies]
4 oz. [$\frac{1}{2}$ cup] castor sugar
8 egg yolks

$\frac{1}{2}$ oz. gelatine, dissolved in 2 tablespoons water
$1\frac{1}{2}$ lb. fresh raspberries, hulled, washed and drained
$1\frac{1}{4}$ pints double cream [3 cups heavy cream], **stiffly whipped**

Line the sides of a 3-pint [$7\frac{1}{2}$-cup] mould with dampened greaseproof or waxed paper. Place a row of sponge fingers upright all around the inside of the mould, with the curved sides of the biscuits against the side. Do not line the bottom of the mould with biscuits.

In a large mixing bowl beat the sugar into the egg yolks with a wire whisk. Continue beating until the mixture is pale yellow and will form a ribbon trail on itself when the whisk is lifted.

Place the mixing bowl over a saucepan of just-simmering water and continue beating, over moderate heat, until the mixture is thick and hot.

Remove the mixing bowl from the heat and stand it in a basin of cold water. Add the dissolved gelatine. Continue to beat the mixture until it is cold. Place the bowl in the refrigerator and leave it to chill for at least 30 minutes.

Sieve 1 pound of the berries into a small bowl and measure out 16 fluid ounces [2 cups] of purée. Place the purée in the refrigerator to chill.

With a metal spoon, fold the chilled berry purée into the chilled egg yolk mixture. Add 1 pint [$2\frac{1}{2}$ cups] of the cream and stir until well blended.

Pour the mixture into the lined mould and arrange the remaining sponge fingers over the top to completely cover the mould. Trim off any protruding sponge fingers.

Cover the mould with greaseproof or waxed paper and refrigerate for at least 6 hours or overnight.

When you are ready to serve the Charlotte, remove the paper from the top and run a knife around the edge of the mould. Place a serving dish over the mould and reverse the two, giving a sharp shake. The Charlotte should slide out easily on to the dish. Decorate with the remaining berries and cream.

Charlotte aux Fraises

ALMOND CREAM WITH STRAWBERRIES

Charlotte aux Fraises (shahr-lot oh frehz) *is a luscious, creamy dessert, grandly suited to the special occasion and well worth the care and effort necessary to prepare it.*

4 SERVINGS

6 fl. oz. [$\frac{3}{4}$ cup] **orange-flavoured liqueur**
3 fl. oz. [$\frac{3}{8}$ cup] **water**
28-30 sponge finger biscuits [cookies]
6 oz. unsalted butter [$\frac{3}{4}$ cup sweet butter], **softened**
4 oz. [$\frac{1}{2}$ cup] **castor sugar**
$\frac{1}{4}$ teaspoon almond essence
3 oz. [$\frac{1}{2}$ cup] **ground almonds**
8 fl. oz. double cream [1 cup heavy cream]
1 lb. fresh or frozen strawberries

Line the bottom of a 2-pint [5-cup] mould with a round of greaseproof or waxed paper. In a small bowl, mix together half of the liqueur and the water. One by one, dip the sponge fingers into the mixture, coating them well. Be careful not to saturate the biscuits or they will be soggy. Line the sides of the mould with the moistened biscuits, reserving the extras to use later. Trim the sponge fingers if they are higher than the mould. Set the mould aside.

In a medium-sized bowl, cream the butter and sugar together with the back of a wooden spoon until the mixture is pale and fluffy. Add the remaining liqueur, the almond essence and the ground almonds and, with the spoon or a wire whisk, beat until all the ingredients are well blended.

In another medium-sized bowl, whip the cream with a whisk until it is thick but not stiff. Beat the cream vigorously into the butter-and-almond mixture and continue beating until a smooth paste is formed. Place the bowl in the refrigerator to chill.

Prepare the strawberries by washing and hulling them if they are fresh, or thawing them if they are frozen. Dry them well on kitchen paper towels. Set them aside, keeping back about 6 strawberries for decoration.

Spoon about one-half of the almond-cream mixture into the mould. Arrange a layer of strawberries on top, followed by a layer of sponge fingers. Repeat the process, finishing with the last of the sponge fingers. Cover the mould with greaseproof or waxed paper and place a large weight or other similarly heavy object (the same diameter as the inside of the mould) on top. Place the mould in the refrigerator for at least 12 hours or overnight.

Remove the weight and the top layer of paper and run a sharp knife around the mould to ease the sides of the Charlotte. Place a serving dish, inverted, over the top of the mould and reverse the two. The Charlotte should slide out on to the dish. Peel off the second round of paper and decorate the top and sides of the Charlotte with the remaining strawberries. Serve very cold.

Charlotte Russe

Charlotte Russe (shahr-lot roose) *was invented by the great French chef Carême, who originally called it Charlotte Parisienne. It is particularly suitable for entertaining as it is best if made the day before.*

4-6 SERVINGS

4 fl. oz. [$\frac{1}{2}$ cup] **fruit-flavoured jelly** [gelatin], **preferably lemon, cool but still liquid**
28-30 sponge finger biscuits [cookies]
10 fl. oz. [$1\frac{1}{4}$ cups] **milk**
1 vanilla pod, split
3 egg yolks
2 tablespoons sugar
1 tablespoon gelatine
3-$3\frac{1}{2}$ fl. oz. [$\frac{3}{8}$ cup] **hot water**
8 fl. oz. double cream [1 cup heavy cream]

Spoon the jelly [gelatin] into a straight-sided charlotte mould. Tip and rotate the mould so that the jelly [gelatin] covers the bottom in a $\frac{1}{2}$- to $\frac{3}{4}$-inch layer. When the jelly [gelatin] is about to set, arrange the sponge fingers around the sides of the mould, fitting them closely together with the bases pressed into the jelly [gelatin]. Place in the refrigerator to set.

In a medium-sized saucepan, warm the milk with the vanilla pod over very low heat. Leave to infuse for 5-7 minutes.

In a large bowl, cream the egg yolks and sugar with a wooden spoon until the mixture is pale and fluffy. Pour in the milk through a strainer, discarding the vanilla pod, and blend well. Return to the pan. Stir the mixture over moderate heat until it thickens, but do not let it boil. Remove the pan from the heat and strain the custard into the large bowl. Place the bowl of custard in a bowl of ice cubes.

In a small saucepan, soak the gelatine in the water until it is quite soft. Then place the pan over low heat to dissolve the gelatine. When it is dissolved, add it to the custard and mix well.

With a large wire whisk, whip the cream until it forms soft peaks but is not too stiff.

When the custard is on the point of setting, fold in the cream. Spoon the cream and custard mixture into the mould and place it in the refrigerator. Leave the Charlotte to set for at least 6 hours or overnight.

To turn the Charlotte out of the mould, dip the mould quickly into hot water. Then place a serving dish, inverted, over the top of the mould and, holding them firmly together, reverse the two. The Charlotte should slide easily out of the mould.

Serve immediately.

For Charlotte Russe, arrange the sponge fingers around the sides of the mould, with the ends in the jelly.

Spoon the cream and custard mixture into the lined mould and place it in the refrigerator until it is set.

Just before serving, trim the ends of the sponge fingers, then dip the mould quickly in hot water and turn out.

An alternative method, which is simpler, is to fill the mould with the cream and custard mixture and, when it is set, turn the Charlotte out and press the sponge fingers around the sides. A ribbon can be tied around the sides to keep the fingers in place.

Chartreuse

Chartreuse (shar-trerz) is a spicy plant liqueur made from 130 herbs and a brandy base. It was originally produced by Carthusian monks at the monastery of the Grande Chartreuse in Grenoble, France, in the early seventeenth century, but it was not commercialized until the middle nineteenth century. Today the order still controls the distillation process of Chartreuse, the secret formula for which is known only by five monks. There are two types of Chartreuse, the green being stronger and drier than the yellow, which is sweeter.

Chartreuse de Pommes

APPLE MOULD WITH REDCURRANT SAUCE

Elegant to serve and economical to make, Chartreuse de Pommes (shahr-trerz d'pohm) *may be accompanied by whipped cream or a thick custard sauce. If they are available, apples of the pippin variety should be used, as apples that pulp quickly when cooked are not successful in this recipe.*

4-6 SERVINGS

- 2 teaspoons vegetable oil
- 4 fl. oz. [$\frac{1}{2}$ cup] water
- 12 oz. [$1\frac{1}{2}$ cups] sugar
- juice of 1 lemon
- $\frac{1}{2}$ teaspoon grated nutmeg
- 2 lb. tart apples, peeled, cored and sliced
- 2 oz. [$\frac{1}{2}$ cup] blanched, slivered almonds
- 2 tablespoons redcurrant jelly
- 2 tablespoons boiling water
- 1 tablespoon brandy

Grease a 1-pint [$2\frac{1}{2}$-cup] mould with the vegetable oil. Set aside.

Put the water with the sugar into a medium-sized saucepan. Stir to dissolve the sugar, then add the lemon juice and nutmeg. Bring the syrup to the boil over moderate heat and boil it for 5 minutes, stirring occasionally with a metal spoon.

Add the apple slices to the syrup and cook them for 10 to 15 minutes, stirring gently from time to time. The syrup should boil briskly and the apples will pull away from the sides of the pan when they are ready.

With a metal spoon, carefully fold the almonds into the apple mixture.

Pour the apple mixture into the mould and place it in the refrigerator for at least 1 hour, or until it is set.

In a cup, combine the redcurrant jelly, the boiling water and the brandy together and stir to melt the jelly. Set the cup aside to allow the sauce to cool.

Turn the chartreuse out of the mould on to a serving dish and spoon the sauce over it. Serve cold.

Chasseur, à la

A la Chasseur (ah lah shah-sur) is a French term meaning 'in the manner of a hunter'. This is a method of cooking game or poultry in which the meat is cooked in white wine with shallots and sautéed mushrooms.

Chasseur Sauce

GAME SAUCE

This is a rich, wine-flavoured sauce prepared from game giblets. Chasseur (shah-sur) *Sauce may be served with any game such as pheasant, grouse, quail, wild boar or venison.*

ABOUT 10 FL. OZ. SAUCE

- wing tips, necks and giblets of the game you are serving
- 1 teaspoon salt
- $\frac{1}{2}$ teaspoon black pepper
- 3 onions, 1 left whole and 2 finely chopped
- 1 tablespoon celery seeds
- 2 oz. [$\frac{1}{4}$ cup] butter
- 3 tomatoes, blanched, peeled, seeded and chopped
- 6 mushroom caps, wiped with a damp cloth and thinly sliced
- 3 tablespoons beurre manié
- 4 tablespoons red wine

Place the wing tips, necks and giblets in a medium-sized saucepan and just cover them with water. Add the salt, pepper, the whole onion and celery seeds to the pan. Place it over high heat. Bring the liquid to the boil and reduce the heat to low. Simmer the stock for $1\frac{1}{2}$ hours.

Remove the pan from the heat and strain the stock into a measuring jug. Discard the bones and flavourings. Check the quantity of strained stock and pour it into a medium-sized saucepan.

Place the pan over high heat and boil the stock until it has reduced to 8 fluid ounces [1 cup].

Remove the pan from the heat and set aside.

In a medium-sized frying-pan, melt the butter over moderate heat. When the foam subsides, add the chopped onions and fry them for 8 to 10 minutes, or until they are soft and transparent.

Add the tomatoes and mushrooms to the pan and cook for a further 2 to 3 minutes.

Using a slotted spoon, transfer the onions, tomatoes and mushrooms to the stock in the saucepan.

Return the pan to low heat, cover and simmer the sauce for $1\frac{1}{2}$ hours, stirring occasionally.

Uncover the pan and stir the beurre manié, in small pieces, into the sauce. Stir in the wine and simmer the sauce for 4 to 5 minutes.

Remove the pan from the heat and pour the sauce into a warmed sauce boat. Serve at once.

Château

Château is the French word for country house, or castle. It is also a culinary term which describes a steak, a method of cooking potatoes and a sauce.

Château steak (*entrecôte château*) is a rather thick slice of porterhouse (from $1\frac{1}{2}$ to 2 pounds in weight), or a slice cut from a rib of beef. It is usually grilled [broiled].

Château potatoes are uncooked potatoes cut into small ovals and sautéed in butter.

Château sauce is a classic accompaniment for Chateaubriand steak and consists of a blend of meat juices, butter, chopped parsley and cayenne pepper.

Château can also mean the homestead on a vineyard and, especially in the Bordeaux area of France, the word is often incorporated into the official name of the wine produced on the surrounding estate. Château Lafite and Château d'Yquem are two of the great wines that follow this procedure. Château-bottled (*mis en bouteille au château*) on the label of a bottle of wine is an indication of authenticity – and quality – and means that the wine has been bottled on the estate.

Chateaubriand

This is a steak of highest quality, cut in a thick slice from the fillet. It is grilled [broiled] and served with Château potatoes and a Château or Béarnaise sauce. It is thought that this steak was named in honour of the French statesman and writer Chateaubriand, having been first prepared by his chef Montmireil.

Château Potatoes

Château potatoes are the traditional accompaniment to Chateaubriand steak. They go equally well, however, with grilled [broiled] *chops or roasted meat.*

4 SERVINGS

1 lb. potatoes
1 teaspoon salt
1 teaspoon black pepper
2 oz. [$\frac{1}{4}$ cup] butter
1 tablespoon chopped parsley

If old potatoes are used, peel and quarter them, rounding off the edges with a potato peeler so that each piece resembles an olive in shape. If new potatoes are used, they should be scraped and left whole. Season the potatoes with salt and pepper.

Melt the butter in a frying-pan over moderate heat. Reduce the heat to low, add the potatoes and, shaking the pan from time to time, cook slowly for 30 to 40 minutes, or until the potatoes are golden in colour.

Arrange the potatoes in a shallow serving dish, sprinkle with chopped parsley and serve immediately.

Chaudfroid

A French term which means 'hot-cold,' Chaudfroid (show-fwah) is the name of a sauce which is used to coat poultry, fish or meat. It can be white or brown and has the addition of aspic jelly to make it thick and shiny. Chaudfroid dishes are served cold and garnished with colourful pieces of vegetables.

Chaudfroid Sauce (White)

This chaudfroid sauce is used to coat cold dishes of chicken, fish, eggs, and similar delicately and lightly flavoured foods. After the cold food has been coated with the chaudfroid sauce it is garnished and covered with aspic jelly. The brown version of this sauce is under BROWN CHAUDFROID SAUCE.

ABOUT 1 PINT

15 fl. oz. [$1\frac{7}{8}$ cups] milk
1 mace blade
1 bay leaf
1 slice of shallot
6 peppercorns
1 tablespoon butter
2 tablespoons flour
2 fl. oz. [$\frac{1}{4}$ cup] aspic jelly
$\frac{1}{4}$ oz. gelatine
3 fl. oz. single cream [$\frac{3}{8}$ cup light cream]
$\frac{1}{2}$ teaspoon salt
$\frac{1}{4}$ teaspoon white pepper

In a small saucepan, heat the milk with the mace blade, bay leaf, shallot and peppercorns over low heat. Leave the milk over the heat for 5 to 7 minutes so that it becomes infused with the flavours. Strain the milk into a bowl or jug and discard the flavourings.

Wash out the saucepan and in it melt the butter over low heat. Remove the pan from the heat and, using a wooden spoon, stir in the flour to make a smooth paste.

Gradually pour in the milk, stirring continuously. When all the milk has been added, return the pan to the heat and bring the sauce to the boil, still stirring. Simmer the sauce for 1 to 2 minutes. Remove the pan from the heat.

In another small saucepan, heat the aspic over low heat until it has melted. Dissolve the gelatine in the aspic and stir it into the sauce. Stir in the cream, salt and pepper. Strain the sauce into a bowl. Stir the sauce as it cools and when it is as thick as double [heavy] cream and on the point of setting it is ready to use.

Chayote

A large, green fruit of the gourd family, the chayote has a firm, white flesh with a delicate and distinctive flavour. It is cooked in a variety of ways, to be served as a vegetable or to be added to soups. If it is cooked with sugar and fresh lime juice, the flavour of the chayote is very similar to stewed apples.

Cheddar Cheese

Perhaps the best-known and most widely used of the English hard, fermented cheeses, Cheddar is also one of the oldest. Made originally in Somerset, Cheddar is also produced in other parts of Britain and made in Canada, New Zealand, Australia and the United States.

Cheddar Spread

A tangy spread, served on buttered toast or crackers, this is suitable for a light supper snack, or for canapés at a buffet or cocktail party.

16 OUNCES

4 oz. [1 cup] Cheddar cheese, grated
6 fl. oz. [$\frac{3}{4}$ cup] sour cream
3 tablespoons sherry

Combine the cheese, sour cream and sherry in a medium-sized bowl. With a wooden spoon, beat vigorously until the mixture is light and fluffy. Seasonings, such as Tabasco sauce, may be added if you like a spicier mixture.

Cheeps

These crispy cheese potatoes make an alternative garnish for fish dishes, and also go well with a soup.

4 SERVINGS

4 large potatoes, scrubbed but not peeled
2 oz. [$\frac{1}{4}$ cup] butter, melted
$\frac{1}{2}$ teaspoon salt
$\frac{1}{4}$ teaspoon onion salt
$\frac{1}{4}$ teaspoon paprika
1 oz. [$\frac{1}{4}$ cup] Parmesan cheese, grated

Cut the potatoes into slices about ½ inch thick and then into ½-inch wide strips. Soak the strips in iced water for 30 minutes, then drain in a colander and dry on kitchen paper towels.

Preheat the oven to very hot 450°F (Gas Mark 8, 230°C). With 1 tablespoon of the butter grease a baking sheet.

Place the potato strips on the sheet in a single layer and brush them generously with the remaining melted butter. Sprinkle with the salt, onion salt and paprika.

Put the potato strips into the oven and bake for 30 minutes, turning the strips occasionally, until the potatoes are crisp and golden outside. Remove the potato strips from the oven and sprinkle them with the Parmesan, shaking the pan so that the potatoes are coated on all sides. Serve the cheeps hot.

Cheese

WHAT CHEESE IS

The making of cheese was originally a method of preserving milk, but became popular for its own sake early in history. Cheese has kept its popularity ever since, being an inexpensive, versatile and nourishing food. Cheese is a valuable protein food, containing high proportions of protein and fat.

Cheese is made by curdling milk by adding a preparation of rennet or a

***A wonderful and delicious variety of cheeses from England, Scotland, Wales, France, Holland, Switzerland, Denmark and Italy — choose a colourful selection from these to serve after your next dinner party.* 1. Edam 2. Gouda 3. Danish Blue 4. Havarti 5. Samsoe 6. Esrom 7. Gruyère 8. Emmenthal 9. Caerphilly 10. Lancashire 11. Cheshire 12. Sage Derby 13. Caboc 14. Stilton 15. Dunlop 16. Cheddar 17. Derby 18. Roquefort 19. Port Salut 20. Camembert 21. Brie 22. Marc de Raisin 23. Parmesan 24. Mozzarella 25. Gorgonzola 26. Bel Paese.**

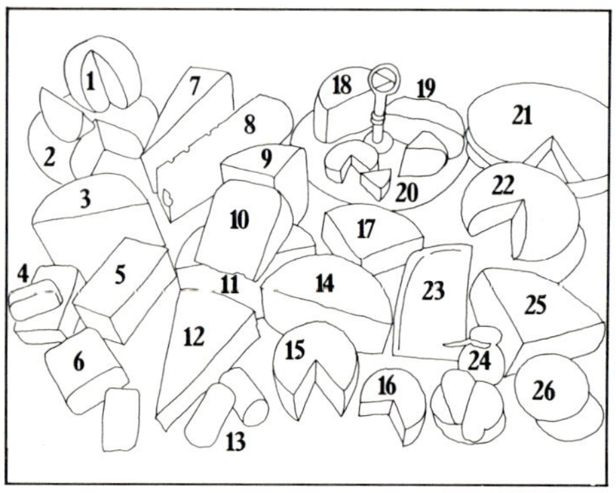

ROQUEFORT
CHEESE
SOCIÉTÉ
PORT SALUT
MOZZARELLA
FORMAGGIO DEL BEL PAESE
S.p.A. GALBANI MELZO ITALY

particular starter culture which changes the milk into lactic acid during the cheese-making process. The curds are separated from the liquid whey and are then ripened in various ways. The milk used in Europe and America is usually that of cows, goats or ewes. The processes used in the cheese-making and the climate and vegetation that produced the milk vary so greatly that many cheeses cannot be reproduced outside their original districts. Others are more easily reproduced and are made commercially in large quantities.

THE COUNTRIES THAT PRODUCE CHEESE

The United States is the world's largest producer of cheese, making twice as much as France, its nearest rival. There are, however, only two well-known American cheeses, the rest being either processed cheeses, or imitations of foreign varieties, although some of these are considered to be as good as, or even better than, their originals.

Liederkranz and Brick are the only well known originally American cheeses. Liederkranz, aromatic and acid, was invented accidentally by Emil Frey, a New York cheese-maker. He was trying to duplicate a German cheese, but produced Liederkranz instead. He named his invention after a local singing society (the word means 'wreath of song').

Brick is little known outside the Middle West – it originated in Wisconsin, the leading American dairy state. When new it is mild in flavour, but it strengthens as it ages. A mature Brick is excellent with a glass of beer.

Britain produces several fine cheeses, of which the best-known are Cheddar, Cheshire and Stilton – one of the world's finest blue-veined cheeses. Cheddar – perhaps the most famous and versatile cheese in the world – is now produced commercially in large quantities all the year round and all over the world. Cheshire, the oldest English cheese, has a nutty, slightly salty flavour, and is rarely imitated successfully. Stilton, traditionally eaten with port and walnuts after a meal, is mellow and rich and has a dark, wrinkled skin.

There are several other well-known cheeses. Caerphilly is one of these – a very soft, easily digested cheese, now made in the West of England, although it was originally Welsh. Derby, a white, mild, open-textured cheese, is sometimes found in the form of Sage Derby, a variety with the white cheese layered or mottled with green coloured cheese that is flavoured with sage. Lancashire cheese is white and crumbly, excellent for toasting or sprinkling over soups. Leicester is a bright orange coloured cheese, with a creamy and tangy flavour and is very good for adding colour to cheese dishes, particularly in Welsh rarebit and cheese sauces.

Dunlop is one of the Scottish cheeses, although it is said to have been originally Irish, introduced during the seventeenth century by a fugitive from religious persecution. It is similar in texture to Cheddar but milder in flavour.

Denmark produces several copies of foreign cheeses, such as Brie, Camembert, Emmenthal and Gorgonzola, but the best-known of its original cheeses are Danish Blue, a blue-veined, salty but creamy cheese, Samsoe which has a slightly sweet flavour and Havarti which is a mild cheese.

Of the Dutch cheeses the best-known are Gouda and Edam. Gouda is strong, with a few small holes and a yellow rind. It is wheel-shaped, while Edam is round with a red skin when the cheese is exported.

Emmenthal and Gruyère are the best-known of the Swiss cheeses, and are both used in cookery, particularly in the making of *fondue*, the traditional Swiss dish of melted cheese. Emmenthal has large holes and is creamy in taste while Gruyère has smaller holes and is tangier in flavour. A third well-known Swiss cheese is Appenzeller, a firm cheese with a spicy flavour and tiny holes.

France produces the widest range of cheeses in the world – nearly every village has its own speciality – of every shape, taste and texture. One of the most popular is Camembert, a pale yellow cheese of soft, creamy texture. Its rind is orange-yellow with a powdery white crust. Next in popularity is Brie, very similar to Camembert in texture, but with its own distinctive flavour.

Roquefort, a salty cheese made from ewes' milk, has a greyish crust and is flecked inside with green-blue, from the action of a mould similar to penicillin which is found in the caves where the cheese is stored.

Port Salut was originally made by Trappist monks, and is a semi-hard cheese, mild and fresh in flavour and in texture rather like butter. It is one of the best all-round French cheeses. Fromage au Marc de Raisin is a sweet, cream cheese rolled in a crust of grape seeds. These are only a very few of the 400 to 500 cheese of France, most of which are local specialities.

Cheese is a fundamental ingredient in Italian cooking, and may be classified according to its use – grating, cooking and for the table.

The hard Italian cheeses for grating are Parmigiano Reggiano, the original Parmesan, and Pecorino Romano, a sharp cheese made from fresh ewes' milk.

The most important cooking cheese in northern Italy is *grana*, of which Parmesan is the best-known variety. In the south, Mozzarella is the chief cooking cheese, very often used in pizzas. Mozzarella is ideally made from buffalo milk but most often from cows' milk. Ricotta is a fresh, moist, unsalted cottage cheese much used in Italian cooking.

Of the eating cheeses, the best-known are Gorgonzola and Bel Paese. Gorgonzola is a blue-veined cheese, spiced and sharp in flavour. Bel Paese is rubbery, mild and soft.

TYPES OF CHEESE FOR COOKING

Wherever cheeses are produced, they can generally be classified under three types: cream, soft and hard. All cheeses are suitable for eating on their own and some are more suitable for use in cooking than others.

Soft and semi-soft cheeses can be used in cooking but tend to be sticky. Hard cheeses – Cheddar, Edam, Gruyère, Emmenthal, Cheshire, Parmesan, Lancashire, Leicester, Derby, Mozzarella – are ideal for cookery. Very hard cheeses, such as Parmesan, are generally grated before using.

Whatever type of cheese is used in cooking, it should never receive more heat than is necessary to melt and if necessary brown it, because overcooking makes it tough and indigestible. When cheese is being grated prior to cooking, a fine grater should be used for hard cheese, while a soft cheese should be shredded. Very soft cheese can simply be sliced thinly.

STORING CHEESE

Once cut, cheese deteriorates fairly rapidly, and it is advisable to buy only enough for a few days or for a week at most, and to store it in a cool place, such as a cold larder. It should be covered loosely, but not so as to make it airtight. If it is airtight it may become mouldy, while if it is entirely exposed to the air it will become hard and dry. Cheese can be stored in the refrigerator for about one week but should be wrapped in waxed paper or aluminium foil, otherwise it will dry too rapidly.

Cheese can be hardened and dried by hanging it in a cheesecloth bag where the air can circulate around it. Dried, grated cheese can be stored in a screw-top jar for several weeks. If you have a home freezer, freshly grated cheese, packed in polythene bags, is a useful standby to have to add to sauces and savoury dishes.

This savoury Cheese Charlotte, topped with crisply fried bacon, makes a light and tasty supper dish.

Cheese Charlotte

This savoury charlotte makes a light and tasty supper dish, and is delicious garnished with crisply fried bacon and parsley.

4 SERVINGS

- 1 thick slice white bread, cut into cubes
- 7 fl. oz. [7/8 cup] milk
- 8 slices of white bread, crusts removed
- 1½ oz. [3 tablespoons] butter
- 3 eggs, separated
- 1½ tablespoons flour
- 8 oz. [2 cups] Cheddar cheese, grated
- ½ teaspoon salt
- ¼ teaspoon grated nutmeg
- 4 fl. oz. single cream [½ cup light cream]

Preheat the oven to moderate 350°F (Gas Mark 4, 180°C).

Put the bread cubes in a shallow dish and sprinkle over half of the milk. In another dish, spread out the bread slices and sprinkle them with the remaining milk. Leave the cubes and slices to soak.

In a large bowl, cream the butter with a wooden spoon and mix in the egg yolks, one at a time. Stir in the flour. Add the soaked bread cubes, cheese, salt and nutmeg. Blend well and stir in the cream.

In a medium-sized bowl, beat the egg whites with a wire whisk until they are stiff. Fold them into the cheese mixture.

Line a greased straight-sided, flameproof dish or casserole with the soaked bread slices. Pour the cheese mixture into the dish. Bake in the oven for 35 to 40 minutes. Serve the Charlotte immediately.

Cheese and Chive Spread

This quick and easy-to-make cream cheese spread is delicious served in baked potatoes or sandwiches, or an accompaniment to steak. It may also be served as a cocktail party dip with celery stalks.

ABOUT 8 OUNCE SPREAD

- 8 oz. cream cheese
- 3 tablespoons chopped fresh chives
- 2 tablespoons single [light] cream
- ⅛ teaspoon salt
- ¼ teaspoon black pepper
- ⅛ teaspoon cayenne

Combine all the ingredients together in a medium-sized mixing bowl and using a wooden spoon mix them to a soft cream.

Chill slightly before serving.

Cheese and Ham Soufflé

A light but satisfying dish for a family supper, this Cheese and Ham Soufflé may be served with a green salad or buttered asparagus and crusty bread.

4 SERVINGS

- 4 oz. [½ cup] butter
- 2 tablespoons fine dry white breadcrumbs
- 3 oz. [¾ cup] flour
- 16 fl. oz. [2 cups] milk, scalded
- 4 oz. [1 cup] Cheddar cheese, grated
- 3 oz. cooked ham, finely chopped
- 6 eggs, separated
- ½ teaspoon salt
- ½ teaspoon paprika
- ⅛ teaspoon cayenne

Preheat the oven to fairly hot 375°F (Gas Mark 5, 190°C). Place a double piece of greaseproof or waxed paper around the outside of a 2-pint [5-cup] soufflé dish and tie with string. The paper should come 2-inches higher than the rim of the dish. Butter the paper and the dish with one-quarter of the butter, then dust lightly with the breadcrumbs, shaking out the excess. Set the dish aside.

In a large saucepan, melt the remaining butter over moderate heat. With a wooden spoon, stir in the flour and cook, stirring constantly, for 1 minute.

Remove the pan from the heat and gradually stir in the scalded milk. Add the cheese and ham to the mixture and stir until the cheese has melted.

In a small mixing bowl, lightly beat the egg yolks with a fork. Add about one-quarter of the hot cheese mixture to the egg yolks and stir well until the ingredients are blended.

Slowly return the egg yolks mixture to the saucepan, stirring constantly. Season the mixture with the salt, paprika and cayenne. Set the pan aside to allow the mixture to cool slightly.

In a medium-sized mixing bowl, beat the egg whites with a wire whisk or rotary beater until they form stiff peaks.

With a metal spoon, gently fold the egg whites into the cooled cheese and ham mixture.

Pour the mixture into the soufflé dish. Place the dish in the oven and bake for 35 minutes, or until the top is puffed up and lightly browned.

Remove the soufflé from the oven. Remove the paper collar and serve.

Cheese Logs

These savoury Cheese Logs, served piping hot, are ideal to serve with pre-dinner drinks.

8 LOGS

- **8 thin slices white bread, crusts removed**
- **8 thin slices Gruyère or Cheddar cheese**
- **3-4 teaspoons anchovy paste or prepared mustard**
- **2 oz. [¼ cup] butter, melted**

Preheat the grill [broiler] to medium.

On each slice of bread place a slice of cheese, which should not quite cover the bread. Spread a little anchovy paste or mustard over each slice of cheese. Roll up the bread and fasten with wooden cocktail sticks. Using a pastry brush, coat the ends and cover the outside of each log with melted butter. Toast the rolls until golden brown on all sides. Serve at once.

Cheese and Onion Pie

This economical pie can be served as an hors d'oeuvre, or as a light luncheon or supper dish with a tossed, mixed salad.

4 SERVINGS

- **8 oz. [2 cups] flour**
- **1 teaspoon salt**
- **2 oz. [¼ cup] plus 1½ oz. [3 tablespoons] butter**
- **2 oz. [¼ cup] vegetable fat**
- **2 tablespoons iced water**
- **3 medium-sized onions, finely chopped**
- **2 garlic cloves, crushed**
- **8 oz. [2 cups] Cheddar cheese, grated**
- **1 egg, lightly beaten**
- **½ teaspoon white pepper**

Make the pastry by sifting the flour and half the salt into a medium-sized mixing bowl. Put in 2 ounces [¼ cup] of the butter and the vegetable fat and cut it into small pieces with a table knife. With your fingertips, rub the fat into the flour until the mixture resembles fine breadcrumbs. Add 2 tablespoons of iced water and, using the knife, mix it into the flour mixture. With your hands, mix until a smooth dough is formed. Add more water if the dough is too dry. Form the dough into a ball and wrap it in greaseproof or waxed paper. Chill the dough in the refrigerator for 20 minutes.

Preheat the oven to fairly hot 400°F (Gas Mark 6, 200°C). Grease a medium-sized pie dish with 1 tablespoon of the butter and set it aside.

In a frying-pan, melt the remaining 2 tablespoons of butter over moderate heat. Add the chopped onions and garlic, reduce the heat to low and cook the mixture gently for about 10 minutes, stirring occasionally and taking care not to let the onions brown. When the onions are soft and translucent, remove the pan from the heat.

In a medium-sized mixing bowl, combine the onion mixture with the grated cheese. Add most of the beaten egg (keep a little to glaze the pie crust), remaining salt and the pepper and, with a fork, beat to blend well. Set aside.

Divide the dough ball into two portions, one slightly larger than the other. On a lightly floured surface, roll out the larger portion of dough until it is quite thin and is large enough to overlap the sides of the pie dish. Line the pie dish, and trim off the excess dough with a knife. Spoon the cheese-and-onion mixture into the dish, spreading it evenly over the bottom.

Roll out the other portion of dough on the floured board to a circle slightly larger than the pie dish. Place the circle of dough on top of the filling. Fold under the overhanging dough and press the edges together with your fingertips. With a pastry brush, coat the surface with the remaining beaten egg. Bake in the centre of the oven for about 35 minutes, or until the pastry is deep golden. Serve either hot or cold.

Cheese Soufflé

A perfect soufflé is generally considered to be a tricky, temperamental dish to make, but this recipe for Cheese Soufflé is very easy to prepare. It is advisable to serve the

For Cheese Soufflé, stir the flour into the butter, to make a roux.

Remove the pan from the heat and beat the egg yolks into the hot sauce.

Gently, but quickly, fold the beaten egg whites into the cooled sauce.

soufflé as soon as it is cooked, otherwise it will sink. Serve it with a crisp green salad, or a green vegetable such as courgettes [zucchini], *and French bread.*

4 SERVINGS

2 tablespoons grated Parmesan cheese
2 oz. [$\frac{1}{4}$ cup] butter, plus extra for greasing
2 oz. [$\frac{1}{2}$ cup] flour
9 fl. oz. [$1\frac{1}{8}$ cups] milk
$\frac{1}{2}$ teaspoon made mustard
$\frac{1}{8}$ teaspoon cayenne pepper
$\frac{1}{8}$ teaspoon grated nutmeg
5 large egg yolks, lightly beaten
5 oz. [$\frac{5}{8}$ cup] mature Cheddar cheese, grated
$\frac{1}{4}$ teaspoon salt
$\frac{1}{4}$ teaspoon pepper
6 egg whites

Low Cal

Butter a 3-pint soufflé dish and then sprinkle it with the Parmesan cheese. Preheat the oven to fairly hot 400°F (Gas Mark 6, 200°C) and place a shelf in the centre.

Melt the butter in a medium-sized saucepan and then stir in the flour. Cook over a low heat, stirring the mixture continuously, until smooth.

Remove from the heat and gradually stir in the milk. Return to the heat and stir until the mixture thickens and bubbles. Cool slightly.

Stir in the mustard, cayenne and nutmeg, then add the egg yolks. Stir in the Cheddar cheese and season to taste.

Whisk the egg whites until stiff. Fold one quarter into the cheese mixture with a large metal spoon or spatula. Fold in the remaining egg whites and mix until just evenly blended.

Turn into the soufflé dish and bake for 30-35 minutes until the soufflé is puffed and golden and quivers slightly in the centre when shaken gently. Serve at once.

The basic mixture can be prepared up to the point where the egg whites are added. Cover the surface closely with cling film and keep in the refrigerator. Warm the mixture gently, stirring, before folding in the egg whites.

If the centre of the cooked soufflé quivers slightly, the inside will be creamy

in texture; if a completely dry inside is preferred, then leave the soufflé in the oven for 2-3 minutes longer.

If Parmesan cheese is not available, use Cheddar as a substitute.

For a Cheese and Mushroom Soufflé, sauté 8 oz. [$1\frac{1}{4}$ cups] finely chopped mushrooms in 1 oz. [2 tablespoons] butter for 2-3 minutes and then mix in to the sauce.

Cheese Soup

This unusual and warming winter soup is especially good with hot crusty bread and lots of butter.

4 SERVINGS

2 oz. [$\frac{1}{4}$ cup] butter
2 medium-sized onions, chopped
2 tablespoons flour
4 fl. oz. [$\frac{1}{2}$ cup] chicken stock
$1\frac{1}{2}$ pints [$3\frac{3}{4}$ cups] milk
12 oz. [3 cups] Cheddar cheese, grated
3 oz. [$\frac{3}{4}$ cup] Gruyère cheese, grated
$\frac{1}{2}$ teaspoon prepared mustard
$\frac{1}{2}$ teaspoon salt
$\frac{1}{4}$ teaspoon black pepper
$1\frac{1}{2}$ teaspoons paprika
1 teaspoon Worcestershire sauce

In a large heavy saucepan, melt the butter over moderate heat. When the foam subsides, add the onion and cook for 6 to 8 minutes or until they are golden. Stir in the flour and cook, stirring, for 2 to 3 minutes. Remove the pan from the heat and gradually stir in the stock. When the mixture is smooth and blended, stir in the milk.

Add the cheese and the mustard. Return the pan to low heat. Cook, stirring, until the cheese melts. Do not allow the soup to reach boiling point. Remove the pan from the heat. Season with salt, pepper and paprika. The amount of seasoning depends on the strength of the cheese, and it is advisable to taste and season as the soup requires. Add the Worcestershire sauce and serve.

Cheese Spread

This spread, for toasted sandwiches or biscuits, will keep for a week or more stored in a screw-top jar in the refrigerator.

10 OZ. SPREAD

4 fl. oz. [$\frac{1}{2}$ cup] milk
1 egg, lightly beaten
$\frac{1}{4}$ teaspoon dry mustard
$\frac{1}{2}$ teaspoon salt
12 oz. [3 cups] Cheddar cheese, diced or grated

In a double saucepan or in a bowl placed over a pan of simmering water, scald the milk (bring it to just below boiling point). Add the egg, mustard, salt and cheese and cook over hot water for 15 minutes, stirring constantly. Remove the pan or bowl from the heat and allow the cheese mixture to cool. Use as required.

Cheese Straws

These light savoury biscuits are especially popular served with apéritifs.

ABOUT 30 STRAWS

4 oz. [1 cup] flour
$\frac{1}{4}$ teaspoon salt
$\frac{1}{8}$ teaspoon cayenne pepper
3 oz. unsalted butter [$\frac{3}{8}$ cup sweet butter] cut into small pieces
4 tablespoons finely grated Cheddar cheese
1 egg yolk, lightly beaten
1 tablespoon iced water

In a medium-sized bowl, sift together the flour, salt and cayenne. Add the butter and rub it into the flour with your fingertips until the mixture resembles fine breadcrumbs. Stir in the grated cheese.

In a teacup, mix together the egg yolk and water. Add the liquid to the butter-and-flour mixture and, with a fork or spoon, mix well until a fairly stiff dough is formed. Roll the dough into a ball and wrap it in greaseproof or waxed paper. Place it in the refrigerator to chill for 1 hour.

Preheat the oven to fairly hot 400°F (Gas Mark 6, 200°C).

On a lightly floured surface, roll out the chilled dough into a rectangle about $\frac{1}{4}$ inch thick. Cut the dough into strips about 2 inches long and $\frac{1}{4}$ inch wide.

Arrange the strips on an ungreased baking sheet and bake in the centre of the oven for about 15 minutes, or until the straws are very light brown in colour.

Remove the baking sheet from the oven and allow the straws to cool before serving.

Cheese Toasties

These tangy Cheese Toasties are the perfect ending to a meal. Alternatively, the toast may be cut into quarters and served as a hot appetizer.

4 SERVINGS

8 oz. [2 cups] Cheddar cheese, grated
2 tablespoons beer
1 teaspoon prepared mustard
$\frac{1}{4}$ teaspoon black pepper
2 tablespoons chutney
4 slices hot toast, with crusts removed
$\frac{1}{4}$ teaspoon paprika

In a medium-sized saucepan, melt the cheese with the beer over low heat, stirring continuously with a wooden spoon. As soon as the cheese has melted and the mixture is thick and creamy, stir in the mustard, pepper and chutney. Continue to cook for 3 to 4 minutes more.

Remove the pan from the heat and spread the mixture on the toast. Sprinkle each slice with paprika. Serve piping hot.

Cheesecake

This popular sweet-sour confection probably originated in Greece and is now world famous. There are hundreds of variations, but the basic ingredients are similar, cottage, curd or cream cheese, eggs and a thickening such as flour, cornflour [cornstarch], *semolina or ground nuts. Extra ingredients are added for flavour; fresh or dried fruits, essences and spices being the most usual. Cheesecake generally has a pastry or biscuit* [cookie] *crust as a base and some recipes require baking and others just chilled in the refrigerator.*

Cheesecake is eaten more in the United States than any other country and lots of the recipes come from the many people from other countries who settled there. A well known Italian cheesecake is Crostata di Ricotta — rich and creamy with ricotta cheese, Kasekuchen from Germany has a lemon and nut flavoured filling in a crisp cinnamon base and in Britain the little Maids of Honour have a creamy cheese filling. This cheesecake is easy to make, it is rich and makes an excellent dessert.

ONE 9-INCH CAKE

3 oz. [$\frac{3}{8}$ cup] plus 1 teaspoon butter, melted
6 oz. digestive biscuits [3 cups graham crackers] crushed
2 tablespoons sugar

FILLING

$1\frac{1}{2}$ lb. full fat cream cheese
3 oz. [$\frac{3}{8}$ cup] castor sugar
3 eggs, separated
1 teaspoon grated lemon rind
1 tablespoon cornflour [cornstarch] mixed with 2 tablespoons lemon juice
2 oz. [$\frac{1}{3}$ cup] currants
$1\frac{1}{2}$ oz. [$\frac{1}{4}$ cup] glacé cherries, chopped

---

Rich and luscious, this Cheesecake is sure to become a favourite with your family, and guests as well.

5 fl. oz. [$\frac{5}{8}$ cup] sour cream
2 teaspoons castor sugar
$\frac{1}{2}$ teaspoon vanilla essence

Preheat the oven to moderate 350°F (Gas Mark 4, 180°C).

With the teaspoon of butter grease a 9-inch loose-bottomed cake tin. Set it aside.

In a medium-sized mixing bowl combine the crushed digestive biscuits [graham crackers], sugar and remaining butter with a wooden spoon. Spoon the mixture into the cake tin and press it firmly, covering the bottom of the tin.

In a large mixing bowl, combine the cream cheese and sugar with a wooden spoon. Add the egg yolks and beat the mixture until it is smooth. Stir in the lemon rind, cornflour and lemon juice, currants and glacé cherries.

In another large mixing bowl, beat the egg whites with a wire whisk or rotary beater until they are stiff.

With a metal spoon, fold the egg whites into the cheese mixture.

Spoon the mixture into the prepared tin. Bake in the centre of the oven for 30 minutes or until the centre is firm when pressed with a finger-tip.

In a mixing bowl, combine the sour cream, castor sugar and vanilla essence and beat well with a wooden spoon.

Remove the tin from the oven and, using a palette knife, spread the sour cream mixture over the top of the cake. Return the cake to the oven and bake for a further 5 minutes.

Remove the tin from the oven and set aside to cool. When cool remove the cake from the tin and chill it in the refrigerator before serving.

Chelsea Buns

☆ ① ⧗ ⧗ ⧗

London's Old Chelsea Bun House was a favourite meeting place in the 18th and 19th centuries, where visitors would enjoy the famous yeasted fruit buns. Although the house was destroyed in 1839, these buns are still popular.

15 BUNS

18 oz. [$4\frac{1}{2}$ cups] strong flour, plus extra for dusting
1 teaspoon salt
1 sachet easy-blend dried yeast
11 fl. oz. [$1\frac{3}{8}$ cups] milk
2 oz. [$\frac{1}{4}$ cup] butter, cut into small pieces
1 egg, beaten

FILLING
6 oz. [1 cup] mixed dried fruit
2 oz. [$\frac{1}{2}$ cup] mixed chopped peel
4 oz. [$\frac{1}{2}$ cup] dark soft brown sugar
4 oz. [$\frac{1}{2}$ cup] butter, melted

GLAZE
2 tablespoons sugar
1 tablespoon milk

Sift the flour and salt into a large bowl, stir in the yeast and make a well in the centre.

Gently warm the milk and butter until

the butter has just melted. Pour into the dry ingredients and add the egg.

With a wooden spoon draw the dry ingredients into the liquids, then mix well to make a soft dough.

Transfer the dough to a lightly floured work surface and knead for about 10 minutes until smooth and elastic.

Place the dough in a large lightly oiled polythene [plastic] bag and leave in a warm place until doubled in size, about $1\text{-}1\frac{1}{2}$ hours.

Lightly grease a 13 × 9-inch Swiss roll tin [jelly roll pan] with oil. Mix the dried fruit with the peel and sugar.

Remove the risen dough from the polythene bag, knock down and then knead for 1 minute. Roll out to a 20-× 15-inch rectangle. Brush the surface with the melted butter and sprinkle evenly with the dried fruit mixture.

Roll up the dough from a long side, like a Swiss [jelly] roll. Finish with the seam underneath. Cut the dough into 15 even-sized pieces and arrange in the tin, leaving a small space between them to allow room for them to rise and spread.

Place the tin in a lightly oiled polythene bag and leave in a warm place until the dough has doubled in size, about 30 minutes.

Preheat the oven to fairly hot 400°F (Gas Mark 6, 200°C) and place a shelf above centre.

Bake for 25-30 minutes, until well risen and golden. Meanwhile, prepare the glaze. Dissolve the sugar in the milk, bring to the boil and boil 2 minutes. Remove the buns from oven and brush with the glaze. Transfer to a wire rack and leave until cold.

Break the buns apart to serve.

Orange buns can be made by substituting candied orange peel and grated rind of 1 orange for the mixed chopped peel.

Add $1\frac{1}{2}$ teaspoons ground cinnamon or mixed spice to the filling.

Instead of the glaze, the tops can be brushed with a thin icing [frosting], flavoured with lemon juice, and sprinkled with chopped nuts.

The dough can be kneaded in a food processor for 2-3 minutes.

The dough can be left to rise in a cool or cold place but it will take considerably longer to double in size.

Cherry

The cherry is a small round stone-fruit found in innumerable varieties, of which there are two main types – sweet and sour.

The best-known varieties of the sweet cherries are Geans, Hearts and Dukes. Geans are soft and sweet, and either black or red in colour. Hearts are known according to the colour of their skins: white hearts, black hearts, etc. Duke cherries are hybrids of sweet and sour, and are sometimes called May Queen in Britain and the United States. Sweet cherries may be eaten raw by themselves or in fruit salads, or may be made into jams, pie fillings, syrups and puddings. They may be preserved in spirits or by drying, crystallizing or freezing.

Of the sour cherries, Amarelles are pale red, with colourless juice, sharp but not acid in taste, and may be eaten as dessert fruit. Morellos are either black or red, and always bitterly acid. They are used in cooking. The Damasca is a very small bitter cherry, from which the liqueur Maraschino is made.

Glacé [candied] cherries are used in the making of cakes, puddings, biscuits [cookies], sweets and so on, both as an ingredient and as a decoration. Cherries which have been pitted, cooked in sugar syrup and flavoured with Maraschino may be used as a cocktail garnish or as an ingredient in cakes, biscuits [cookies], etc.

Cherry Brandy

A fruit liqueur, rather than a brandy in the true sense, cherry brandy is distilled from cherries and their stones. The oil given off by the crushed stones during fermentation gives the liqueur its distinctive bitter-sweet vaguely almond flavour.

Cherry Heering, a Danish liqueur manufactured by the Heering family for over 150 years, is one of the most popular types of cherry brandy. Kirsch, or *kirschwasser,* always white in colour, is also made from cherries.

Cherry Compôte

Cherry Compôte may be served either as a dessert with cream, or as an accompaniment to cold ham, chicken or duck. It should be served very cold.

6 SERVINGS

14 oz. canned unsweetened, stoned cherries
3 tablespoons sugar
$\frac{1}{2}$ teaspoon grated orange rind
1 tablespoon unsweetened orange juice
1 tablespoon redcurrant jelly

Drain the cherries and set them aside, reserving 8 fluid ounces [1 cup] of the fruit syrup.

In a medium-sized pan, heat the cherry syrup with the sugar, orange rind and orange juice over moderate heat, stirring constantly to dissolve the sugar. Bring the liquid to the boil. Add the cherries, reduce the heat to very low and simmer the mixture for 5 minutes. Remove the pan from the heat and stir in the redcurrant jelly.

Place the cherry compôte in a serving bowl and chill for at least 1 hour before serving.

Cherry Jam

Cherries contain very little acid and pectin and, consequently, cherry jam is considered difficult to make successfully. Duke cherries have been found to be the best kind for jam-making, but Morello cherries and other acid varieties are also very good. Black cherries make a very sweet jam and are better for bottling or freezing. If you use Morello cherries, halve the quantity of lemon juice. Whatever kind of cherries you are using, they should always be fresh, firm and slightly under-ripe.

ABOUT 12 LB. JAM

10 lb. stoned cherries (about 11 lb. before stoning), stones reserved
juice of 5 lemons
7 lb. sugar

In a large preserving pan put the cherries and lemon juice. Put the cherry stones in a cheesecloth bag and add it to the pan.

Place the pan over low heat, bring to the boil and simmer for 30 minutes, or until the cherries are tender. With tongs, remove the bag of stones from the pan and discard it.

Add the sugar to the pan and stir, over low heat, until it has dissolved. Increase the heat to moderate, bring to the boil and cook briskly until the mixture sets. To test if the jam is set remove the pan from the heat, take a teaspoonful of jam from the pan and place it on a cold saucer. When it is cool, push the jam with your finger. If it wrinkles, setting point has been reached. If not, return the pan to the heat and continue cooking.

With a slotted spoon dipped in boiling water and dried, quickly remove the scum from the surface of the jam. Allow the jam to cool in the pan until a thin skin forms on the surface. Stir the jam gently and pour it into clean, dry, warm jars. Fill the jars to the top to allow for shrinkage. Press a circle of waxed paper on to the surface of the jam in each jar. Cover with jam covers and secure with rubber bands.

Label the jars and place them in a cool, dry, dark place until ready to use.

Cherries Jubilee

A colourful, flamboyant dessert that takes only a few minutes to prepare, Cherries Jubilee makes a splendid end to any dinner party. It is traditionally served with vanilla ice-cream.

6 SERVINGS

14 oz. canned unsweetened, stoned black cherries
$\frac{1}{8}$ teaspoon ground cinnamon
1 tablespoon castor sugar
2 teaspoons arrowroot
2 fl. oz. [$\frac{1}{4}$ cup] Cognac

Low Cal

Drain the cherries and set them aside, reserving approximately 8 fluid ounces [1 cup] of the fruit syrup.

In a medium-sized saucepan, heat the reserved cherry syrup with the cinnamon, sugar and arrowroot over very low heat, stirring constantly with a wooden spoon. Cook for 3 to 4 minutes, or until all the ingredients have blended well and the juice is just warm. Add the cherries to the mixture and heat gently for another 1 to 2 minutes. Pour the cherries and juice into a serving bowl or chafing dish and set aside.

In a small saucepan, warm the Cognac over very low heat. Pour the Cognac over the cherries and ignite it. Serve as soon as the flames have died away.

Cherry Pie

This juicy Cherry Pie may be served as a dessert with fresh cream or a light custard sauce or as a very special coffee-time treat.

6 SERVINGS

8 oz. [2 cups] flour
$\frac{1}{4}$ teaspoon salt
4 teaspoons castor sugar
2 oz. [$\frac{1}{4}$ cup] plus 1 tablespoon butter
2 oz. [$\frac{1}{4}$ cup] vegetable fat
2 egg yolks
2 tablespoons iced water
2 lb. canned stoned cherries
3 tablespoons granulated sugar
$\frac{1}{4}$ teaspoon vanilla essence
1 tablespoon cornflour [cornstarch]
1 egg white, lightly beaten

Sift the flour and salt into a medium-sized mixing bowl. Add the castor sugar and stir to mix. Using a knife, cut 2 ounces [$\frac{1}{4}$ cup] of the butter and the vegetable fat

Black cherries flavoured with Cognac and cinnamon, Cherries Jubilee makes a luscious end to a superb dinner.

A filling and nourishing dessert for a winter's meal, Cherry Tapioca is quick, easy and economical.

into the flour. Using your fingertips, rub the fat into the flour until the mixture resembles fine breadcrumbs. Make a well in the centre of the mixture and add the egg yolks mixed with 1 tablespoon of iced water. With the knife, mix the flour mixture with the egg yolks, then use your hands to mix the ingredients until a smooth dough is formed. Add more iced water if the pastry is too dry. Pat the pastry into a ball, wrap it in greaseproof or waxed paper and refrigerate for 15 minutes.

Preheat the oven to fairly hot 375°F (Gas Mark 5, 190°C). Grease a medium-sized pie dish with the remaining butter and set it aside.

Drain the cherries, reserving 6 fluid ounces [$\frac{3}{4}$ cup] of the fruit syrup, and set them aside. In a medium-sized saucepan, heat the cherry syrup with the granulated sugar and vanilla essence over moderate heat until the mixture comes to the boil. Add the cherries and cook for 1 to 2 minutes longer, or until the cherries are heated through. Remove the pan from the heat and stir in the cornflour [cornstarch]. Mix gently until the cornflour [cornstarch] has completely dissolved and the liquid has thickened. Set the pan aside in a cool place.

Remove the dough from the refrigerator and divide it in two, one piece slightly larger than the other. On a lightly floured surface, roll out the larger piece of dough until it is quite thin. Line the pie dish with this dough. Spoon in the cherry filling, spreading it out evenly in the dish.

Roll out the remaining dough on the floured surface to a circle slightly larger than the pie dish. Place this dough over the cherry filling, folding under the overhanging dough and pressing the edges of the dough together with your fingertips. Make two or three slits in the pastry lid. With a pastry brush, lightly brush the egg white over the pastry. Bake in the centre of the oven for about 40 minutes, or until the pastry is deep golden brown. Serve either hot or cold.

Cherry Salad

This light and special tasting Cherry Salad particularly complements rich game dishes or roasts.

6 SERVINGS

1 lb. sweet black cherries, halved and stoned
3 tablespoons blanched, slivered almonds
4 tablespoons sour cream
3 teaspoons white wine vinegar
1 teaspoon lemon juice
2 teaspoons sugar
1 teaspoon salt
$\frac{1}{2}$ teaspoon white pepper

Low Cal

In a salad bowl, mix together the cherries and almonds. Set aside.

In a small bowl, mix the sour cream, vinegar, lemon juice, sugar, salt and pepper together, beating briskly with a fork or small wooden spoon until the ingredients are thoroughly blended.

Add the sour cream dressing to the cherry and almond mixture, toss well to coat and chill in the refrigerator until ready to serve.

Cherry Soup

Cold fruit soups are relatively unknown in English-speaking countries but they make a refreshing and unusual start to a meal. In the summer especially, they are much lighter and easier to digest than cooked hors d'oeuvre or hot soup.

4 SERVINGS

1 lb. canned stoned Morello cherries
8 fl. oz. [1 cup] red wine
1 cinnamon stick
1 teaspoon grated lemon rind
$\frac{1}{2}$ teaspoon lemon juice
1 tablespoon cornflour [cornstarch]
2 tablespoons water
2 tablespoons sugar
2 tablespoons sour cream

Drain the cherries, reserve the syrup, and set them aside.

In a large saucepan, heat the cherry syrup, red wine, cinnamon stick, lemon rind and lemon juice together over moderate heat until the mixture comes to the boil. Add the cherries, reduce the heat to very low and cook for 15 minutes. Remove the pan from the heat and remove and discard the cinnamon stick.

In a teacup, mix the cornflour [cornstarch] and water to a paste. Add this paste to the cherry mixture and stir with a wooden spoon to blend the ingredients well. Stir in the sugar.

Pour the cherry mixture into a deep serving bowl and place it in the refrigerator to chill for 1 hour. The soup should be served very cold. Just before serving, spoon the sour cream over the top of the soup.

Cherry Tapioca

A filling and nourishing dessert for a winter's meal, Cherry Tapioca is both economical and simple. It may be decorated with whipped cream or fresh cherries.

4 SERVINGS

14 oz. canned sweetened, stoned cherries, drained
2 tablespoons brandy (optional)
10 fl. oz. [1$\frac{1}{4}$ cups] milk
8 fl. oz. single cream [1 cup light cream]
2 oz. [$\frac{1}{3}$ cup] **tapioca**
$\frac{1}{2}$ teaspoon vanilla essence
$\frac{1}{2}$ teaspoon grated lemon rind
$\frac{1}{2}$ teaspoon grated nutmeg

Place the cherries in a medium-sized baking dish and moisten them with the brandy if used. Set the dish aside.

Preheat the oven to warm 325°F (Gas Mark 3, 170°C).

In a medium-sized saucepan, heat the milk and cream (bring to just under boiling point) over low heat. Add the tapioca, vanilla essence, lemon rind and nutmeg and, stirring constantly with a wooden spoon, simmer the mixture for 3 to 4 minutes, or until it thickens.

Pour the tapioca mixture over the cherries. Bake in the oven for 45 minutes, or until the tapioca is brown on top. Remove the dish from the oven and let it stand for 5 minutes before serving.

Chervil

Chervil is often used in French and Italian cooking but is relatively unknown in Britain and the United States. In appearance, it resembles parsley with its lacy leaves and very small flowers. It has a delicate taste, rather like aniseed.

Chervil is best used in dishes requiring little cooking since it quickly loses its flavour, and it is therefore a popular garnish, chopped or whole, for salads, cheese or egg dishes. It is also used to season soups and sauces, and goes particularly well with beef.

Chervil Avocado Salad

This is an unusual and refreshing accompaniment to a hot main dish such as baked ham or roast leg of lamb. It may also be served as a light, summery first course.

4 SERVINGS

4 ripe avocados, peeled and stoned
4 fl. oz. [$\frac{1}{2}$ cup] fresh lemon juice
$\frac{1}{2}$ teaspoon salt
$\frac{1}{2}$ teaspoon black pepper
1 tablespoon chopped fresh chervil

With a small, sharp knife, cut the avocados lengthways into thin slices and place them on a shallow glass dish. Cover them with lemon juice and season with salt and pepper.

Cover the dish and marinate the avocado in the refrigerator for at least 1 hour.

Remove the dish from the refrigerator and, with a slotted spoon, transfer the avocado slices to a chilled serving dish, discarding the lemon juice. Sprinkle the avocado with the chervil and serve at once.

Chervil and Leek Soup

This is a warm winter soup that is especially superb when served with crusty French bread. It is economical to make and easy to prepare.

4 SERVINGS

3 oz. [$\frac{3}{8}$ cup] butter
3 large leeks, thoroughly washed and chopped
1 medium-sized carrot, scraped and chopped
3 medium-sized potatoes, peeled and diced
2 pints [5 cups] chicken stock
1 teaspoon salt
$\frac{1}{2}$ teaspoon black pepper
1 bunch chervil, washed and finely chopped, or 2 tablespoons dried chervil
4 fl. oz. single cream [$\frac{1}{2}$ cup light cream]

In a large saucepan, melt 2 ounces [$\frac{1}{4}$ cup] of butter over moderate heat. When the foam subsides, add the chopped leeks, carrot and potatoes. Fry the vegetables for 10 to 12 minutes, stirring occasionally to prevent them from sticking to the bottom of the pan.

Pour in the stock. Add the salt, pepper and chervil to the pan and bring to the boil over high heat. Reduce the heat to low, cover and simmer the soup for 40 minutes.

Remove the pan from the heat and strain the soup into a bowl. Alternatively, purée the soup in a blender.

Return the strained or puréed soup to the saucepan. Bring it to the boil over moderate heat and cook for 5 minutes. Add the cream and swirl the remaining butter into the mixture, stirring until it melts.

Transfer the soup to a warmed tureen and serve immediately.

Cheshire Cheese

The oldest English cheese, Cheshire is a hard, rather crumbly cheese, of which there are two varieties—white and red, the latter being the milder, and artificially coloured. Occasionally red Cheshire accidentally develops a system of blue veins which give it its much appreciated texture and flavour. This 'blue' Cheshire is rare and much sought-after. Cheshire, unlike Cheddar and Stilton is not successfully copied. This is due to the excess salt in Cheshire soil and therefore the unusually saline composition of the milk.

Chestnut

The chestnut is the large brown nut of the *castenea* tree, the best known species being the sweet or Spanish chestnut and the Japanese chestnut. The American species, which once grew extensively in North America, was wiped out by a blight at the end of the nineteenth century. Chestnuts grown in Britain are small and hard to peel and therefore most of the chestnuts sold in the shops are imported from either France or Italy. They are in season during the winter months.

Sweet and floury when cooked, chestnuts are used boiled, puréed or roasted in soups and sauces, for stuffings and garnishings and as a sweet in cake fillings, puddings and ices. When steeped and cooked in syrup, they are called *marrons glacés,* an expensive delicacy.

To remove the shells from chestnuts, make a small slit in the hard skin at the pointed end of the nut with a sharp knife. Put the chestnuts into a saucepan and cover with cold water. Put the pan over high heat and bring the water to the boil. Boil the nuts for 2 minutes and remove the pan from the heat. With a slotted spoon take out the nuts, two at a time, and peel them, removing the inner skins as well while they are still warm. If they become cool and difficult to peel, bring the water to the boil again but do not let it continue boiling. When all the chestnuts are peeled, put them back in the saucepan, cover them with fresh water and simmer gently over low heat for about 45 to 60 minutes or until they are tender.

Another way to peel chestnuts is to put them in an ovenproof dish with a little water after they have been slit and to bake them in the oven preheated to a hot 425°F (Gas Mark 7, 220°C) for 8 minutes. Peel and cook them as above.

Drain the chestnuts and serve them immediately. If you wish to glaze the chestnuts, reserve the cooking liquid. To glaze 1 pound of boiled chestnuts, in a small bowl, blend 6 fluid ounces [$\frac{3}{4}$ cup] of the cooking liquid with $1\frac{1}{2}$ tablespoons of arrowroot until the mixture is smooth.

Pour the mixture into a large, deep frying-pan and bring it to simmering point over moderate heat. Simmer the mixture for 2 minutes, stirring constantly.

Add the chestnuts to the pan. Stir and cook the chestnuts for 3 to 4 minutes or until they are thoroughly heated. Add more of the cooking liquid if the glazing mixture is too thick.

Remove the pan from the heat and stir 2 tablespoons of butter into the chestnuts. Stir the chestnuts until the butter has melted. Turn the chestnuts into a warmed serving dish and serve at once.

To roast chestnuts, slit the pointed ends and roast in front of an open fire, under a hot grill [broiler] or in the oven preheated to hot 400°F, (Gas Mark 6, 200°C) for about 20 minutes or until the shells split open and the chestnuts are deep brown.

Chestnut Compôte

This is a rich dessert which may be served with whipped cream and sponge finger biscuits [cookies]. *For a pleasant variation substitute a tablespoon of Maraschino liqueur for the vanilla essence, but add it after the chestnuts have been cooked.*

4 SERVINGS

6 oz. [¾ cup] sugar
1 pint [2½ cups] water
½ teaspoon vanilla essence
1 lb. chestnuts, peeled

In a medium-sized saucepan, dissolve the sugar in the water over moderate heat, stirring continuously with a metal spoon. Mix in the vanilla essence, increase the heat to high and boil the syrup for 5 minutes. Add the chestnuts, cover the pan and reduce the heat to low. Simmer for 45 to 60 minutes, or until the chestnuts are tender and the syrup thick.

Remove the pan from the heat and when the chestnuts are cool pour them and the syrup into a glass serving dish.

Place the dish in the refrigerator and chill well before serving.

Chestnut Sauce

This sauce is the traditional accompaniment to roast turkey served at Christmas.

1 PINT

2 oz. [¼ cup] butter
1 small onion, finely chopped
1 carrot, scraped and finely sliced
3 fl. oz. [⅜ cup] sherry
2 tablespoons flour
12 fl. oz. [1½ cups] chicken stock
bouquet garni, consisting of 4 parsley sprigs, 1 thyme spray and 1 bay leaf tied together
½ teaspoon salt
¼ teaspoon freshly ground black pepper
8 oz. chestnuts (weighed after peeling), boiled and chopped

In a medium-sized saucepan, melt three-quarters of the butter over moderate heat. Add the onion and carrot, reduce the heat to low and cook the vegetables for 8 minutes, stirring occasionally.

Add the sherry and simmer for 5 minutes, or until it reduces a little in volume. Stir in the flour and cook gently for 5 minutes. Add the stock, bouquet garni, salt and pepper. Simmer gently for 20 minutes. Add the chopped chestnuts and cook for 10 minutes more.

Taste and add more salt and pepper if necessary. Remove and discard the bouquet garni.

Rub the mixture through a strainer placed over a saucepan, or purée it in blender. Place the saucepan over low heat and cook the sauce, stirring constantly, for 2 to 3 minutes. Just before serving, stir in the remaining butter and serve immediately.

Chestnut and Sausage Stuffing

This is the traditional stuffing for turkey. It is simple to make and adds a delicious flavour to the bird.

STUFFING FOR ONE 10-12 LB. TURKEY

1¼ lb. chestnuts, peeled
1 pint [2½ cups] beef stock
1 celery stalk, chopped
½ teaspoon salt
¼ teaspoon pepper
2 tablespoons butter
1 large onion, finely chopped
8 oz. pork sausage meat
3 oz. [1½ cups] fresh white breadcrumbs
2 eggs, lightly beaten

Put the chestnuts, stock, celery, salt and pepper in a medium-sized saucepan over moderate heat. Simmer for 1 hour, or until the chestnuts are tender and have absorbed all the stock. Transfer the chestnuts and celery to a medium-sized mixing

Chestnuts in syrup, Chestnut Compôte makes a rich dessert, served with sponge fingers and whipped cream.

bowl and allow to cool. Crumble the chestnuts into small pieces, or mash through a coarse strainer.

In a small saucepan, melt the butter over moderate heat. Add the onion and sausage meat and cook for 8 minutes. Remove the pan from the heat and allow the sausage mixture to cool. Add the breadcrumbs and eggs to the chestnuts along with the onion and sausage meat and mix well with a spoon.

Use the stuffing as required.

Chestnut Soup

This thick and creamy soup, garnished with fried apple slices and parsley, makes a warming dish for winter.

4 SERVINGS

$1\frac{1}{2}$ lb. chestnuts, peeled
1 small onion, sliced
1 carrot, scraped and sliced
$1\frac{1}{2}$ pints [$3\frac{3}{4}$ cups] chicken stock
$\frac{1}{2}$ teaspoon salt
$\frac{1}{4}$ teaspoon freshly ground black pepper
1 teaspoon cornflour [cornstarch] mixed with 1 tablespoon milk
2 tablespoons single [light] cream
1 tablespoon butter
1 cooking apple, peeled, cored and sliced
1 tablespoon chopped parsley

Place the chestnuts in a large saucepan with the onion, carrot, stock, salt and pepper. Cover the pan and simmer over low heat for 1 hour, or until the chestnuts are completely soft.

Strain the chestnut mixture, mashing it through the strainer with a wooden spoon, and return it to the saucepan. Alternatively, purée the mixture in a food mill or blender.

If the soup is too thin, add the cornflour [cornstarch] mixture and stir in well. Add the cream and reheat the soup slowly over low heat.

To make the garnish, melt the butter in a medium-sized frying-pan over moderate heat. Add the apple slices and fry them until they are golden brown. Add them to the soup, and sprinkle the top with the parsley.

Serve at once.

Chianti

Chianti, the best-known and most popular of the Italian wines, is produced in Tuscany, a region in Central Italy about 100 miles to the north of Rome. Both red and white wines are produced, although only the red is, by law, now permitted to call itself Chianti. (The white is officially designated Toscano Bianco.)

Chianti is robust and, like BEAUJOLAIS, should be drunk young. It is usually bottled in the well known straw flasks that seem to be popular for using as lamp bases afterwards.

A great deal of Chianti is produced each year and the quality of the wine can therefore vary quite widely. The best of it is called Chianti Classico and is produced in a legally defined area between the mediaeval cities of Florence and Siena. It is beautifully balanced and mellow to taste and, unlike most Chianti, ages well. Chianti Classico can be identified by its special black cockerel trade-mark.

Chianti complements any of the slightly heavier, meaty pasta dishes and can be particularly recommended for lasagne and spaghetti alla carbonara.

Chicken

This is one of a group of poultry (others are duck, goose, guinea fowl and turkey) that are domestic birds specially reared for the table. The very small chickens (poussins) weigh about 1 to $1\frac{1}{4}$ pounds and are usually 6 weeks old.

Spring chickens are 3 months old and weigh between 2 to $2\frac{1}{2}$ pounds. The larger roasting chickens are up to one year old and weigh 3 to 4 pounds.

Boiling fowl are larger, older birds which are tougher and therefore require longer, slower cooking, such as boiling or braising.

Capons are castrated young cocks which have been specially fattened. Their flesh is white and delicate and they usually weigh from 6 to 10 pounds.

At one time chicken was expensive and considered a luxury dish, but now, with the introduction of broiler house reared birds, chickens are in greater supply and are an economical buy.

Chickens are usually sold trussed, that is, ready for the oven. A good chicken has tender firm flesh and should have a plump breast. Many oven-ready chickens are frozen, in which case it is important that the bird is completely thawed before cooking.

If you buy an untrussed bird, look for a really fresh one. The signs to look for are the same as for a trussed bird, but check that the feet are black or white (depending on the breed of bird). A yellow colour is a give-away to an old tough one.

Chicken may be cooked in a variety of ways—roasted, braised or casseroled, and small pieces are ideal for frying or grilling [broiling]. The giblets (excluding the liver) and bones make excellent chicken stock. If the stock is not required immediately, it can be frozen in a home freezer for future use. For this pour the cooled stock into plastic containers leaving a $\frac{1}{2}$ inch space between the top of the stock and the lid. Cool the stock to room temperature, skim off the excess fat, then cover.

Chicken livers are delicious served on their own either grilled [broiled] or fried, and also make superb pâté, risotto or after dinner savouries.

TRUSSING A CHICKEN

A chicken is trussed so that it keeps its shape during cooking and is therefore easier to carve.

The simplest way to truss a bird is with a skewer and a piece of string. Push the skewer right through the bird just below the thigh bone. Turn the bird on to its breast. Catch in the wing pinions with the string, pass the string under the ends of the skewer and cross it over the back. Turn the bird over, pass the string over the drumsticks and tie under the parson's nose.

To truss a chicken in the traditional way it is necessary to have a long trussing needle and strong fine string.

1. Place the flap of skin neatly over the back of the neck and fold the pinions or ends of the wings backwards over the flap to hold it in position.
2. Put the chicken on its back with the breast away from you. Press the legs well into the sides, as this raises and plumps the breast. Thread the needle and push it through the lower part of the carcass.
3. Pass the string over one drumstick, through the tip of the breastbone and over the other drumstick. Tie firmly.

4. Re-thread the needle and thrust it through the carcass where the drumstick and the second joint meet and then out the other side.
5. Turn the chicken over and push the needle through the wing, the neck flap on either side of the back bone, and then the other wing. Tie firmly.

ROAST CHICKEN I
Rub salt, pepper and 1 tablespoon of butter all over and inside a medium-sized chicken. Stuff it, if liked. Place it in a roasting tin in the oven preheated to hot 425°F (Gas Mark 7, 220°C) for 15 minutes. Reduce the temperature to moderate 350°F (Gas Mark 4, 180°C) and roast the chicken, basting every 10 minutes with 2 tablespoons of melted butter mixed with 1 tablespoon of vegetable oil, until it is tender. After the first 15 minutes of cooking, turn the bird on its side and, after a further 15 minutes, on its other side. When the chicken is cooked, remove it from the tin, cut and remove the trussing string and keep the chicken hot on a serving dish or board. Leave it for 5 minutes at room temperature before carving.
Roasting Times: A 2-pound oven-ready chicken takes from 50 to 60 minutes to roast. Add between 10 and 15 minutes for every additional pound.

ROAST CHICKEN II
Rub salt and pepper all over a $3\frac{1}{2}$-pound chicken, inside and out. Place half an onion, a garlic clove, a parsley sprig, a bay leaf and a thyme spray inside the bird. Truss the bird. Melt 4 ounces [$\frac{1}{2}$ cup] of butter in a shallow flameproof dish over moderate heat. Put the chicken into the melted butter and turn it so that it is well coated all over. Place it in the oven preheated to very hot 450°F (Gas Mark 8, 230°C) and baste it with the butter in the dish every 7 minutes during the whole of the cooking time. Turn the bird on its side after 20 minutes and on its other side after a further 15 minutes. A medium-sized bird of $3\frac{1}{2}$ pounds will take about 1 to $1\frac{1}{2}$ hours. By this time the chicken will be golden brown. When the chicken is cooked, remove it from the dish, cut off the trussing string, place the chicken on a serving dish and keep it hot. Put the cooking dish over high heat. Add 4 fluid

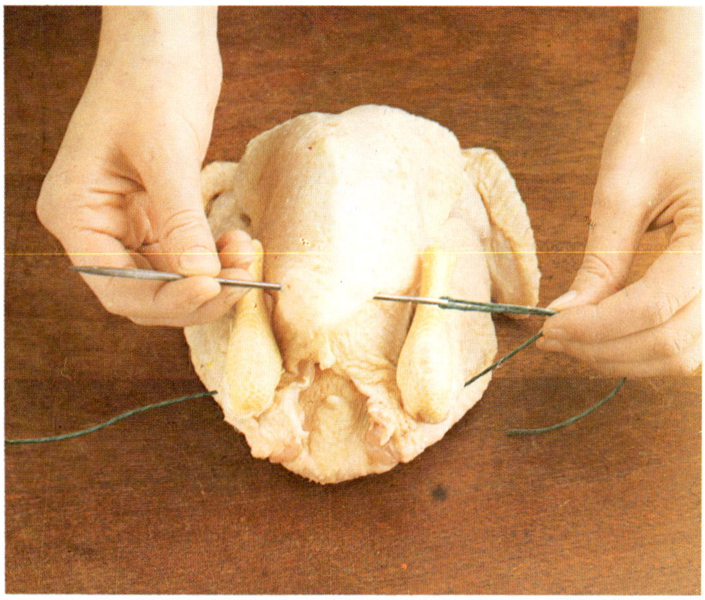

Push a threaded trussing needle through the lower part of the carcass. Pass the string over one drumstick, through the tip of the breastbone and over the other drumstick. Tie firmly.

Then re-thread the needle and thrust it through the top of the carcass, above the wings, where the drumstick and the second joint meet and then out the other side.

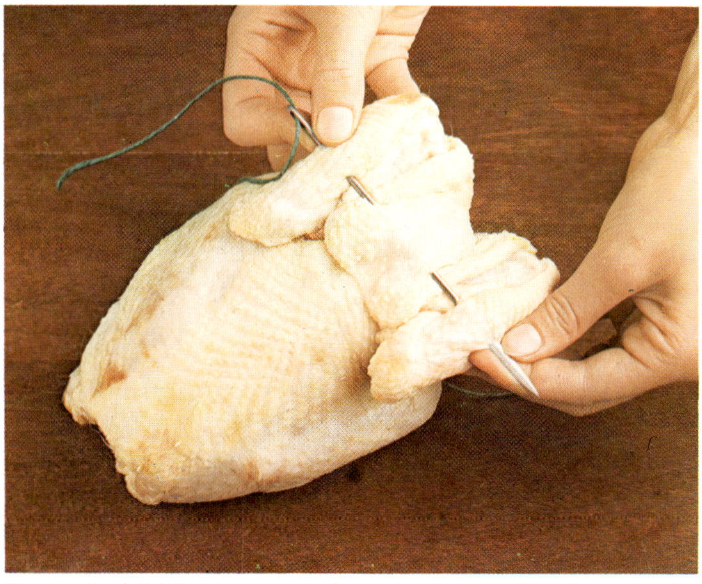

Turn the chicken over and push the needle through the wing, the neck flap on either side of the back bone, and then the other wing. Tie firmly.

Tie the string ends firmly together. Rub salt and pepper all over the skin of the chicken. It is now ready to be roasted, braised or casseroled.

ounces [$\frac{1}{2}$ cup] of wine or stock to the cooking juices and bring it to the boil. Boil briskly for 1 minute, stirring constantly. Taste the sauce and add more salt and pepper if necessary. Strain the sauce into a sauceboat.

BOILED CHICKEN

Put the chicken into a pan with enough cold salted water to just cover the bird. Add a sliced onion and carrot and a bouquet garni. Place the pan over high heat and bring to the boil. Cover the pan, reduce the heat to very low and simmer gently until the chicken is tender, skimming occasionally.

The chicken will take from 45 minutes to $1\frac{1}{2}$ hours to cook, depending on the size of the bird. These timings relate only to young birds, since older boiling fowls require at least 2 to 3 hours. To test the bird to see if it is cooked, pierce the thigh with a sharp knife. If the liquid that oozes out is clear, then the bird is cooked.

Chicken Breasts en Papillote

CHICKEN BREASTS COOKED IN A PARCEL

The chicken breasts in this recipe are covered with a creamy, spicy sauce, wrapped in envelopes of foil and then baked. They should be served still wrapped in the foil. Accompanied by spinach and rice, they make a delicious meal.

3 SERVINGS

- 6 chicken breasts, skinned and boned
- 2 tablespoons lemon juice
- 4 oz. [$\frac{1}{2}$ cup] butter
- 2 tablespoons flour
- 8 fl. oz. [1 cup] chicken stock
- 4 fl. oz. [$\frac{1}{2}$ cup] dry white wine
- 1 egg yolk, lightly beaten
- $\frac{1}{2}$ teaspoon salt
- $\frac{1}{2}$ teaspoon black pepper
- $\frac{1}{4}$ teaspoon cayenne
- $\frac{1}{4}$ teaspoon grated nutmeg
- 4 oz. mushrooms, wiped and finely chopped
- 1 teaspoon chopped spring onions [scallions]

Low Cal

Sprinkle the chicken breasts with the lemon juice and set them aside for 15 minutes to absorb the flavour.

In a medium-sized frying pan melt half the butter over moderate heat. When the foam subsides add the chicken breasts to the pan and cook for 8 minutes on each side, or until they are lightly browned. Remove the breasts from the heat and set aside.

Preheat the oven to fairly hot 400°F (Gas Mark 6, 200°C).

Cut 6 pieces of aluminium foil, each large enough to enclose a breast half. Grease the pieces of foil with half the remaining butter.

In a small saucepan, melt the rest of the butter over moderate heat. With a wooden spoon, stir in the flour and cook, stirring, for 1 minute. Remove the pan from the heat.

Add the chicken stock gradually, stirring constantly. When all the stock has been absorbed, return the pan to the heat and, stirring continuously, bring the sauce to the boil. Remove the pan from the heat and gradually stir in the wine. When all the wine has been added, return the pan to the heat again and, stirring continuously, cook the sauce until it is thick. Beat 4 tablespoons of the hot sauce, a spoonful at a time, into the beaten egg yolk.

Stir the egg mixture into the hot sauce. Place the pan over very low heat and continue cooking and stirring until the sauce has thickened. Do not let it boil or it will curdle.

Remove the pan from the heat and add the salt, pepper, cayenne, nutmeg, mushrooms and spring onions [scallions].

Place half a chicken breast in the middle of each piece of foil and spoon the sauce over it. Bring together the edges of the foil and seal the parcel by folding the edges over.

Arrange the parcels on a baking sheet and bake in the oven for 30 to 40 minutes, or until the chicken is very tender. Serve at once.

Chicken Breasts with Tarragon

White wine, cream and tarragon are essential ingredients in many famous French dishes. Here they combine to make a rich, creamy sauce served with succulent chicken breasts. This dish may be accompanied by glazed carrots and creamed potatoes.

3 SERVINGS

- 6 chicken breasts, skinned and boned
- 4 tablespoons seasoned flour, made with 4 tablespoons flour, $\frac{1}{2}$ teaspoon salt and $\frac{1}{2}$ teaspoon black pepper
- 2 oz. [$\frac{1}{4}$ cup] butter
- 2 shallots or spring onions [scallions] finely chopped
- 3 fl. oz. [$\frac{3}{8}$ cup] dry white wine
- 1 teaspoon chopped fresh tarragon
- 2 fl. oz. [$\frac{1}{4}$ cup] chicken stock, made from the giblets or a stock cube
- 2 fl. oz. double cream [$\frac{1}{4}$ cup heavy cream]

Coat the chicken breasts thoroughly with half the seasoned flour. Reserve the remaining flour.

In a large, deep frying-pan, melt three-quarters of the butter over moderate heat. When the foam subsides, add the chicken breasts to the pan and brown them for 5 to 7 minutes on both sides. With tongs, transfer the breasts from the pan to a heated dish.

Add the shallots or spring onions [scallions] to the pan and fry them for 4 to 5 minutes. Pour in the wine and stir to blend it with the pan juices.

Increase the heat to high and boil the wine, stirring, until it has reduced to about half the original quantity.

Remove the pan from the heat and stir in the remaining seasoned flour to make a thick paste.

Return the pan to low heat and add the tarragon and chicken stock.

Return the chicken to the pan, cover and cook for about 25 minutes, or until the chicken is tender.

With tongs, remove the chicken breasts from the pan and place them in a warmed serving dish. Keep hot.

Add the remaining butter and cream to the pan and cook, stirring occasionally, for 2 to 3 minutes.

Remove the pan from the heat and pour the sauce over the chicken breasts. Serve at once.

Chicken Chablis

This smooth, sophisticated dish may be served with buttered noodles and a green salad. It should be accompanied by a well-chilled Chablis.

4-6 SERVINGS

- 4 oz. [1 cup] flour
- 2 teaspoons salt
- 1 teaspoon freshly ground black pepper
- 1 x 4-lb. chicken, cut into six serving pieces (wings, legs, breasts)
- 4 fl. oz. [$\frac{1}{2}$ cup] olive oil
- 8 oz. canned tomatoes
- 2 tablespoons butter
- 12 fl. oz. [$1\frac{1}{2}$ cups] Chablis
- 8 oz. mushrooms, sliced and sautéed in 2 tablespoons butter with 1 crushed garlic clove

In a shallow dish, mix together half the flour with half the salt and pepper. Coat the chicken pieces with this seasoned flour.

In a medium-sized flameproof casserole, heat the oil over moderate heat. Add the chicken pieces and brown them for 2 to 3 minutes on each side. Reduce the heat to low, cover the casserole and cook the chicken pieces for 10 minutes.

Remove the casserole from the heat. With tongs, remove the chicken pieces from the casserole and set them aside. Cover the chicken pieces with aluminium foil to keep them warm. Pour off the excess oil from the casserole and add the tomatoes. Return the casserole to moderate heat and bring the tomatoes to the boil.

In a small bowl, mix the remaining flour with the butter to make a smooth paste (beurre manié).

Gradually stir the beurre manié into the tomato liquid. Cook, stirring, until the mixture thickens. Slowly add the wine, stirring constantly. When the sauce is well blended, add the remaining salt and pepper and return the chicken pieces to the casserole with the garlic-flavoured mushrooms. Reduce the heat to low, cover the casserole and cook for 25 minutes, or until the chicken is tender. Remove the casserole from the heat and serve hot.

Chicken Chaudfroid

Cold chicken breasts coated in a creamy white sauce, attractively garnished with tomatoes and green pepper and glazed with aspic, Chicken Chaudfroid (show-fwah) *makes an impressive dish for a buffet party. It may be prepared the day before and kept in the refrigerator until just before serving.*

6 SERVINGS

- 6 chicken breasts, skinned and boned
- 1 teaspoon lemon juice
- $\frac{1}{4}$ teaspoon salt
- $\frac{1}{4}$ teaspoon white pepper
- 2 oz. [$\frac{1}{4}$ cup] butter
- $\frac{1}{4}$ green pepper
- 1 tomato
- 15 fl. oz. [$1\frac{7}{8}$ cups] white chaudfroid sauce, cool and on the point of setting
- $1\frac{1}{2}$ pints [$3\frac{3}{4}$ cups] aspic jelly, cool and on the point of setting
- watercress

Preheat the oven to fairly hot 400°F (Gas Mark 6, 200°C).

On a wooden board, rub the chicken breast halves all over with the lemon juice, salt and pepper.

In a large, shallow, flameproof casserole, melt the butter over moderate heat. When the foam subsides, add the chicken breasts, turning them with tongs to coat them well with the butter. Place a piece of aluminium foil over the chicken, cover the casserole and place it in the oven. Bake the chicken breasts for 15 to 20 minutes, or until they are tender. Remove them from the oven and leave them to cool.

While the chicken is baking, remove the seeds and core from the green pepper and cut the pepper into triangles. Slice the tomato and cut each slice in half.

When the chicken breasts are cool, place them on a wire rack with a piece of aluminium foil underneath. Using a spoon, lightly coat each chicken breast with chaudfroid sauce. Leave the chicken breasts until the sauce is firm and set, then coat them a second time.

When the second coating of chaudfroid has set, arrange the chicken pieces on a flat serving dish. Place the tomatoes and green pepper on each piece of chicken to form an attractive pattern.

Cold chicken breasts glazed with aspic, Chicken Chaudfroid is a superb dish for a buffet party.

Cover the decorated chicken with the nearly setting aspic, spooning on an extra coat if necessary after the first has set. Put the dish in the refrigerator to chill until the aspic has completely set.

Allow the remaining aspic to set completely and chop it into cubes. Arrange the cubes round the chicken. Garnish the dish with the watercress, cover and place it in the refrigerator until you are ready to serve it.

Chicken Curry

All curries are good party dishes as they can be made well in advance, the previous day if necessary, and reheated just before serving. If you like a mild curry, omit the green chilli and halve the amount of chilli powder. Serve the curry with plain boiled rice, a bowl of yogurt, various fresh chutneys and poppadums. Wine should not be served with a curry but a well-chilled lager is just right.

4 SERVINGS

3 lb. chicken pieces (at least 2 pieces per person)
2 teaspoons salt
3 teaspoons turmeric
4 tablespoons vegetable oil
1 large onion, finely chopped
2 garlic cloves, finely chopped
2-inch piece root ginger, peeled and finely chopped
1 green chilli, finely chopped
3 teaspoons ground coriander
1½ teaspoons ground cumin
1 tablespoon garam masala
1 teaspoon chilli powder
1 lb. canned peeled tomatoes, drained and sieved
½-inch slice of creamed coconut
1 tablespoon chopped coriander leaves

Dry the chicken pieces with kitchen paper towels. Combine 1 teaspoon salt and 2 teaspoons turmeric on a plate. Rub the chicken pieces all over with this mixture.

Heat the oil in a large, deep frying-pan or saucepan over high heat. Add the chicken pieces, reduce the heat to moderate and fry them lightly on all sides for about 5 minutes, using tongs to turn them. Remove the chicken pieces and set them aside on a plate.

Add the onion to the casserole or pan, adding more oil if necessary. Fry the onion, stirring occasionally, for about 8 minutes or until it is soft and lightly coloured. Add the garlic, ginger and green chilli and fry for a further 4 minutes.

Put the ground coriander, cumin, garam masala, chilli powder and the remaining teaspoon of turmeric in a cup with 2 tablespoons of water and mix to a paste. Add the paste to the frying-pan and, stirring frequently, fry the spices for 8 minutes. If the mixture becomes too dry, add 2 to 3 tablespoons of water.

Add the sieved tomatoes and the remaining teaspoon of salt. Stir to mix and put in the chicken pieces. Lower the heat, cover the pan and simmer for 40 to 45 minutes or until the chicken pieces are tender.

Add the creamed coconut and stir until it has completely dissolved. Cook for 10 minutes. Stir the curry and taste it, then add salt and a teaspoon of sugar, if necessary. Stir in the chopped coriander leaves and serve hot with plain boiled rice.

Chicken, English-Style

This is one of the best ways to cook an older, tougher chicken. The addition of vegetables, as well as the long, slow cooking makes the chicken tender and flavourful.

6 SERVINGS

1 x 5 lb. boiling chicken
2 large leeks, sliced
2 carrots, scraped and sliced
1 small turnip, peeled and quartered
8 peppercorns
bouquet garni, consisting of 4 parsley sprigs, 1 thyme spray and 1 bay leaf tied together
12 parsley sprigs
1 teaspoon salt
1 oz. [2 tablespoons] butter
2 tablespoons flour
2 fl. oz. single cream [¼ cup light cream]
4 streaky bacon slices, rind removed and halved

Put the chicken in a large saucepan and pour over enough water to cover the bird. Add the leeks, carrots, turnip, peppercorns and bouquet garni. Place the pan over high heat and bring the water to the boil. Cover the pan, reduce the heat to low and simmer the chicken for about 2½ hours, or until it is tender. Remove the pan from the heat and strain off 1¼ pints [3 cups] of the stock into a small saucepan. Leave the chicken in the remaining stock in the pan and keep warm.

Place the small saucepan over moderate heat and boil the stock until it has reduced by about one-third. Remove the pan from the heat and allow the stock to cool. Skim off the fat from the surface and set the pan aside.

Put the parsley in a medium-sized saucepan with the salt. Pour in a little water—just enough to cover the parsley—and place the pan over moderate heat. Bring the water to the boil. Cover the pan, reduce the heat to low and simmer the parsley for 8 minutes, or until it is tender. Drain the parsley thoroughly and squeeze out the moisture. Press the parsley through a strainer, using the back of a wooden spoon, into a bowl. Set the parsley purée aside.

Chicken Florentine is a delicious dish of chicken breasts and spinach.

In a small saucepan, melt the butter over low heat. Remove the pan from the heat and, with a wooden spoon, stir in the flour. Gradually add the cooled and skimmed stock from the small saucepan, stirring constantly. Return the pan to moderate heat and bring the sauce to the boil. Boil for 1 minute, stirring constantly. Remove the pan from the heat and stir in the parsley purée. Beat the sauce for 2 minutes, then stir in the cream. Cover the pan and return it to very low heat to keep warm.

Preheat the grill [broiler] to high. Roll up each bacon slice half and secure it with a wooden cocktail stick. Grill [broil] the bacon rolls for 6 to 7 minutes, turning them occasionally. When they are cooked, set them aside and keep warm.

Remove the chicken from the pan and discard the remaining stock, flavourings and vegetables.

Carve the chicken and arrange it on a warmed serving platter. Spoon over a little of the parsley sauce and serve the rest in a sauce boat. Garnish the chicken with bacon rolls.

Chicken Florentine

CHICKEN BREASTS WITH SPINACH

A delectable combination of tender, Parmesan-coated chicken breasts and spinach, Chicken Florentine may be accompanied by herb-flavoured rice and a light, white wine such as a Soave.

6 SERVINGS

- **4 oz. [1 cup] Parmesan cheese, grated**
- **4 oz. [$1\frac{1}{4}$ cups] dry white breadcrumbs**
- **6 chicken breasts, boned and skinned**
- **3 tablespoons seasoned flour, made with 3 tablespoons flour,**
- **1 teaspoon salt and**
- **$\frac{1}{2}$ teaspoon black pepper**
- **1 egg, lightly beaten with 1 tablespoon water**
- **6 oz. [$\frac{3}{4}$ cup] butter**
- **5 lb. spinach, well washed and coarse stalks removed or 2 large packets frozen spinach**
- **1 teaspoon salt**
- **$1\frac{1}{2}$ tablespoons lemon juice**
- **$1\frac{1}{2}$ lb. mushrooms, wiped clean and sliced**
- **1 lemon, sliced**

Mix the cheese and breadcrumbs together in a shallow bowl. Roll the chicken breasts in the seasoned flour to coat them all over. Then dip them in the beaten egg mixture and then in the cheese and breadcrumbs. Place the well-coated chicken breasts in the refrigerator and leave them to chill for at least 1 hour.

In a large frying-pan, melt two-thirds of the butter over moderate heat. When the foam subsides, add the chicken breasts and brown them on both sides.

Reduce the heat to low, cover the pan and cook the chicken for about 25 to 30 minutes, or until it is tender.

While the chicken is cooking, put the washed spinach into a large pan with the salt. Place the pan over moderate heat and cook the spinach until it is tender. There will be enough water left on the leaves after washing for the spinach to cook. If using frozen spinach cook according to the directions on the packets.

When the spinach is cooked, press it between two plates to squeeze out the moisture. Chop it coarsely. Arrange the chopped spinach on a large flat serving dish and sprinkle it with the lemon juice.

With tongs, remove the chicken breasts from the frying-pan and place them on top of the spinach. Cover and keep hot.

Add half the remaining butter to the frying-pan and melt it over moderately high heat. Add the mushrooms and sauté them for 4 to 5 minutes.

With a slotted spoon, remove the mushrooms from the pan and arrange them around the chicken.

Place the remaining butter in the frying-pan and, over moderately high heat, cook the butter until it is brown.

Remove the pan from the heat and strain the butter over the chicken breasts.

Garnish with the lemon slices.

Chicken with Ginger

A simple yet elegantly rich dish, Chicken with Ginger can be served on a bed of cooked rice and accompanied by a green vegetable. Chilled lager would go well with this dish, or, if a wine is preferred, a light Alsatian Sylvaner.

4 SERVINGS

Low Cal

- **4 chicken quarters**
- **$\frac{1}{2}$ teaspoon salt**
- **$\frac{1}{2}$ teaspoon black pepper**
- **4 oz. [$\frac{1}{2}$ cup] butter**
- **1 garlic clove, finely chopped**
- **10 fl. oz. [$1\frac{1}{4}$ cups] chicken stock**
- **2 pieces preserved [candied] ginger, chopped**
- **2 teaspoons lemon juice**
- **1 tablespoon cornflour [cornstarch]**
- **3 tablespoons cold water**
- **2 tablespoons chopped parsley**

On a chopping board, rub the chicken pieces with salt and pepper.

In a large frying-pan melt the butter over moderate heat. When the foam subsides add the chicken pieces. Cook them for 5 to 7 minutes on each side until golden brown.

Reduce the heat to low. Add the garlic

Easy to prepare, Chicken with Herbs is a fragrant and delicious casserole.

to the pan and stir in the stock. Cover the pan and cook the chicken for about 30 to 35 minutes or until the chicken is tender.

Transfer the chicken to a warmed serving dish and cover with aluminium foil to keep it warm. Mix the chopped ginger and lemon juice into the juices in the pan. Cook very gently for about 1 minute.

In a teacup, mix together the cornflour [cornstarch] and water to form a smooth paste. Add this paste to the mixture in the pan, stirring until it dissolves and the sauce thickens. Add the parsley.

Return the chicken to the frying-pan and cook for a further 5-8 minutes.

Transfer the chicken to a warmed serving dish and serve immediately.

Chicken and Ham Paste

This paste will keep well for up to a week in the refrigerator, and is suitable for sandwiches or for canapés.

1 POUND

- 8 oz. cooked chicken
- 8 oz. lean, cooked ham
- 6 oz. [$\frac{3}{4}$ cup] butter, softened
- $\frac{1}{2}$ teaspoon salt
- $\frac{1}{4}$ teaspoon freshly ground black pepper
- $\frac{1}{2}$ teaspoon grated nutmeg
- 4 oz. [$\frac{1}{2}$ cup] clarified butter

Put the chicken and ham through a food mill or mincer [grinder] twice. When the chicken and ham are finely minced [ground] transfer them to a medium-sized mixing bowl. With a wooden spoon, beat in the butter. Alternatively, the meat may be chopped and puréed with the butter in a blender.

Season the purée with salt, pepper and nutmeg. Spoon the mixture into small pots and pour over the clarified butter to seal the paste.

Leave the paste until the butter has set, then use as required.

Chicken with Herbs

The herbs in this recipe give the chicken a fragrant and delicious flavour. Serve with Brussels sprouts and buttered noodles or rice and, to drink a light Alsatian wine.

4-6 SERVINGS

- 2 oz. [$\frac{1}{4}$ cup] butter
- 1 x 4-lb. chicken, cut in serving pieces

- 10 fl. oz. [$1\frac{1}{4}$ cups] chicken stock
- 2 garlic cloves, crushed
- 2 tablespoons chopped parsley
- 2 tablespoons chopped spring onions [scallions]
- 1 tablespoon dried tarragon
- 1 teaspoon dried marjoram
- 4 oz. mushrooms, sliced
- juice of 1 lemon
- $\frac{1}{2}$ teaspoon salt
- $\frac{1}{4}$ teaspoon black pepper

Low Cal

Preheat the oven to warm 325°F (Gas Mark 3, 170°C).

In a large saucepan or flameproof casserole melt the butter over moderate heat. When the foam subsides, place the chicken pieces in the pan and brown them on all sides, turning them with two large spoons.

Remove the chicken from the pan and arrange the pieces on the bottom of a medium-sized casserole.

Add the stock to the pan and stir well to mix. Bring the liquid to the boil over high heat. Add the garlic.

Add the parsley, spring onions [scallions], tarragon, marjoram, mushrooms, lemon juice, salt and pepper to the casserole and pour the stock mixture over the chicken. Be sure the chicken is not completely covered by the liquid.

Cover the casserole tightly and place it in a large roasting tin. Pour boiling water into the tin to a depth of 2 inches. Bake for 2 hours, or until the chicken is tender.

Remove the casserole from the oven and serve.

Chicken Juniper

This is a succulent and aromatic dish. The sweet, sharp flavour of juniper berries gives the chicken a subtle and unusual flavour. Serve with fluffy mashed potatoes and a crisp green salad.

4 SERVINGS

- 2 oz. [$\frac{3}{4}$ cup] white breadcrumbs
- $1\frac{1}{2}$ oz. [$\frac{1}{4}$ cup] oatmeal
- 1 teaspoon dried basil
- $\frac{1}{2}$ teaspoon dried sage
- $\frac{1}{2}$ teaspoon dried thyme
- 12 juniper berries, crushed with the back of wooden spoon
- 1 teaspoon grated lemon rind
- $\frac{1}{2}$ teaspoon salt
- $\frac{1}{4}$ teaspoon black pepper
- 2 tablespoons butter, melted
- 1 egg yolk
- 1 x 4 lb. chicken
- 10 fl. oz. [$1\frac{1}{4}$ cups] dry white wine
- 3 carrots, scraped and thinly sliced
- 4 shallots or spring onions [scallions] thinly sliced

Preheat the oven to fairly hot 375°F (Gas Mark 5, 190°C).

In a medium-sized bowl, mix together the breadcrumbs, oatmeal, basil, sage, thyme, juniper berries, lemon rind, salt and pepper. Add 1 tablespoon of the butter and the egg yolk and mix well. With a spoon, place the stuffing into the breast cavity of the chicken. Fold the flap of skin over the back of the neck and truss or secure with a metal skewer.

Place the chicken in a roasting tin and brush it with the remaining melted butter. Pour in the wine and add the carrot and shallots or spring onions [scallions]. Cover the bird loosely with aluminium foil and roast in the oven for 1 to 1½ hours or until the chicken is tender.

Place the chicken on a warm serving dish and pour the juices and vegetables over it. Serve immediately.

Chicken Kiev

This classic Russian dish, Chicken Kiev, is succulent chicken breasts stuffed with a savoury butter, then coated in egg and crumbs and fried until crisp and golden brown. Serve it with peas and allumettes potatoes.

4 SERVINGS

- 4 oz. [½ cup] butter
- 1 tablespoon chopped fresh parsley
- 1 tablespoon chopped fresh chives
- 1 garlic clove, crushed
- ½ teaspoon salt
- ½ teaspoon freshly ground black pepper
- 8 chicken breasts, skinned and boned
- 2 oz. [½ cup] flour
- 2 eggs, lightly beaten
- 6 oz. [2 cups] fine dry white breadcrumbs
- sufficient vegetable oil for deep-frying

In a medium-sized mixing bowl, cream the butter with a wooden spoon When it is soft, beat in the parsley, chives, garlic, salt and pepper. Divide the butter mixture into eight pieces (one for each breast half) and shape them into small, oval pieces. Place the pieces of butter mixture in the refrigerator.

Place one chicken breast half between 2 sheets of greaseproof or waxed paper on a chopping board and pound it thin with a mallet or similar heavy object. Flatten the remaining chicken breast halves in the same way.

Remove the greaseproof or waxed paper and wrap the chicken breast halves around the butter mixture envelope-fashion so that each piece is tubular in shape with the butter sealed in.

Put the flour, beaten eggs and breadcrumbs into three separate shallow bowls and set them side by side on the kitchen table. Dip the chicken breasts, one by one, first into the flour, then into the egg (make sure that each piece is thoroughly coated with the egg mixture) and, finally, into the breadcrumbs. Each piece should have a fairly thick layer of breadcrumbs. Refrigerate the chicken breasts for 1 hour before frying.

Just before frying, preheat the oven to very cool 250°F (Gas Mark ½, 130°C).

In a large pan suitable for deep-frying, heat the oil until it reaches 360°F on a fat thermometer, or until a small piece of dry bread dropped into the hot oil turns golden in 50 seconds.

Use a frying basket if you have one; this makes it easier to remove the chicken breasts the moment they are ready. Fry the breasts two at a time, for about 5 to 6 minutes each, or until they are golden brown in colour. As each batch is cooked, place them on a baking sheet lined with kitchen paper towels and then put them in the oven to keep warm.

Serve as soon as all the chicken breasts are cooked.

For Chicken Kiev, wrap the flattened chicken breasts around the butter mixture, envelope-fashion.

Dip the stuffed breasts first into the flour, then into the beaten eggs and, finally, into the breadcrumbs.

After deep-frying the stuffed chicken breasts, place them on kitchen paper towels to drain any excess oil.

Chicken à la King

This is an excellent recipe for using cooked chicken and makes an ideal dish for a buffet party. Plain boiled rice makes a good accompaniment.

4 SERVINGS

- 2 tablespoons butter
- 1 green pepper, white pith removed, seeded and finely chopped
- 6 oz. button mushrooms, finely sliced
- 1 tablespoon flour
- 1 teaspoon salt
- 10 fl. oz. single cream [1¼ cups light cream]
- 10 fl. oz. [1¼ cups] milk
- 1½ lb. cooked chicken, diced
- 3 egg yolks
- 2 teaspoons lemon juice
- 1 tablespoon paprika
- 2 teaspoons chopped parsley
- 3 tablespoons sweet sherry

In a medium-sized saucepan, melt the butter over moderate heat. When the foam subsides add the green pepper and, stirring occasionally with a wooden spoon, cook gently for 6 minutes. Add the mushrooms and cook for a further 4 minutes. Stir in the flour and salt and cook for 2 minutes longer. Gradually add the cream and milk, stirring continuously. Bring the mixture to the boil, reduce the heat to low and cook for 3 minutes. Stir in the chicken and reduce the heat to very low so that, though the mixture continues to cook, it does not even simmer.

In a small bowl, beat the egg yolks, lemon juice, paprika and parsley together with a wooden spoon. Add 4 tablespoons of the hot sauce, a spoonful at a time, to the egg mixture and stir well to mix. Pour this mixture into the pan, stir to mix and cook gently for 4 minutes. Do not let it boil or the sauce will curdle. Mix in the sherry and serve.

Chicken and Leek Pie

This crisp golden pastry-topped pie with a filling of chicken and leeks makes a tasty lunch or supper dish. When cold, a piece of it is ideal for a packed lunch.

Chicken and Leek Pie, topped with crisp, golden pastry, makes a tasty lunch or supper dish for the family.

6 SERVINGS

1 x 5 lb. chicken
2 medium-sized onions, halved
2 celery stalks, quartered
bouquet garni, consisting of 4 parsley sprigs, 1 thyme spray and 1 bay leaf tied together
$2\frac{1}{2}$ teaspoons salt
4 pints [5 pints] water
$2\frac{1}{2}$ lb. leeks, including 2 inches of the green stems, thoroughly washed and cut into $\frac{1}{2}$ inch slices
1 teaspoon sugar
4 oz. cooked ham, thinly sliced
1 tablespoon chopped parsley
4 tablespoons double [heavy] cream

PASTRY
6 oz. [$1\frac{1}{2}$ cups] flour
$\frac{1}{8}$ teaspoon salt
5 oz. [$\frac{5}{8}$ cup] butter, cut into walnut-sized pieces
3-4 tablespoons iced water
1 egg, lightly beaten

Place the chicken, onions, celery, bouquet garni and 2 teaspoons of salt in a large saucepan. Pour over the water. The chicken should be completely covered with water, so add more if necessary.

Place the pan over high heat and bring the water to the boil. With a metal spoon, skim off any scum that rises to the surface. Reduce the heat to low, partly cover the pan, with the lid on a slant, and simmer for 1 to $1\frac{1}{2}$ hours, or until the chicken is tender.

Meanwhile, prepare the pastry. Sift the flour and salt into a medium-sized mixing bowl. Add the butter and the iced water. With a knife, mix quickly to a firm dough which should be lumpy.

On a lightly floured surface, roll out the dough into an oblong shape. Fold it in three and turn it so that the open edges face you. Roll out again into an oblong shape and proceed as before. Repeat this once again to make three turns in all. Wrap the dough in greaseproof or waxed paper and put it in the refrigerator to chill.

Remove the pan from the heat and transfer the chicken to a wooden board or platter. Strain the stock into a measuring jug. Discard the vegetables and flavourings. Return 16 fluid ounces [2 cups] of the stock to the saucepan and add the leeks. Place the pan over high heat. Bring the stock to the boil. Reduce the heat to low, partially cover the pan and simmer the leeks for 15 to 20 minutes, or until they are tender.

Preheat the oven to fairly hot 400°F (Gas Mark 6, 200°C).

With a small, sharp knife, detach the chicken meat from the skin and bones. Discard the skin and bones. Cut the meat into bite-sized pieces and put them in a deep pie dish spreading them out over the base of the dish. Pour the leeks and stock into the dish. Sprinkle the sugar and remaining salt over the leeks and chicken.

Arrange the slices of ham in a layer over the leeks, leaving a small gap in the middle. Sprinkle the ham with the parsley. Set the dish aside.

Remove the dough from the refrigerator. If it looks streaky, roll it out into an oblong shape and fold it in three once again. On a floured surface, roll out the dough to 1-inch larger than the top of the pie dish. With a knife cut a $\frac{1}{2}$-inch strip around the pastry. Dampen the rim of the dish with water and press the pastry strips on top of the rim. With a pastry brush dipped in water, lightly moisten the strips.

Using the rolling pin, lift the dough on to the dish. With a knife, trim the dough and, with your fingers, crimp the edges to seal them to the strips already in the dish. With a sharp knife, cut a fairly large cross in the middle of the pastry. With a pastry brush, coat the surface of the pastry with beaten egg.

Roll out the trimmings and use to make a decoration for the top of the pie.

Place the pie in the oven and bake for 1 hour, or until the top is golden brown. Remove the pie from the oven.

In a small saucepan, heat the cream over low heat. Open up the cross in the pastry and pour in the warmed cream.

Chicken Mayonnaise

This delicious recipe for cold chicken makes an attractive summer lunch dish. Bought mayonnaise may be used instead but a home-made one gives the dish a much richer flavour.

4 SERVINGS

MAYONNAISE

- 2 egg yolks
- $\frac{1}{2}$ teaspoon salt
- $\frac{1}{2}$ teaspoon castor sugar
- 1 teaspoon mustard
- 10 fl. oz. [$1\frac{1}{4}$ cups] olive oil
- 1 to 2 tablespoons wine vinegar
- 1 tablespoon chopped parsley
- $\frac{1}{2}$ teaspoon dried tarragon
- 1 large, crisp Cos [Romaine] lettuce, washed and chilled
- 1 x 4 lb. cooked chicken, the meat removed from the bones and cut into pieces

GARNISH

- 2 hard-boiled eggs, quartered
- 1 tablespoon capers
- 1 canned pimiento, cut into strips

First make the mayonnaise sauce. Put the egg yolks in a small mixing bowl with the salt, sugar and mustard. Using a wire whisk or wooden spoon, whisk or beat them until well mixed.

Add 2 tablespoons of the olive oil, drop by drop, beating continuously. Then add the remaining oil in a thin stream, beating all the time. If the sauce becomes too thick and difficult to beat, add a few drops of vinegar to thin it.

When all the oil has been beaten in, stir in the vinegar. Taste the mayonnaise and adjust the seasoning by adding more salt, sugar, mustard or vinegar, if necessary. Stir in the parsley and tarragon. Cover the bowl and put it in the refrigerator to chill for 30 minutes.

Arrange the lettuce on a serving platter. Put the chicken pieces on top.

Cover the chicken pieces with the chilled mayonnaise. Garnish with the hard-boiled eggs, capers and pimiento.

Chicken Mousse

This smooth, decorative Chicken Mousse is an attractive addition to a cold buffet table. It may be served with a tomato and chicory salad tossed in vinaigrette dressing.

8-12 SERVINGS

- 1 lb. cooked chicken meat, cold
- 2 oz. [$\frac{1}{4}$ cup] butter, softened
- 15 fl. oz. [$1\frac{7}{8}$ cups] béchamel sauce, cold
- $\frac{1}{2}$ oz. gelatine, dissolved in 2 tablespoons water
- $\frac{1}{2}$ teaspoon salt
- $\frac{1}{2}$ teaspoon white pepper
- $\frac{1}{8}$ teaspoon cayenne pepper
- 4 tablespoons double [heavy] cream, lightly whipped
- 4 fl. oz. [$\frac{1}{2}$ cup] aspic jelly, cooled but not set
- $\frac{1}{4}$ cucumber, peeled and thinly sliced

Put the chicken through a mincer [grinder] twice and place it in a medium-sized mixing bowl. With a wooden spoon, beat the butter into the chicken. Gradually beat in the béchamel sauce until the mixture is smooth and creamy.

Lightly stir the dissolved gelatine into the mixture. Add the salt, pepper and cayenne. Gently fold in the cream.

With cold water, rinse out a 2-pint [5-cup] soufflé dish. Turn the chicken mixture into the dish. With a knife, smooth the top of the mousse and cover it with half the aspic jelly.

Leave the aspic to set. Arrange the sliced cucumber over the top of the mousse and cover it with the remaining aspic.

Place the mousse in the refrigerator and leave it until the aspic is completely set.

Chicken Paprikash

A richly coloured Hungarian dish, Chicken Paprikash may be served with a cucumber salad and boiled rice. A light, white Hungarian wine like Gabor goes well with this dish.

6 SERVINGS

- 6 chicken pieces
- 1 teaspoon salt
- $\frac{1}{2}$ teaspoon black pepper
- 1 oz. [2 tablespoons] butter
- 2 large onions, chopped
- 1 large garlic clove, crushed
- $1\frac{1}{2}$ tablespoons paprika
- 10 fl. oz. [$1\frac{1}{4}$ cups] stock, prepared from chicken giblets or stock made from a stock cube
- 2 green peppers, white pith removed, seeded and sliced
- 4 tomatoes, blanched, peeled and chopped
- $1\frac{1}{2}$ tablespoons flour
- 5 fl. oz. [$\frac{5}{8}$ cup] sour cream

On a wooden board, rub the chicken pieces with the salt and pepper. Set them aside.

In a large saucepan, melt the butter over moderate heat. When the foam subsides, add the onions and garlic and fry them for 8 to 10 minutes, or until they are lightly coloured.

Stir the paprika into the onions and garlic and cook for a further 2 to 3 minutes.

Pour in the stock and add the chicken pieces, peppers and tomatoes to the pan. Cover the pan, reduce the heat to low and cook for 1 hour, or until the chicken is tender.

In a teacup, blend the flour with 2 tablespoons of the sour cream until the mixture is smooth.

Pour the flour and cream mixture into the saucepan and stir to mix. Increase the heat to moderate, bring to the boil and cook for 2 minutes. Pour in the rest of the cream, stir to mix and serve immediately.

Chicken Parmigiana

A casserole good enough for a party yet inexpensive enough for an everyday meal, Chicken Parmigiana is good served with buttered noodles or rice.

4 SERVINGS

- 1 x 4 lb. chicken, cut into serving pieces
- 1 teaspoon salt
- 1 teaspoon freshly ground black pepper
- 4 fl. oz. [$\frac{1}{2}$ cup] olive oil
- 4 oz. mushrooms, wiped clean and sliced
- 1 medium-sized green pepper, white pith removed, seeded and finely sliced
- 3 medium-sized onions, finely sliced
- 2 garlic cloves, finely chopped
- 1 teaspoon dried thyme
- 1 lb. tomatoes, peeled, seeded and chopped or 14 oz. canned tomatoes
- 4 tablespoons dry, pale sherry
- 3 oz. [$\frac{3}{4}$ cup] Parmesan cheese, grated

Preheat the oven to moderate 350°F (Gas Mark 4, 180°C).

On a chopping board, rub the chicken pieces with salt and pepper and set aside.

Chicken Paprikash is a colourful dish of chicken, tomatoes and peppers.

In a large flameproof casserole heat the olive oil over moderate heat. Add the chicken pieces and brown them for 5 to 7 minutes on both sides. Add the mushrooms, green pepper, onions, garlic, thyme, tomatoes and sherry and bring to the boil.

Cover the casserole and place it in the centre of the oven to bake for $1\frac{1}{2}$ to $1\frac{3}{4}$ hours, or until the chicken is tender when pierced with a fork.

Sprinkle about one-third of the Parmesan cheese on top of the dish and serve the rest as an accompaniment.

Chicken Pulao

A spicy mixture of rice and chicken, Chicken Pulao makes an exotic and attractive centrepiece for a buffet party. It needs only a mixed salad and some well chilled white wine to complete the meal.

6 SERVINGS

1 x 3 lb. chicken, cut into serving pieces
1 bay leaf
6 peppercorns
1 teaspoon salt
12 oz. [2 cups] Basmati (long-grain) rice, washed, soaked in water for 30 minutes and drained
$\frac{1}{2}$ teaspoon chilli powder
1 teaspoon turmeric
$\frac{1}{2}$ teaspoon ground cumin
2 garlic cloves, crushed
5 fl. oz. [$\frac{5}{8}$ cup] yogurt
6 tablespoons vegetable oil
$\frac{1}{2}$ teaspoon saffron threads
1 large onion, sliced
2 tablespoons boiling water
2 tablespoons butter

GARNISH

1 onion, sliced
3 oz. [$\frac{1}{2}$ cup] seedless raisins
3 oz. [$\frac{5}{8}$ cup] almonds, blanched and quartered

Put the chicken pieces, bay leaf, peppercorns and $\frac{1}{2}$ teaspoon of the salt into a medium-sized pan. Add enough water to half cover the chicken and bring to the boil over high heat. Cover the pan, lower the heat and simmer for 40 minutes or until the chicken is nearly but not quite cooked.

While the chicken is cooking, parboil the rice. In a medium-sized saucepan, bring 3 pints [$7\frac{1}{2}$ cups] of water to the boil. Add the remaining salt and the drained rice.

After the water comes to the boil again, boil the rice for 1 minute. Remove the pan from the heat and drain the rice through a strainer. Set aside.

When the chicken is cooked, remove the pieces from the pan. Strain the stock and reserve 10 fluid ounces [$1\frac{1}{4}$ cups].

In a shallow bowl, mix the chilli powder, turmeric, cumin, garlic and yogurt together. Coat the chicken pieces well with this mixture.

In a large frying pan, heat 4 tablespoons of the oil. Add the chicken pieces and fry them over moderate heat for 10 minutes, or until they are lightly coloured on all sides. Remove the chicken pieces with tongs and set them aside on a plate.

In the same frying pan, fry the onion over moderate heat for 5 to 6 minutes or until it is golden brown.

Preheat the oven to moderate 350°F (Gas Mark 4, 180°C).

In a cup, soak the saffron threads in the water for 5 minutes. Divide the rice into 2 equal parts. Put one half in a bowl and pour the saffron over it. Mix well so that the rice is quite yellow.

In a large flameproof dish, melt the butter over moderate heat. Put in a layer of half the yellow rice, pressing it down with the back of a spoon. Spread half of the onion on top and then place a layer of half the white rice. Put half the chicken on top. Layer again in the same order but leave a little of both the yellow and the white rice to just cover the last layer of the chicken.

Bring the reserved stock to the boil and pour it carefully over the rice and chicken. Cook for 2 minutes on top of the stove, cover the dish and place it in the oven. Bake for 30 to 40 minutes, or until the rice is quite cooked and all the liquid absorbed.

Meanwhile prepare the garnish. In a small frying-pan heat the remaining 2 tablespoons of oil over moderate heat. Add the onion and fry, stirring frequently, for 5 minutes. Add the raisins and almonds and fry for a further 5 minutes or until the onions are brown, the almonds golden and the raisins puffed up.

When the rice is ready, remove the dish from the oven. If you intend to serve directly from the flameproof dish, just sprinkle the top with the garnish and serve. Alternatively, spoon the rice and chicken, including the crusty base, on to a heated serving dish. Sprinkle the garnish on top and serve.

Chicken with Rice and Cherries

An exotic and unusual combination of tastes, Chicken with Cherries is an adaptation of a traditional Irani dish. It is a meal in itself and need be accompanied only by a tossed mixed salad. A medium sweet white wine, such as Graves or a well chilled rosé, would go well with this dish.

4 SERVINGS

1 x 3 lb. chicken, cut into 8 serving pieces
2 teaspoons salt
1 teaspoon black pepper
4 tablespoons olive oil
2 medium-sized onions, finely sliced
3 fl. oz. [$\frac{3}{8}$ cup] chicken stock
$1\frac{1}{2}$ lb. fresh black Morello cherries or 2 lb. canned, stoned Morello cherries, drained
2 oz. [$\frac{1}{4}$ cup] sugar
2 tablespoons water
12 oz. [2 cups] long-grain rice, washed and drained
4 oz. [$\frac{1}{2}$ cup] butter, melted
$\frac{1}{2}$ teaspoon crushed saffron threads, dissolved in 1 tablespoon hot water

On a chopping board, sprinkle the chicken pieces with the salt and pepper and set aside.

In a large frying-pan heat the oil over moderate heat. When it is hot, add the chicken pieces, a few at a time. Cook them for 5 to 7 minutes on each side or until they are evenly and thoroughly browned. As the chicken is browned, transfer it to a heated plate. Add the onions to the oil remaining in the frying-pan and fry them for 6 minutes, or until they begin to brown slightly.

Return the chicken pieces to the frying-pan, pour in the chicken stock and bring the mixture to the boil. Reduce the heat to low, cover the pan and cook the chicken for 30 minutes, or until it is tender when pierced with a fork.

While the chicken is simmering, combine the cherries, sugar and water together in a medium-sized saucepan over low heat. Stirring frequently, simmer uncovered for 5 minutes or until the sugar has dissolved and the cherries have given off most of their liquid. Remove the pan from the heat and set aside.

In a large saucepan, bring $1\frac{1}{2}$ pints [$3\frac{3}{4}$ cups] of water to the boil over moderate heat. Add the rice and boil for 5 minutes. Remove the pan from the heat and drain the rice through a strainer. Set aside.

Transfer the chicken pieces to a plate, reserving about 2 tablespoons of the cooking liquid and the browned onion slices.

Put the reserved cooking liquid and half the melted butter into a large flameproof casserole and mix well. Place half of the rice on the bottom of the casserole, spreading it out evenly and cook over moderate heat for 8 minutes. Remove the casserole from the heat. Add the chicken pieces, onions and about half of the cherries. Arrange the remainder of the rice on top of the mixture. Pour in the remaining cherries with their cooking liquid, cover the casserole and simmer over very low heat for 15 minutes or until the rice is tender.

Remove about 4 ounces [1 cup] of the cooked rice from the casserole and place it in a medium-sized bowl. Add the remainder of the melted butter and the dissolved saffron threads to the rice, stirring until the mixture is bright yellow. Set aside.

Arrange half of the remaining rice in the casserole on the base of a serving platter and place the chicken pieces with the onions on top. Cover the meat with the cherries and the remaining rice and sprinkle the saffron rice on top and around the edge.

An unusual combination of flavours, Chicken with Rice and Cherries is a beautiful dish for a dinner party.

Chicken Riviera

CHICKEN SALAD WITH WALNUTS, CHERRIES AND TARRAGON

This is an excellent and unusual chicken salad with an interesting contrast in textures and flavours. If you like, the chicken may be roasted the day before and kept, wrapped in aluminium foil, in the refrigerator.

4 SERVINGS

1 x 4 lb. chicken
$\frac{1}{2}$ teaspoon salt
3 tarragon sprigs
2 tablespoons butter
8 fl. oz. [1 cup] water
1 large Cos [Romaine] lettuce, washed and drained
2 oz. [$\frac{1}{2}$ cup] walnuts, quartered

SAUCE

1 teaspoon mustard
$\frac{1}{2}$ teaspoon sugar
$\frac{1}{2}$ teaspoon freshly ground black pepper
$\frac{1}{2}$ teaspoon salt
6 tablespoons olive oil
2 tablespoons vinegar
2 fl. oz. single cream [$\frac{1}{4}$ cup light cream]
14 oz. canned, stoned cherries, drained
1 teaspoon dried tarragon

Preheat the oven to moderate 350°F (Gas Mark 4, 180°C).

Rub the chicken, inside and out, with the salt. Put the tarragon and 1 tablespoon of the butter inside the bird. Rub the remaining butter over the bird. Place the chicken in a roasting tin and pour the water around it. Put the pan in the oven

Chicken salad with cherries and walnuts in a cream dressing, Chicken Riviera makes an excellent summer lunch.

and roast the chicken for $1\frac{1}{2}$ to 2 hours or until the chicken is tender. Test it by piercing the thigh with a skewer—the juice that runs out should be clear. Baste frequently and, halfway through the cooking, turn the chicken over so that it browns on all sides.

When the chicken is cooked, remove it from the oven. Allow it to cool completely and then carve it into 8 serving pieces. Refrigerate the chicken pieces for about 30 minutes, so that they will be very cold.

Skim any fat from the surface of the cooking juices in the roasting pan. Pour the juices through a strainer into a jug. Reserve 5 fluid ounces [$\frac{5}{8}$ cup].

To make the sauce, put the mustard, sugar, pepper and salt in a small bowl. With a fork, beat in the oil and vinegar. Stir in the cream and the reserved cooking juices. (If the juices have jellied, melt them over very low heat and allow to cool slightly.) Add the cherries and the tarragon.

Put the lettuce leaves on a serving dish or 4 individual dishes. Remove the chicken pieces from the refrigerator and arrange them on the bed of lettuce. Spoon the sauce over the top. Garnish with the walnuts and serve.

Chicken Salad with Avocados and Russian Dressing

A chicken salad is an ideal party dish as it can be prepared in advance. If you do prepare the salad beforehand, make the dressing and prepare the chicken and olives but add the avocados at the last moment, or they will discolour and spoil the look of the dish.

4-6 SERVINGS

1 x 4 lb. cooked chicken, cold
2 avocados
10 large black olives, stoned and cut in half

RUSSIAN DRESSING

2 egg yolks
$\frac{1}{2}$ teaspoon salt
$\frac{1}{2}$ teaspoon sugar
1 teaspoon prepared French mustard
10 fl. oz. [$1\frac{1}{4}$ cups] olive oil
1 to 2 tablespoons vinegar
$\frac{1}{8}$ teaspoon cayenne pepper
$\frac{1}{2}$ teaspoon chilli sauce
1 hard-boiled egg, finely chopped
1 shallot, finely chopped
1 teaspoon chopped parsley

First make the dressing. Put the egg yolks in a small mixing bowl with the salt, sugar and mustard. Using a wire whisk or wooden spoon, whisk or beat until well mixed. Add 3 tablespoons of the olive oil drop by drop, beating continuously. Then gradually add the remaining oil in a thin stream, beating all the time. If the sauce becomes too thick and difficult to beat, add a few drops of the vinegar to thin it. When all the oil has been beaten in, stir in the vinegar. Taste the dressing and adjust the seasoning by adding more salt, sugar, mustard or vinegar, if necessary. Stir in the cayenne, chilli sauce, hard-boiled egg, shallot and parsley. Cover the bowl and put it in the refrigerator to chill for 15 minutes.

On a wooden board cut the chicken into pieces and detach the meat from the skin and bones. Discard the skin and bones. Cut the meat into bite-sized pieces and place them in a serving bowl.

Cut the avocados in half lengthways, remove the stones and then peel and dice the halves. Add the diced avocados and olives to the chicken.

Pour the chilled dressing over the chicken mixture and toss well with a fork. Serve at once.

Chicken Salad with Bean Sprouts and Olives

This is a deliciously crisp, crunchy, chicken salad that makes an attractive centrepiece for a buffet party.

6-8 SERVINGS

1 x 4 lb. cooked chicken, cold
8 oz. bean sprouts (fresh or canned and drained)
4 celery stalks, finely chopped
1 teaspoon salt
$\frac{1}{2}$ teaspoon black pepper
1 Webb [iceberg] lettuce, washed and chilled
12 black olives, stoned

FRENCH DRESSING

3 tablespoons olive oil
1 tablespoon wine vinegar
$\frac{1}{4}$ teaspoon salt
$\frac{1}{4}$ teaspoon black pepper

MAYONNAISE

1 egg yolk
$\frac{1}{4}$ teaspoon salt
$\frac{1}{4}$ teaspoon black pepper
$\frac{1}{2}$ teaspoon prepared mustard
$\frac{1}{4}$ teaspoon sugar
6 fl. oz. [$\frac{3}{4}$ cup] olive oil
1 tablespoon wine vinegar
$\frac{1}{2}$ teaspoon soy sauce

On a wooden board cut the chicken into pieces and, with a small, sharp knife, detach the meat from the skin and bones. Discard the skin and bones. Cut the chicken meat into strips and put them into a medium-sized mixing bowl.

In a medium-sized bowl, mix together the ingredients for the French dressing. Mix in the bean sprouts and the celery. When the dressing is well mixed, pour it over the chicken mixture and toss well.

Cover the bowl and put it in the refrigerator to chill for about 30 minutes.

Meanwhile prepare the mayonnaise. With a wire whisk or fork, beat the egg yolk in a small mixing bowl with the salt, pepper, mustard and sugar. Add 3 tablespoons of olive oil, drop by drop, beating continuously. When the sauce is thick, the rest of the oil may be added a little more quickly. If the sauce becomes too thick and difficult to beat, add a few drops of the vinegar to thin it. When all the oil has been beaten in, stir in the remaining vinegar and the soy sauce. Taste the mayonnaise and adjust the seasoning by adding more salt, mustard, sugar or pepper, if necessary.

Arrange leaves of lettuce on each plate and spoon the chicken mixture into the centre. Spoon over the mayonnaise and garnish with the olives.

Chicken Salad with Sour Cream Dressing

The secret of this dish is in the attractive presentation. The colourful ingredients make it look pretty as well as tasty to eat.

4-6 SERVINGS

1 x 4 lb. cooked chicken, cold
6 hard-boiled eggs
2 green peppers, white pith removed, seeded and finely shredded
4 tablespoons stuffed olives, sliced
1 lb. grapes, peeled and seeded
4 oz. [$\frac{4}{5}$ cup] blanched almonds
$\frac{1}{2}$ teaspoon black pepper

FRENCH DRESSING

3 tablespoons white wine vinegar
2 teaspoons prepared mustard
$\frac{1}{2}$ teaspoon salt
6 tablespoons olive oil

SOUR CREAM DRESSING

6 tablespoons white wine vinegar
10 fl. oz. [$1\frac{1}{4}$ cups] sour cream
2 teaspoons sugar
$\frac{1}{2}$ teaspoon salt
$\frac{1}{2}$ teaspoon white pepper

On a wooden board, carve the chicken into pieces and, with a small, sharp knife, detach the meat from the skin and bones. Discard the skin and bones. Cut the meat into strips and put it into a salad bowl.

Separate the yolks from the whites of the hard-boiled eggs. Finely chop the whites and add to the chicken. Keep the yolks aside on a plate. Add the peppers, olives, grapes and almonds. Do not mix or toss the ingredients.

Prepare the French dressing. In a small mixing bowl, combine the vinegar, mustard and salt. Mix well and stir in the oil. Pour the dressing over the ingredients in the bowl.

Press the egg yolks through a fine strainer or push them through a garlic press over the chicken mixture. Toss the salad to mix the ingredients well. Sprinkle the black pepper over the top. Cover the salad bowl and keep it in the refrigerator until you are ready to serve it.

Lastly prepare the sour cream dressing. In a small mixing bowl, slowly beat the vinegar into the sour cream. Add the sugar, salt and pepper and mix well. Taste the dressing and add more salt, sugar or vinegar, if necessary. Pour the dressing into a sauce boat or small bowl.

Chicken Salad with Sour Cream Dressing is an attractive buffet dish.

Chicken San Marino

FRIED CHICKEN BREASTS WITH MUSHROOMS AND MOZZARELLA

This Italian recipe for chicken makes a truly delectable supper party dish served with risotto and a light chilled Soave wine.

4-6 SERVINGS

- 8 chicken breasts, skinned and boned
- 4 tablespoons seasoned flour, made with 4 tablespoons flour,
- 1 teaspoon salt and
- 1 teaspoon freshly ground black pepper
- 4 oz. [$\frac{1}{2}$ cup] butter
- 8 large button mushrooms, wiped and sliced
- 8 slices mozzarella cheese

On a chopping board, place the chicken breasts between 2 pieces of greaseproof or waxed paper and, with a mallet or rolling pin, pound them until they are thin.

Put the seasoned flour on a large plate and, one by one, dip the chicken breasts in the mixture until they are well coated. Set them aside.

In a large frying-pan melt three-quarters of the butter over moderate heat. When the foam subsides, add the chicken pieces and cook, a few pieces at a time, for 10 to 12 minutes. Transfer the chicken pieces to a shallow flameproof casserole.

Preheat the grill [broiler] to high.

Melt the remaining butter in the same frying-pan and add the mushroom slices, sautéeing them for 1 to 2 minutes until they have been just coated with the butter. Arrange the mushroom slices on top of the chicken and cover each piece with a slice of mozzarella cheese.

Put the chicken under a hot grill [broiler] for about 3 minutes, or until the mozzarella has melted and is beginning to brown. Serve very hot.

Chicken Sauté

This dish is ideal for an informal lunch party, because it needs little preparation. Serve it with crusty French bread, a crisp green salad and chilled dry white wine.

4 SERVINGS

- 1 x 3$\frac{1}{2}$ lb. chicken, cut into 4 serving pieces
- $\frac{1}{2}$ teaspoon salt
- $\frac{1}{2}$ teaspoon black pepper
- 3 oz. [$\frac{3}{8}$ cup] butter
- 1 tablespoon vegetable oil
- 2 fl. oz. [$\frac{1}{4}$ cup] dry white wine
- 1 tablespoon chopped parsley

Sprinkle the chicken pieces with the salt and pepper. In a large, heavy frying-pan, melt the butter and oil over moderate heat. When the foam subsides, add the chicken pieces and brown them for 8 to 10 minutes on both sides.

Reduce the heat to low, cover the pan and cook slowly for 10 minutes. Uncover the pan and continue cooking for 30 to 40 minutes or until the chicken pieces are tender but not dry. When the chicken pieces are cooked, transfer them with tongs to a serving dish. Cover and keep warm.

Increase the heat to moderate and add the white wine to the pan. Stir well to mix. Stir in the parsley. Cook the sauce for 2 to 3 minutes. Taste the sauce and add more salt if necessary. Pour the sauce over the chicken pieces and serve immediately.

Chicken Sauté Marengo

After the Battle of Marengo, which was a victory for the French army, Napoleon asked his chef, Dumand, to prepare a special dinner. Food was in short supply but, with a great chef's ingenuity, Dumand prepared a dish with all the ingredients he had on hand. Tradition has it that the dish was garnished with crayfish, but mushrooms are used in this recipe, which is closely associated with the original. The dish was such a success that Napoleon named it after the battle and it is now part of classic French Cuisine. A good wine to serve with this is Gevrey Chambertin (Napoleon's favourite red burgundy) or a white burgundy such as Pouilly Fuissé or Puligny Montrachet.

6 SERVINGS

- 1 x 5 lb. chicken, cut into 6 serving pieces
- 1 teaspoon salt
- $\frac{1}{2}$ teaspoon black pepper
- 3 fl. oz. [$\frac{3}{8}$ cup] olive oil
- 2 garlic cloves, finely chopped
- 4 medium-sized tomatoes, blanched, peeled, seeded and chopped
- 2 teaspoons tomato purée
- 4 fl. oz. [$\frac{1}{2}$ cup] brandy
- 2 tablespoons butter
- 20 to 24 button mushroom caps, wiped clean
- fried croûtons [to garnish]
- 6 fried eggs

On a chopping board, season the chicken pieces with the salt and pepper.

In a large frying-pan heat the olive oil over moderate heat. Add the chicken pieces and brown them for 5 to 7 minutes on each side. When the chicken is deep golden on all sides, reduce the heat to low and add the garlic. Cover the pan and continue to cook the chicken for about 45 minutes, or until it is tender, turning the pieces at least once during the cooking period. Transfer the chicken pieces to a warm serving dish, cover with aluminium foil and keep warm.

Pour off as much oil as possible from the pan, leaving about 3 tablespoons of the sediment. Add the chopped tomatoes and tomato purée to the pan. Stir well and add the brandy. Cook the mixture over very low heat for 2 to 3 minutes, until the ingredients are thoroughly blended and the mixture has reduced. Pour the sauce over the chicken pieces.

In a small saucepan, melt the butter over moderate heat. When the foam subsides add the mushroom caps and sauté them for 4 to 5 minutes, shaking the pan from time to time. Add the mushrooms to the chicken and sauce as a garnish, and serve surrounded by fried croûtons and fried eggs.

Chicken in Sherry and Cream

This rich dish of chicken baked in cream and flavoured with sherry may be served with rice cooked with peas or with tomatoes to add a touch of colour. A variation on this recipe is to bake the chicken in sour cream. Use 8 fluid ounces [1 cup] of sour cream diluted with the same amount of water. Omit the sherry and substitute 8 ounces of sliced mushrooms and $\frac{1}{2}$ teaspoon thyme.

4 SERVINGS

- 2 oz. [$\frac{1}{4}$ cup] butter
- 1 x 4 lb. chicken, cut into serving pieces
- $\frac{3}{4}$ tablespoon flour
- 16 fl. oz. single cream [2 cups light cream]
- 3 tablespoons sherry
- 1 teaspoon salt
- $\frac{3}{4}$ teaspoon black pepper

Preheat the oven to moderate 350°F (Gas Mark 4, 180°C).

In a large, deep frying-pan, melt three-quarters of the butter over moderate heat. When the foam subsides, place the chicken pieces in the pan and brown them on all sides.

With tongs, transfer the chicken pieces from the pan to a medium-sized oven-proof casserole.

In a medium-sized saucepan, melt the remaining butter over moderate heat. Remove the pan from the heat. With a wooden spoon, stir the flour into the

Chicken Sauté Marengo is a classic French dish of sautéed chicken in a brandy-flavoured tomato sauce, garnished with fried eggs and mushrooms.

butter. Pour in the cream and stir well to mix. Then add the sherry, salt and pepper. Return the pan to the heat and bring the sauce to the boil. Pour it over the chicken pieces in the casserole.

Cover the casserole and place it in the oven. Bake for 40 to 45 minutes, or until the chicken is tender when tested with a fork.

Remove the casserole from the oven and serve at once.

Chicken Siena

This lightly flavoured chicken dish makes an easily prepared lunch or dinner meal. Serve it with a mixed salad and to drink a white Toscano Bianco.

Low Cal

4-6 SERVINGS

- 8 chicken breasts, skinned and boned
- $\frac{1}{2}$ teaspoon salt
- $\frac{1}{2}$ teaspoon black pepper
- 3 oz. [$\frac{3}{8}$ cup] butter
- 1 tablespoon olive oil
- 3 tablespoons lemon juice
- 4 tablespoons chopped fresh parsley
- 1 tablespoon chopped fresh basil, or 1 teaspoon dried basil

Sprinkle the chicken breast halves with the salt and pepper.

In a large frying-pan heat the butter and olive oil together over moderate heat. When the foam subsides add the chicken pieces and cook them for 15 minutes, turning each piece at least once during the cooking period. Transfer them to a warmed serving dish.

Add the lemon juice to the juices in the pan and stir well. Add the parsley and basil and cook for 1 to 2 minutes, stirring constantly. Pour the sauce over the chicken and serve hot.

Quick and easy to prepare, Chicken Spanish Style is the ideal dish to serve for an informal dinner party.

Chicken Soufflé

This superbly light soufflé is an unusual way to use up chicken leftovers. It is ideal to serve as a main supper dish for the family with fried potatoes and a salad. It also makes a tempting meal for invalids.

4 SERVINGS

- 3 tablespoons butter
- 8 to 10 oz. finely minced [ground] cooked chicken
- 8 fl. oz. [1 cup] thick béchamel sauce, cooled
- ½ teaspoon salt
- ½ teaspoon freshly ground black pepper
- 4 egg yolks
- 5 egg whites

Low Cal

Preheat the oven to fairly hot 375°F (Gas Mark 5, 190°C). Grease a 2-pint [5-cup] soufflé dish with 1 tablespoon of the butter. Tie a piece of greaseproof or waxed paper around the outside of the dish, allowing it to project 2 inches above the rim.

In a medium-sized saucepan, combine the chicken with the béchamel sauce. Add the remaining butter and the salt and pepper. Place the pan over low heat and heat the mixture gently, stirring constantly. Remove the pan from the heat and allow the mixture to cool slightly. Add the egg yolks one at a time, beating well between each addition.

Put the egg whites in a bowl and beat them with a wire whisk or rotary beater until they form stiff peaks. With a metal spoon, very lightly fold and cut the whites into the chicken mixture.

Pour this mixture into the prepared soufflé dish and bake in the centre of the oven for 30 minutes or until the soufflé has puffed up and is lightly browned on top. Serve immediately.

Chicken, Spanish Style

This is a marvellous dish for a dinner party, since it is so quick and easy to prepare and will keep without spoiling in a warm oven for up to an hour should your guests be late. It may be accompanied by rice or boiled new potatoes and a green salad. A Spanish burgundy is a good wine to serve with this casserole.

6 SERVINGS

- 2 oz. [½ cup] seasoned flour, made with 2 oz. [½ cup] plain [all-purpose] flour, 1 teaspoon salt and ½ teaspoon black pepper
- 1 x 4½ to 5 lb. chicken, cut into serving pieces
- 2 fl. oz. [¼ cup] olive oil
- 1 large onion, finely chopped
- 2 garlic cloves, crushed
- 1 red pepper, white pith removed, seeded and chopped
- 1 green pepper, white pith removed, cored, seeded and chopped
- 10 fl. oz. [1¼ cups] chicken stock, prepared from the giblets or from a stock cube
- 2 tablespoons butter
- 8 oz. mushrooms, sliced
- 6 tomatoes, sliced
- 10 stuffed olives, cut in half
- 10 black olives, stoned

Low Cal

Preheat the oven to warm 325°F (Gas Mark 3, 170°C).

Put the seasoned flour on a plate and roll the chicken pieces in it until they are well coated.

In a large frying-pan heat the oil over moderate heat. Add the chicken pieces and fry them for 5 to 7 minutes on each side, or until they are lightly browned.

Using tongs, transfer the chicken pieces to a large ovenproof casserole.

Add the onion, garlic and peppers to the pan and fry them, stirring, for 5 to 6 minutes. Spoon the vegetables over the chicken pieces in the casserole.

In a small saucepan, bring the stock to the boil over moderately high heat. Remove the pan from the heat and pour the stock into the casserole.

Cover the casserole and place it in the oven. Bake for 1 to 1½ hours, or until the chicken is tender when pierced with a fork.

Ten minutes before the end of the cooking, melt the butter in a small frying-pan over moderate heat and cook the mushrooms and tomatoes for about 5 minutes. Add the mushrooms, tomatoes and olives to the casserole. Serve hot, straight from the casserole.

Chicken and Spring Vegetable Soup with Dumplings

This soup with tiny dumplings is a tasty, simple and satisfying meal which is ideal for a cold winter day.

4 SERVINGS

SOUP
3½ pints [8¾ cups] cold water
2 medium-sized onions, quartered
6 carrots, scraped, 3 coarsely chopped and 3 cut into matchstick shapes
4 celery stalks with leaves, cut in halves
6 peppercorns
2 teaspoons salt
2 bay leaves
1 x 3½ lb. chicken, with the giblets (except the liver)

DUMPLINGS
4½ oz. [1 cup plus 2 tablespoons] flour
1 teaspoon baking powder
½ teaspoon salt
½ egg, lightly beaten
2 fl. oz. [¼ cup] milk

To make the soup, in a large, heavy saucepan, bring the water to the boil over high heat. Add the onions, the coarsely chopped carrots, celery, peppercorns, salt and bay leaves to the pan. Bring the water to the boil again. Place the chicken and giblets in the pan. Cover the pan, reduce the heat to moderately low and simmer the chicken for about 2 hours.

Remove the pan from the heat. Transfer the chicken to a wooden chopping board. Strain the soup into another large saucepan, discarding the vegetables and seasonings. Strip the chicken meat from the bones. Discard the skin, bones and gristle. Chop the meat into bite-sized pieces and keep it warm.

Cool the soup until the fat solidifies on top. With a metal spoon, remove the fat. Put the pan over high heat and bring the soup to the boil. Add the carrot matchsticks to the soup and reduce the heat to moderately low. Simmer for 10 minutes, or until the carrots are tender.

Meanwhile, prepare the dumplings. Sift 4 ounces [1 cup] of the flour, the baking powder and salt into a medium-sized mixing bowl. In a cup, mix together the beaten egg and milk. Gradually stir the egg and milk mixture into the flour with a wooden spoon. Add only enough liquid to make a firm dough—it should not be too wet. Sift the remaining flour over the dough and with your fingers, form small balls about the size of walnuts.

When the carrots are cooked, increase the heat under the saucepan to high. When the soup is boiling rapidly, drop the balls of dough into the soup. Cook the dumplings for 4 to 5 minutes, or until they are fluffy and have risen to the top of the soup. Be careful not to overcook the dumplings or they will be heavy. Stir in the reserved chicken pieces and simmer for 1 minute. Ladle the soup and dumplings into a warmed tureen or individual bowls and serve immediately.

Tasty and easy to prepare, Chicken Soup with Dumplings makes a satisfying meal for a cold winter's day.

Chicken Stock

A well-flavoured home-made chicken stock is invaluable. It forms the basis for so many sauces and soups and is used in a wide variety of dishes. The flavour of home-made chicken stock can never be matched by a stock cube.

2½ PINTS

carcass, bones and giblets (excluding the liver) of a cooked or raw chicken
1 carrot, scraped and sliced
4 celery stalks, sliced
1 onion stuck with 2 cloves
bouquet garni, consisting of 4 parsley sprigs, 1 thyme spray and 1 bay leaf tied together
grated rind of ½ lemon
1 teaspoon salt
10 peppercorns
3 pints [7½ cups] water

Put the carcass, bones and giblets (if available) into a large saucepan with the carrot, celery, onion, bouquet garni, lemon rind, salt, peppercorns and water.

Place the pan over high heat and bring the liquid to the boil. With a metal spoon, remove any scum that rises to the surface. Half cover the pan with the lid, reduce the heat to low and simmer the stock gently for about 2 hours.

Remove the pan from the heat and strain the liquid into a bowl. Discard the bones, vegetables and seasonings. Allow the stock to cool before covering the bowl with a large plate or piece of aluminium foil. If you are not using the stock immediately, put it in the refrigerator. Remove the fat from the surface just before using the stock.

Chicken Sultan

A tempting dish for any occasion, Chicken Sultan is relatively quick to cook and is guaranteed to be a favourite. It can be served with rice and buttered asparagus tips, and accompanied by a Chablis or one of those light, fragrant wines of the Rheingau, such as Rüdesheimer or Johannisberger.

4 SERVINGS

1 x 4 lb. chicken, cut into serving pieces
$1\frac{1}{2}$ teaspoons salt
$1\frac{1}{2}$ teaspoons black pepper
2 oz. [$\frac{1}{4}$ cup] butter
1 medium-sized onion, finely sliced
2 garlic cloves, finely chopped
1 tablespoon tomato purée
2 tablespoons flour
6 fl. oz. [$\frac{3}{4}$ cup] chicken stock
6 fl. oz. [$\frac{3}{4}$ cup] white wine
3 tablespoons slivered almonds
1 teaspoon dried tarragon
6 fl. oz. [$\frac{3}{4}$ cup] sour cream

Sprinkle the chicken pieces with 1 teaspoon salt and $\frac{1}{2}$ teaspoon pepper and set aside.

In a large frying-pan melt the butter over moderate heat. When the foam subsides add the chicken pieces. Cook them for 5 to 7 minutes or until they are brown all over. Remove the chicken pieces from the pan and keep warm.

Add the onion and garlic to the pan, and, stirring occasionally, cook for 3 to 4 minutes. Add the tomato purée and flour, and stir well for a few seconds before adding the stock and wine. Stirring constantly, bring the mixture to the boil.

Return the chicken pieces to the pan and add the almonds and tarragon. Mix well and baste them with the sauce. Cover the pan and reduce the heat to low. Cook for 50 minutes, or until the chicken pieces are tender.

Transfer the chicken pieces to a warmed serving dish. Add the remaining $\frac{1}{2}$ teaspoon salt and pepper to the sauce and stir in the sour cream, blending thoroughly. Pour the sauce over the chicken and serve immediately.

Chicken in Sweet Red Wine

This easy-to-prepare baked chicken is ideal for an elegant dinner party or a special occasion family lunch or supper.

4 SERVINGS

1 x 5 lb. chicken, cut into serving pieces
3 oz. [$\frac{3}{4}$ cup] seasoned flour made from 3 oz. plain flour [$\frac{3}{4}$ cup all-purpose flour], 2 teaspoons salt and 1 teaspoon freshly ground black pepper
3 oz. [$\frac{3}{8}$ cup] butter
1 large onion, sliced
15 fl. oz. [$1\frac{7}{8}$ cups] sweet, red dessert wine
8 oz. mushrooms, sliced

Preheat the oven to very hot 450°F (Gas Mark 8, 230°C).

Coat the chicken pieces with the seasoned flour.

Melt the butter in a large, heavy, shallow flameproof casserole over moderate heat. When the foam subsides add the chicken pieces, 2 or 3 at a time, turning them frequently so that they brown evenly. When the chicken pieces are brown, remove them with a slotted spoon and set them aside on a plate.

Remove the casserole from the heat and pour off all but 2 tablespoons of the fat in the pan. Add the onion and fry over moderate heat for 5 minutes. Return all the chicken pieces to the casserole and pour in the wine. Scatter over the mushrooms.

Increase the heat to high and bring the wine to the boil.

This unusual American Chicken Tamale Pie is subtly flavoured with garlic, chilli powder and herbs.

Place the casserole in the oven and bake for 30 minutes or until the chicken is tender. Baste frequently.

Remove the casserole from the oven and serve.

Chicken Tamale Pie

This unusual American chicken pie with subtle spicy flavourings is a dish that may be served for a family meal or dinner party. If the pie has to be kept waiting, just turn off the oven and leave the pie inside with the door closed.

6 SERVINGS

- **1 x 5 lb. chicken**
- **3½ teaspoons salt**
- **10 peppercorns**
- **1 teaspoon celery seed**
- **1 bay leaf**
- **2 oz. [⅓ cup] cornmeal**
- **1 teaspoon chilli powder**
- **2 tablespoons butter**
- **1 green pepper, white pith removed, seeded and sliced**
- **1 large onion, chopped**
- **1 garlic clove, finely chopped**
- **3 large tomatoes, blanched, peeled, seeded and chopped**
- **¼ teaspoon Tabasco sauce**
- **⅛ teaspoon dried oregano**
- **⅛ teaspoon dried thyme**
- **⅛ teaspoon dried tarragon**
- **10 oz. whole-kernel sweet corn, fresh, frozen and thawed or canned and drained**
- **2 oz. [½ cup] Parmesan cheese, grated**

Place the chicken in a large saucepan and cover it with water. Add 2 teaspoons of salt, the peppercorns, celery seed and bay leaf.

Place the pan over high heat and bring the water to the boil. Reduce the heat to low, cover the pan and simmer for 1 to 1½ hours, or until the chicken is tender when prodded with a fork. Skim any fat off the surface occasionally with a slotted spoon.

Remove the pan from the heat and allow the chicken to cool in the liquid to room temperature.

Remove the chicken from the pan and place it on a wooden board. With a small sharp knife, carefully detach the meat from the skin and bones. Discard the skin and bones.

With a slotted spoon, skim any fat off the surface of the stock in the pan and pour it through a strainer into a measuring jug. Reserve 16 fluid ounces [2 cups] of the stock.

In a medium-sized saucepan, bring 12 fluid ounces [1½ cups] of the strained stock to the boil over high heat.

In a cup, mix the cornmeal with another 4 fluid ounces [½ cup] of the reserved stock. Pour it into the boiling stock in the pan and stir to combine. Add 1 teaspoon of salt and ½ teaspoon chilli powder. Cook for 15 minutes, or until the mixture is very thick.

Preheat the oven to moderate 350°F (Gas Mark 4, 180°C).

Remove thc pan from the heat and line the sides and bottom of a 5-pint [3-quart] casserole with the cornmeal mixture.

In a small frying-pan, melt the butter over moderate heat. When the foam subsides, add the green pepper, onion and garlic and fry them for 8 to 10 minutes, or until the onion is soft and transluscent but not brown.

Add the tomatoes, Tabasco sauce, oregano, thyme, tarragon and remaining chilli powder to the pan and reduce the heat to low. Simmer gently for 2 to 3 minutes. Add the corn kernels and the remaining salt. Remove the pan from the heat.

Place the chicken in the bottom of the lined casserole and cover it with the tomato and corn mixture. Sprinkle the top of the dish with the Parmesan cheese and place it in the oven. Bake for 30 minutes.

Chicken Tetrazzini

CASSEROLE OF CHICKEN AND NOODLES

Named after the famous Italian soprano, Chicken Tetrazzini is an interesting combination of chicken and noodles, with a subtle flavouring of sherry. There is really no need for any vegetable to accompany this magnificent dish, but a crisp green salad may be served afterwards.

6 SERVINGS

- **1 x 5 lb. chicken**
- **1 onion, studded with 4 cloves**
- **3 celery stalks**
- **2½ teaspoons salt**
- **1 bay leaf**
- **2 carrots, scraped**
- **3 pints [7½ cups] water**
- **4 oz. [½ cup] plus 1 tablespoon butter**
- **2 tablespoons flour**
- **½ teaspoon Tabasco sauce**
- **1 egg yolk**
- **1½ tablespoons sherry**
- **4 fl. oz. single cream [½ cup light cream]**
- **8 oz. mushrooms, sliced**
- **8 oz. flat noodles (tagliatelli)**
- **4 oz. [1 cup] Parmesan cheese, grated**

Put the chicken, onion, celery, 2 teaspoons salt, bay leaf, carrots and water in a large saucepan. The bird should almost be covered with water, so add more if necessary. Place the pan over high heat and bring the water to the boil.

Reduce the heat to low, cover the pan and simmer the chicken for 1½ to 2 hours, or until the chicken is tender when prodded with a fork.

Remove the pan from the heat and let the chicken cool in the cooking liquid. When it is cool, take the chicken out of the pan and place it on a wooden board. Remove all the meat from the bones and discard the carcass and skin. Strain the cooking liquid into a measuring jug. Reserve 16 fluid ounces [2 cups] of the stock and refrigerate it until the fat solidifies on the top. Skim off the fat.

With 1 tablespoon of butter, grease a large, shallow flameproof casserole and set it aside.

In a small saucepan, bring the reserved cooking liquid to the boil over high heat.

In a large saucepan, melt half the remaining butter over moderate heat. Remove the pan from the heat and, with a wooden spoon, stir in the flour.

Stir the cooking liquid slowly into the butter and flour roux in the large saucepan. Replace the pan on the heat and bring the sauce to the boil. Cook for 1 minute or until the sauce is thick and smooth. Add the Tabasco sauce and remaining salt. Remove the pan from the heat.

In a small mixing bowl or teacup, lightly beat the egg yolk with a fork. Beat 2 tablespoons of the hot sauce into the egg yolk.

Add the egg yolk mixture to the hot sauce, stirring continuously. Stir in the sherry, cream and chicken.

Return the pan to moderately low heat and cook until the mixture is thoroughly heated, stirring constantly. Do not boil.

In a saucepan melt 2 tablespoons of the butter over moderate heat. When the foam subsides sauté the mushrooms for 4 to 5 minutes, shaking the pan from time to time. Add the mushrooms to the chicken mixture.

Boil the noodles in plenty of salted water for 12 to 15 minutes, or until they are just tender.

Preheat the grill [broiler] to high.

Place alternate layers of the chicken mixture and noodles in the buttered casserole. Sprinkle the top of the dish with Parmesan and dot with the remaining butter.

Place the casserole under the grill [broiler] until the top has browned. Remove the casserole from the heat and serve at once.

Chicken Valentine

This is a simple but very delicious dish which is excellent served with rice and a crisp green salad or mashed potatoes and French beans. Serve with a well-chilled, fresh-tasting Moselle wine.

6 SERVINGS

1 x 5 lb. chicken
1 onion
1 bay leaf
¼ teaspoon dried rosemary
6 peppercorns
2 carrots, scraped and halved
2 celery stalks, sliced
1 garlic clove
1½ teaspoons salt
1½ oz. [3 tablespoons] butter
3 tablespoons flour
8 fl. oz. single cream [1 cup light cream]
1 egg yolk
1 tablespoon lemon juice
⅛ teaspoon cayenne pepper
¼ teaspoon black pepper

Put the chicken in a large saucepan with the onion, bay leaf, rosemary, peppercorns, carrots, celery, garlic and 1 teaspoon salt. Pour in enough water to cover the chicken and put the pan over high heat. When the water comes to the boil, reduce the heat to low and simmer for 1 to 1½ hours or until the chicken is tender when pierced with the point of a sharp knife.

Transfer the chicken to a warm dish. Cover the dish with aluminium foil and keep hot. Strain the stock and put it back in the pan. Place it over moderate heat and bring to the boil. Cook for 15 minutes.

In a small saucepan, melt the butter over low heat. Remove the pan from the heat and mix in the flour using a wooden spoon. Slowly add 12 fluid ounces [1½ cups] of the boiling stock, stirring rapidly. Return the pan to the heat and simmer over very low heat for 10 minutes or until the mixture is thick and smooth. Stir the cream into the sauce.

Cook gently for a further 10 minutes, stirring frequently. Remove the pan from the heat. Put the egg yolk in a small bowl. Beat it lightly with a fork or spoon. Add 3 or 4 tablespoons of hot sauce, a spoonful at a time, beating continuously. Pour the egg and sauce mixture into the pan, stirring rapidly. Add the lemon juice, cayenne and pepper. Taste the sauce and add more salt if necessary. Remove the aluminium foil from the chicken and pour a little sauce over the bird. Carve the chicken at the table and serve the rest of the sauce in a warmed sauce-boat.

Chicken Livers in Aspic

This is a tasty appetizer, simple to prepare and delicious to eat. The aspic is unmoulded and garnished with shredded lettuce.

6 SERVINGS

1 pint [2½ cups] aspic jelly, melted
6 whole chicken livers
2 tablespoons butter
1 large onion, finely chopped
¼ teaspoon salt
⅛ teaspoon white pepper
4 fl. oz. [½ cup] sherry
1 crisp lettuce, washed and shredded

Into a 1½-pint [3¾-cup] mould, pour enough aspic jelly to make a ½-inch layer on the bottom. Place the mould in the refrigerator to chill until the jelly is set.

Dry the chicken livers with kitchen paper towels.

In a medium-sized frying-pan, melt the butter over moderate heat. When the butter foam subsides, add the chicken livers and fry them, shaking the pan, until the livers are lightly browned all over. Add the onion, and cook, stirring, for 5 seconds. Sprinkle the salt and pepper over the livers.

Pour the sherry into the pan, cover and simmer over low heat for 10 minutes. Using a slotted spoon, remove the chicken livers from the pan and set them aside. Increase the heat to high and boil the liquid in the pan until it is syrupy. Remove the pan from the heat. Coat the livers with the syrup and set them aside.

When the syrup coated livers have cooled, place them in the mould on top of the aspic, which should have set. Fill up the mould with the remaining jelly and put it back in the refrigerator. Leave to set for 1 hour.

Unmould the chicken livers in aspic on to a flat serving dish and surround with the shredded lettuce.

Chicken Livers with Ham and Sherry

This tempting combination of Chicken Livers, Ham and Sherry is best served with boiled rice and a green vegetable. A strong, dry red wine, such as Châteauneuf du Pape, would be an ideal accompaniment.

4 SERVINGS

3 oz. [⅜ cup] butter
6 slices bread, crusts removed and cut into 12 triangles
1½ lb. chicken livers, cut in halves
½ teaspoon salt
¼ teaspoon black pepper

½ teaspoon dried rosemary
3 slices smoked ham, diced
2 fl. oz. [¼ cup] sweet sherry

In a large, heavy frying-pan, melt 1 tablespoon of the butter over moderate heat. Add the bread triangles to the pan and fry them for 5 minutes on each side, or until they are crisp. With a slotted spoon, remove them from the pan and place them to one side on kitchen paper towels to drain.

Add 2 ounces [¼ cup] of the butter to the frying-pan and melt it over moderate heat. Add the chicken livers, salt, pepper, rosemary and ham to the pan. Simmer the mixture for 8 minutes, stirring occasionally.

Arrange the fried bread triangles on a warmed serving dish. With a slotted spoon, remove the chicken livers from the pan and arrange them on the fried bread.

Add the sherry to the pan, increase the heat slightly and cook for 3 minutes. With a wooden spoon, stir in the remaining butter. When the butter has melted, pour the sauce over the livers and serve.

Chicken Liver Pâté

☆ ① ⧗ ⧗ ⧗

This superb pâté is ideal to serve as a first course for a dinner party with hot buttered toast, as it may be made a day or two in advance and kept in the refrigerator. Alternatively, it makes an elegant main course accompanied by a fresh mixed salad and crusty French bread.

You will need a food mill or electric blender to make this pâté. To render the chicken fat, place it in the top part of a double boiler, heat it over boiling water until it is melted and then strain it.

APPROX. $1\frac{1}{2}$ LB.

- **2 pints [5 cups] water**
- **2 teaspoons salt**
- **1 celery stalk**
- **3 parsley sprigs**
- **8 peppercorns**
- **1 lb. chicken livers**
- **$\frac{1}{2}$ teaspoon Tabasco sauce**
- **8 oz. [1 cup] butter or rendered chicken fat**
- **$\frac{1}{4}$ teaspoon grated nutmeg**
- **2 teaspoons dry mustard**
- **$\frac{1}{4}$ teaspoon ground cloves**
- **1 medium-sized onion, finely minced**
- **1 garlic clove, finely minced**
- **2 tablespoons brandy or dry sherry**
- **2 oz. [$\frac{1}{4}$ cup] stuffed green olives, sliced**

In a large saucepan, bring the water to the boil over high heat. When the water is boiling, add $\frac{1}{2}$ teaspoon salt, the celery, parsley and peppercorns. Reduce the heat to moderate and simmer for 10 minutes. Add the chicken livers, cover the pan and cook for 10 minutes.

Drain the livers through a strainer and mince [grind] them in a food mill or, a few at a time, in an electric blender. Add the remaining salt, Tabasco sauce, butter or rendered chicken fat, nutmeg, mustard, cloves, onion, garlic and brandy or sherry. Blend the ingredients thoroughly.

Put the pâté into a $1\frac{1}{2}$-pint [$3\frac{3}{4}$-cup] terrine or dish, smooth the top and decorate with the olives. Place in the refrigerator to chill for at least 6 hours.

Home-made pâté is always a delicious first course for a dinner party and this superb Chicken Liver Pâté, garnished with olives, is no exception.

Chicken Liver Risotto

CHICKEN LIVERS COOKED WITH MUSHROOMS AND RICE

Tasty and inexpensive, Chicken Liver Risotto is very simple to prepare and ideal to serve as a main dish for lunch or supper accompanied by a green salad.

4 SERVINGS

- 2 oz. [$\frac{1}{4}$ cup] butter
- 1 medium-sized onion, finely chopped
- 4 oz. mushrooms, wiped clean and sliced
- 10 oz. [$1\frac{2}{3}$ cups] long-grain rice, washed, soaked in water for 30 minutes and drained
- 1 pint [$2\frac{1}{2}$ cups] boiling chicken stock
- 8 chicken livers, cut into small pieces
- 2 tablespoons chopped parsley
- 2 oz. [$\frac{1}{2}$ cup] Parmesan cheese, grated

In a large, heavy saucepan, melt three-quarters of the butter over moderate heat. Add the onion and cook, stirring occasionally, for 8 minutes or until the onion is soft and translucent but not brown. Add the mushrooms and cook for a further 3 minutes.

Add the rice to the saucepan and cook, stirring constantly, for 2 minutes. Pour on the stock and let the rice cook uncovered over high heat for 15 seconds. Cover the saucepan, reduce the heat to very low and simmer gently for 20 minutes, or until the liquid is absorbed and the rice is tender.

While the rice is cooking, prepare the chicken livers. Melt the remaining butter in a medium-sized frying-pan over moderate heat. Add the chicken livers and cook them for 10 minutes, stirring occasionally.

When the rice is cooked, stir in the chicken livers and parsley. Put the mixture into a warmed serving dish and sprinkle on the Parmesan cheese. Serve immediately.

Chicken Livers with Sweet and Sour Sauce

An unusual combination of chicken livers, pineapple, soy sauce and vinegar gives this dish a delicious sweet and sour taste. Ideal accompaniments are boiled rice and green beans or peas.

4 SERVINGS

- 3 tablespoons soy sauce
- 1 lb. chicken livers, cut in halves
- 2 fl. oz. [$\frac{1}{4}$ cup] vegetable oil
- 13 oz. canned pineapple chunks
- 4 oz. [$\frac{2}{3}$ cup] blanched almonds
- 2 fl. oz. [$\frac{1}{4}$ cup] vinegar
- $\frac{1}{4}$ teaspoon salt
- 1 teaspoon sugar
- 2 tablespoons cornflour [cornstarch]

Put 2 tablespoons of the soy sauce in a small bowl. Dip the chicken liver halves in the sauce. Add more soy sauce if necessary. In a large frying-pan, heat the oil over moderate heat. Add the chicken livers and cook them for 10 minutes, stirring occasionally. Drain the pineapple and reserve the syrup. Add the pineapple chunks and almonds, stir to mix and cook for 1 minute. With a slotted spoon, remove the livers, pineapple and almonds and set aside on a plate.

Add cold water to the reserved pineapple syrup to make 10 fluid ounces [$1\frac{1}{4}$ cups]. Put the pineapple syrup, vinegar, remaining soy sauce, salt and sugar into the pan. Blend the cornflour [cornstarch] with 3 tablespoons of water and add to the pan. Cook over low heat, stirring constantly for 10 minutes or until the sauce is thick and smooth. Taste the sauce and add sugar and salt, if necessary. Put the chicken liver and pineapple mixture into a warmed serving dish and pour on the sauce.

Serve immediately.

Chicken Liver Risotto with mushrooms is a tasty and inexpensive dish.

Chicken Livers with Water Chestnuts

This delicious combination of flavour and texture makes Chicken Livers with Water Chestnuts an unusual appetizer at the start of a meal or a hot savoury after the dessert.

4 SERVINGS

- 8 lean bacon slices
- 8 chicken livers
- 8 canned water chestnuts, drained
- $\frac{3}{4}$ teaspoon black pepper
- $\frac{1}{2}$ teaspoon ground ginger
- 4 tablespoons soy sauce

Low Cal

Heat the grill [broiler] to medium.

Wrap each slice of bacon around a chicken liver and a water chestnut. Spear each bacon parcel on to metal skewers, (3 or 4 to each skewer). Sprinkle with pepper and ginger and brush with soy sauce.

Place the skewers under the grill [broiler], and turning them occasionally, cook for 8 to 10 minutes. Brush with soy sauce, remove from skewers and serve.

Chicken Livers in Wine

Perfect for an informal dinner party, this is a quick and easy dish to prepare. It may be served with rice and a crisp, green salad.

6 SERVINGS

- 4 tablespoons plus 1 teaspoon flour
- $\frac{1}{2}$ teaspoon salt
- $\frac{1}{4}$ teaspoon black pepper
- 2 lb. chicken livers
- 2 tablespoons butter
- 1 garlic clove, crushed
- 8 fl. oz. [1 cup] light, sweet, red wine

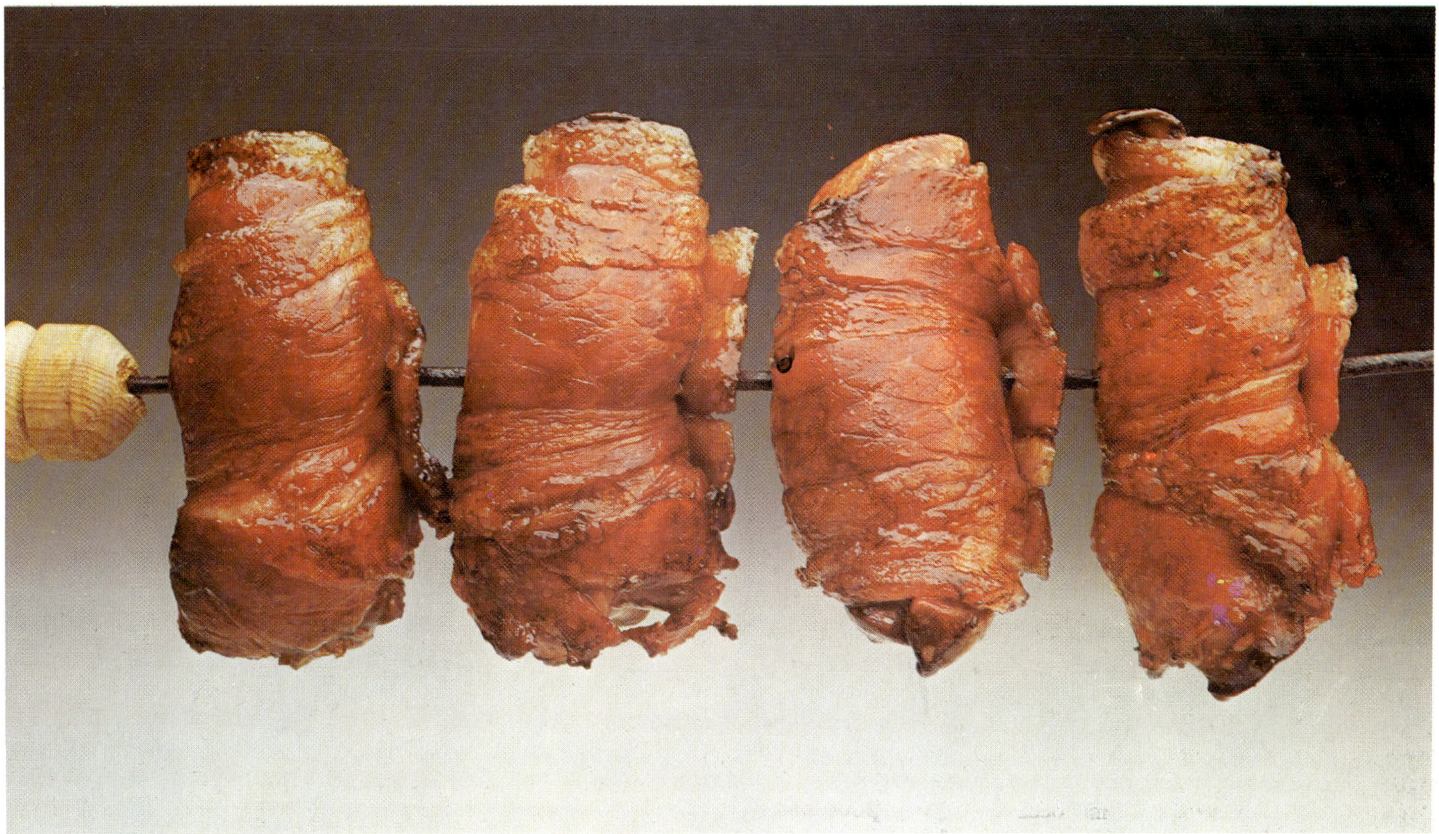

Mix 4 tablespoons of the flour with the salt and pepper on a large plate. Coat the chicken livers lightly in the seasoned flour and shake off any excess flour.

In a medium-sized frying-pan melt the butter over moderate heat. Add the garlic and fry for 1 minute. Add the livers, a few at a time, and fry until crispy and brown but still slightly pink inside. Using a slotted spoon, remove the livers from the fat as they cook and keep on a warm plate.

When all the livers are cooked, reduce the heat to low and add the 1 teaspoon of flour. Stir with a wooden spoon and gradually add the wine. Mix well. Taste and add more seasoning if necessary.

Cook the mixture until it thickens slightly. Return the livers to the pan and stir into the sauce.

Serve immediately.

Chick-pea

This member of the pea family is small, round and corn-coloured. Chick-peas should be soaked overnight, and they require a good hour's cooking. They have an earthy flavour, and are used in south-western France, Spain, particularly in soups, in North Africa, where they are part of the garnish for a classic couscous, in Turkey and in India.

Chick-peas are used both fresh and dry and when roasted and finely ground they have even been used as a substitute for coffee.

Chicken Livers with Water Chestnuts, wrapped in bacon, makes a tempting appetizer or hot savoury.

Chick-peas Catalan

Chick-peas are a favourite ingredient in Spanish cooking, and are often served with the small, spicy sausages known as chorizos. In this dish, chorizos and chick-peas are cooked with bacon to make a tasty and filling meal.

4 SERVINGS

12 oz. [2 cups] dried chick-peas, soaked overnight
2 medium-sized onions, studded with 3 or 4 cloves
2 carrots, scraped and quartered
bouquet garni, consisting of 4 parsley sprigs, 1 thyme spray and 1 bay leaf tied together
1 teaspoon salt
½ teaspoon black pepper
8 oz. streaky bacon
1 lb. chorizos or garlic smoked sausages
2 tablespoons olive oil
4 tablespoons tomato purée
1 garlic clove, crushed

Drain the soaked chick-peas and place them in a large saucepan. Add the onions, carrots, bouquet garni, salt, pepper, bacon and sausages. Pour in enough cold water to completely cover the mixture. Spoon on the olive oil, which should form a layer on the surface. Bring the mixture to the boil over high heat. Cover the pan and reduce the heat to low. Simmer the mixture for 3 hours.

With a slotted spoon, transfer the chick-peas to another saucepan. Lift out the sausages and bacon and cut them into bite-sized pieces. Discard the bouquet garni.

Remove the carrot and onion (take out the cloves) and mash them with a fork. Strain the remaining mixture, reserving 8 fluid ounces [1 cup].

Add the bacon and sausage pieces, onion and carrot purée, tomato purée and crushed garlic to the chick-peas along with the reserved cooking liquid. Cover the pan and bring to the boil over moderate heat. Reduce the heat to low and simmer the mixture for 30 minutes. Remove the pan from the heat and serve immediately.

Chicory

Chicory is a crisp vegetable that is served raw in salads or cooked in various savoury dishes.

Another variety of chicory is wild and the leaves and roots only are used. The leaves can be chopped and added to salads but the roots are usually roasted and ground and added to coffee.

In the United States, chicory is known as French or Belgian endive, and in France it is known simply as endive.

Chicory Braised in butter and lemon juice or vinegar makes an elegant accompaniment to roast meats.

Chicory, Braised

This method of cooking chicory ensures that it is deliciously tender. It makes a sophisticated accompaniment to roasted or grilled [broiled] *meats.*

4 SERVINGS

2 oz. [¼ cup] butter
1½ lb. chicory [French or Belgian endive], trimmed and cleaned
3 tablespoons water
1 teaspoon lemon juice or wine vinegar
½ teaspoon salt
¼ teaspoon black pepper

Low Cal

Preheat the oven to cool 300°F (Gas Mark 2, 150°C).

Rub half of the butter over the bottom of a shallow flameproof casserole large enough to hold all of the chicory [endive] in one layer, and arrange the chicory [endive] heads in the casserole. Cut the remaining butter into small pieces and dot them over the chicory [endive]. Add the water, lemon juice or vinegar and ¼ teaspoon of the salt. Place the casserole over moderate heat and bring the liquid to the boil.

Cover the chicory [endive] with aluminium foil, put the lid on the casserole and place it in the oven. Braise for 1¼ hours, or until the chicory [endive] is tender when pierced with a knife.

Season the vegetable with the remaining salt and the pepper and serve immediately.

Chicory with Cheese and Ham

An appetizing combination of flavour and texture, Chicory with Cheese and Ham is ideal to serve as a light main dish for a family lunch or supper, accompanied by boiled new potatoes.

4 SERVINGS

1 tablespoon lemon juice
1 lb. chicory [French or Belgian endive], trimmed and cleaned
1½ oz. [3 tablespoons] butter
1 tablespoon flour
½ teaspoon salt
¼ teaspoon white pepper
5 fl. oz. [⅝ cup] milk
⅛ teaspoon grated nutmeg
2 oz. [½ cup] Gruyère cheese, grated
8 slices cooked ham
2 tablespoons toasted breadcrumbs

Half-fill a medium-sized saucepan with water. Add the lemon juice, and bring to the boil over moderate heat. Add the chicory [endive], reduce the heat to low and cook, covered, for 20 to 25 minutes, or until the chicory [endive] is tender when pierced with a knife.

Reserve 5 fluid ounces [⅝ cup] of the cooking liquid and thoroughly drain the chicory [endive] in a colander.

To make the sauce, melt 2 tablespoons of the butter in a small, heavy saucepan over low heat. Remove the pan from the heat and stir in the flour, salt and pepper. Return the saucepan to the heat and, beating constantly with a wooden spoon, add the reserved cooking liquid and the milk a little at a time. When both liquids have been added, cook the mixture for a further 3 minutes, stirring constantly until the sauce is smooth and has thickened slightly. Add the nutmeg and three-quarters of the cheese, blending them thoroughly into the sauce. Bring the sauce to the boil. Remove the saucepan from the heat and set aside.

Preheat the grill [broiler] to moderate. Wrap each head of chicory [endive] in a slice of ham and arrange the heads, side by side, in a shallow flameproof baking dish. Pour the sauce over them and sprinkle with the breadcrumbs and the remaining cheese.

Cut the remaining tablespoon of butter

into small pieces and dot them on top of the mixture. Put the dish under the grill [broiler] for 5 minutes or until brown. Serve immediately.

Chicory and Eggs

This is a simple, traditional supper dish that takes only a short time to prepare.

4 SERVINGS

1 large bunch of wild chicory leaves [curly endive]
8 fl. oz. [1 cup] chicken stock
1 teaspoon dried marjoram
½ teaspoon dried thyme
1 teaspoon cornflour [cornstarch]
1 tablespoon milk
4 eggs

Low Cal

Blanch the chicory [endive] leaves by cooking them over moderate heat in boiling water for 5 minutes. Drain well on kitchen paper towels, squeezing out all excess moisture. Chop the leaves into small pieces and place them in a small saucepan with the stock and herbs. Bring to the boil over moderate heat, reduce the heat to low, cover, and simmer for 30 minutes.

In a cup, mix the cornflour [cornstarch] with the milk until it becomes a smooth paste. Add it to the chicory and stir with a wooden spoon until the mixture thickens. Turn the mixture on to a serving dish and keep warm. Poach the eggs and arrange them on top of the chicory [endive]. Serve immediately.

Chicory and Tomato Salad

This refreshing salad with its piquant vinegar and honey dressing makes an unusual accompaniment to cold chicken or beef.

4 SERVINGS

3 heads chicory [French or Belgian endive], trimmed
6 tomatoes, sliced
8 black olives, stoned
2 tablespoons red wine or cider vinegar
1 tablespoon clear honey
1 small onion, finely chopped
3 tablespoons olive oil
2 teaspoons lemon juice
⅛ teaspoon salt
½ teaspoon sugar

Low Cal

With a sharp knife, finely slice the chicory [endive] crosswise and place it in a salad bowl. Add the tomatoes and olives to the bowl.

In a small mixing bowl, combine the vinegar, honey, onion, oil, lemon juice, salt and sugar with a fork. Just before serving, pour the dressing over the chicory, tomatoes and olives and toss well.

Chilean Wines

Chile, a country that stretches along almost the entire west coast of South America, is the sub-continent's largest exporter of wine.

It is one of the few countries to have escaped the phylloxera epidemic that almost wiped out most of the European vineyards in the 19th century and its finer wines, especially whites made from pre-epidemic Riesling grapes, are quite excellent. And, due to recent quality controls imposed on what is still an essentially peasant industry, these wines are improving all the time.

Chile produces red and fortified wines as well as white, although its white wines seem to travel better and it tends to be by its Rieslings or its Pinot Noirs that Chile is judged. Chile's red wines are made from Cabernet grapes and the best of them are not unlike lighter Bordeaux to taste.

Chili con Carne

A dish originating in the southwestern United States which enjoys immense popularity all over the North American continent, Chili con Carne (kon kahr-nee) *is economical to make and ideal for any informal party. Serve with chilled lager.*

6 SERVINGS

2 tablespoons olive oil
2 medium-sized onions, finely sliced
2 garlic cloves, chopped
1½ lb. lean minced [ground] beef
8 oz. canned tomatoes
3 oz. canned tomato purée
1 bay leaf
1 teaspoon ground cumin
1 teaspoon dried oregano
1 teaspoon cayenne pepper
2 teaspoons mild chilli powder
2 teaspoons salt
12 fl. oz. [1½ cups] beef stock
14 oz. canned red kidney beans, drained

In a large frying-pan, heat the oil over moderate heat. Add the onions and garlic and fry them for 5 to 6 minutes, stirring constantly. Add the meat and brown it, stirring from time to time to make sure the meat breaks up properly and does not stick to the pan.

Put the mixture into a large, heavy saucepan and, mixing well, add the tomatoes, tomato purée, bay leaf, cumin, oregano, cayenne pepper, chilli powder, salt and stock. Cover the pan and bring the liquids to the boil over moderate heat. Reduce the heat to low and simmer the mixture, stirring occasionally, for 1 hour. Add the kidney beans, cover the pan again and continue simmering for 30 minutes. Remove the bay leaf and serve.

A famous American dish, Chili con Carne is inexpensive to make and perfect for an informal party.

Chilli
A native of the West Indies and tropical America, the chilli is the pungent pod of various peppers but particularly of the capsicum. There are many varieties differing in pungency, colour and shape. Chillis are used, both fresh and dried, as a condiment in India, South East Asia, Mexico, Latin America and the West Indies.

Chilli Powder
Chilli powder is a pungent condiment made from dried, red chillis and if it is bought ground, it may vary considerably in strength.

Chine
The chine is the bony part which adheres to the fillet of a loin of veal, mutton, lamb or pork, or to the bony part of a rib or sirloin of beef. Chine bone is a joint, usually of beef, consisting of a part of the backbone and its attached flesh. Because of the high proportion of bone, this is an uneconomical cut of beef that is hard to carve.

Chinese Cabbage
In Chinese called *Pe-Tsai,* this is a fairly common variety of cabbage, also sometimes known as celery cabbage. The heart is oval in shape, with very tightly closed, almost white leaves. All methods of preparing green cabbage are suitable for this vegetable. Chinese cabbage may also be used in salads or marinated like red cabbage.

Chinese Fried Rice

A simple dish, Chinese Fried Rice is easy to prepare, and makes an excellent complement to such rich dishes as chicken baked in wine.

4 SERVINGS

2 to 3 teaspoons peanut oil
8 oz. [$1\frac{1}{3}$ cups] long-grain rice, washed, cooked for 11 minutes in boiling salted water, drained and cooled
2 teaspoons soy sauce

In a heavy iron frying-pan, heat the peanut oil over moderately high heat. Add the cold cooked rice and increase the heat to high. Stir to coat the rice with the oil and then add 1 teaspoon of the soy sauce.

Fry the rice, stirring constantly, until it is coloured a light tan. Taste the rice and, if you like, add more soy sauce.

When the rice tastes pleasant, reduce the heat to moderate and cook gently, turning frequently until the rice is moist, hot and steaming. If it seems dry cover the pan tightly, reduce the heat to very low and cook for 2 to 3 minutes.

Serve this dish as quickly as possible as a crust forms if it is allowed to stand.

Chinese Gooseberry
A native of South East Asia, the Chinese gooseberry is also known as carambola and the coromandel gooseberry. A hairy, browned-skinned, green-fleshed fruit the size of a plum, it can be eaten raw but is usually preserved in sugar.

Chinese Roast Pork

This is the roast pork which is served in many Chinese restaurants. It can be eaten either hot or cold, and should be accompanied by Chinese mustard — dry mustard mixed with cold water, which is very hot but an excellent relish for pork, fried rice and fresh pineapple.

4 SERVINGS

3 to 4 lb. loin of pork, boned and trimmed of all fat
2 fl. oz. [$\frac{1}{4}$ cup] soy sauce
2 fl. oz. [$\frac{1}{4}$ cup] molasses or 4 tablespoons brown sugar
$\frac{1}{2}$ teaspoon salt
$\frac{1}{4}$ teaspoon freshly ground black pepper
2 tablespoons sherry
$\frac{1}{2}$-inch piece of fresh root ginger, peeled and sliced

With a sharp knife, cut off the fatty part of the loin, leaving the 'eye' or meaty part. Cut this in half. In a large shallow dish mix together the soy sauce, molasses or sugar, salt, pepper, ginger and sherry. Marinate the pork in this for at least 4 hours, turning the meat over frequently.

Preheat the oven to fairly hot 375°F (Gas Mark 5, 190°C).

Place the pork and marinade in a roasting tin and roast in the oven for 10 minutes. Turn the meat over and increase the heat to very hot 475°F (Gas Mark 9, 240°C). Continue roasting for about 40 minutes, turning and basting frequently. The meat is done when it is no longer pink in the middle.

Preheat the grill [broiler] to high.

Place the meat under the grill [broiler], browning on both sides for 2 to 3 minutes. Remove the meat from the heat and place it on a serving dish, discarding the remaining marinade. Cut it into slices and serve.

Ching-chiao-ch'ao niu-jou
STEAK WITH PEPPER

Simple to prepare, this highly flavoured dish of steak and bean sprouts makes an unusual lunch or supper dish. Serve it with boiled rice or noodles.

4 SERVINGS

1 lb. topside beef [top round], 1-inch thick
6 oz. bean sprouts, fresh or canned and drained
$\frac{1}{2}$ tablespoon cornflour [cornstarch]
2 tablespoons cold water
2 oz. [$\frac{1}{4}$ cup] butter
1 garlic clove, crushed
$\frac{1}{2}$ teaspoon salt
$\frac{1}{2}$ teaspoon freshly ground black pepper
4 tablespoons soy sauce
2 teaspoons sugar
2 tomatoes, blanched, peeled and quartered
2 green peppers, white pith removed, seeded and coarsely diced
4 spring onions [scallions], sliced

Prepare the steak for cooking by cutting it diagonally in short, thin slices. If you are using canned bean sprouts, rinse them in cold water and drain them in a colander. In a cup, mix the cornflour [cornstarch] and water to a paste.

In a heavy frying-pan, melt the butter over moderate heat. When the foam subsides, mix in the garlic, salt and pepper. Add the steak and fry it in the seasoned butter until it is browned all over.

Increase the heat to high. Add the soy sauce and sugar to the pan, cover and cook for 5 minutes. Uncover the pan and add the bean sprouts, tomatoes and green peppers. Cover again and cook for 5 minutes. Stir in the cornflour [cornstarch] paste, mixing with a wooden spoon until the liquid thickens. Transfer the mixture to a heated serving dish. Sprinkle with the sliced onions [scallions] and serve immediately.

Chining
Chining is a method of severing ribs from the backbone in a joint. The ribs are sawn through, rather than chopped. This makes joints, such as loin or neck of lamb, mutton, veal, or pork, easy to carve into convenient chops.

An attractive selection of some of the most popular Chinese dishes: Chinese Roast Pork, Chinese Fried Rice and Ching-chiao ch'ao niu-jou.

simmer, stirring the chocolate with a metal spoon as it melts, so that it becomes smooth. As soon as the chocolate is melted remove the saucepan or bowl from the heat.

Scald the milk in a small saucepan over moderately high heat. Gradually pour one-quarter of the hot milk on to the melted chocolate. Stir vigorously to blend the two. Slowly stir in the rest of the milk, reserving two tablespoons. Set the chocolate-and-milk mixture aside.

In a teacup soak the gelatine in the water. When the water has been absorbed, mix in the remaining 2 tablespoons of hot milk. Stir well to make sure that all the gelatine has melted.

Stir the dissolved gelatine and the coffee into the chocolate-and-milk mixture. In another bowl beat the egg yolks and sugar with a wire whisk until they are thick and frothy. Add the chocolate-and-milk mixture and beat well with the whisk. Put the bowl into the refrigerator to chill.

Pour the cream into a medium-sized mixing bowl. With a whisk, beat the cream until it is almost stiff. Then beat in the vanilla sugar or castor sugar and vanilla essence.

When the chocolate-and-milk mixture starts to set, fold the whipped cream into it with a metal spoon. If necessary, beat the cream into the mixture with a whisk.

Rinse out a large 4-pint mould with cold water and pour the mixture into it. Leave the pudding in the refrigerator overnight.

To turn the pudding out of the mould, loosen the sides with a table knife. Then place a serving platter, inverted, over the top of the mould. Reverse the two and give the mould a good shake. The pudding should slide easily out of the mould on to the plate.

If you like, decorate the pudding with chocolate vermicelli [sprinkles].

Chocolate Mushroom Cake

Don't be put off by the name of this cake. It does not contain mushrooms; it simply looks like a very impressive upturned one. This effect is achieved by piping cocoa-flavoured buttercream icing from the outer edge of the cake to the centre.

ONE 9-INCH CAKE

1 tablespoon butter
3 eggs
3 oz. [$\frac{3}{8}$ cup] sugar
$\frac{1}{4}$ teaspoon almond essence
$2\frac{1}{2}$ oz. [$\frac{5}{8}$ cup] self-raising flour
1 tablespoon cocoa
2 oz. [$\frac{1}{3}$ cup] ground almonds

DECORATION

3 tablespoons sieved apricot jam, warmed
8 oz. [1 cup] almond paste
6 oz. icing sugar [$1\frac{1}{2}$ cups confectioners' sugar]
$\frac{1}{2}$ teaspoon almond essence
3 oz. [$\frac{3}{8}$ cup] butter
1 tablespoon sifted cocoa, dissolved in 2 tablespoons hot water

Preheat the oven to fairly hot 375°F (Gas Mark 5, 190°C).

With the tablespoon of butter, lightly grease an 8-inch cake tin and set aside.

In a medium-sized mixing bowl, beat the eggs, sugar and almond essence with a wire whisk until the mixture is light and fluffy.

Fold the flour, cocoa and ground almonds into the mixture.

Turn the mixture into the prepared cake tin. Place the tin in the oven and bake for 25 minutes or until a skewer inserted into the centre of the cake comes out clean.

Remove the tin from the oven. Run a knife round the edge of the tin and reverse the cake on to a wire cake rack.

When the cake is cool, use a pastry brush to brush the sides of the cake with the sieved jam.

With your hands knead the almond paste for about 3 minutes or until it is soft and pliable. Roll the almond paste into a long thin strip, wide enough to cover the sides of the cake. Press the paste against the sides of the cake and trim it with a sharp knife. Knead the trimmings into a small roll for the stalk. Dust the top of the stalk with a little cocoa. Transfer the cake to an attractive serving dish.

In a medium-sized mixing bowl, gradually beat the icing [confectioners'] sugar and almond essence into the butter with a wooden spoon. Continue beating until the mixture is smooth. If the icing is too thick, add a little milk. Beat in the dissolved cocoa. Fill a forcing bag, fitted with a size No. 21 star nozzle, with the icing and pipe lines from the outer edge of the cake to the centre, completely covering the top of the cake. Place the stalk upright, in the centre.

Chocolate Peppermint Sandwich Cake

An interesting combination of chocolate and peppermint, this elegant sandwich cake may be covered with peppermint-flavoured icing or sprinkled with icing [confectioners'] *sugar.*

ONE 8-INCH CAKE

6 oz. [$\frac{3}{4}$ cup] plus 1 teaspoon margarine, softened
1 tablespoon flour
6 oz. [$\frac{3}{4}$ cup] castor sugar
$\frac{1}{2}$ teaspoon vanilla essence
3 eggs
4 oz. [1 cup] self-raising flour
2 oz. [$\frac{1}{2}$ cup] cocoa
1 tablespoon warm water

FILLING

3 oz. [$\frac{3}{8}$ cup] butter
6 oz. icing sugar [$1\frac{1}{2}$ cups confectioners' sugar]

½ teaspoon peppermint essence
green food colouring

Using the teaspoon of margarine, lightly grease two 7-inch round sandwich tins. Sprinkle the tins with the tablespoon of flour, knocking out any excess.

Preheat the oven to fairly hot 375°F (Gas Mark 5, 190°C).

In a large mixing bowl, cream the margarine and sugar with a wooden spoon, until the mixture is light and fluffy. Beat in the vanilla essence.

Add the eggs, one at a time, beating well after each addition, until the mixture is thick and creamy.

Sift the flour and cocoa into the bowl and fold them into the mixture with a metal spoon. Stir the water in carefully.

Spoon the mixture into the prepared tins. Place the tins in the oven. Bake for 25 to 30 minutes, or until a skewer inserted into the cakes comes out clean.

Remove the cakes from the oven and reverse them on to a wire cake rack. Leave to cool.

To make the icing, in a medium-sized mixing bowl, cream the butter and icing [confectioners'] sugar with a wooden spoon, until the mixture is light and creamy.

Stir in the peppermint essence and a few drops of green food colouring to make the icing a pale green colour.

With a knife, spread the icing over one of the cakes. Place the second cake on top.

An interesting combination of flavours, this attractive Chocolate Peppermint Sandwich Cake is delicious either as a dessert or teatime treat.

Chocolate Pineapple Rings are delicious served as a rich dessert or with morning coffee.

Chocolate Pineapple Rings

A lusciously rich sweet from Germany, Chocolate Pineapple Rings may be served as a dessert or with morning coffee.

10 RINGS

- 5 oz. [$\frac{5}{8}$ cup] butter
- 2 oz. [$\frac{1}{4}$ cup] sugar
- 6 oz. [$1\frac{1}{2}$ cups] flour
- 3 tablespoons ground almonds
- $\frac{1}{4}$ teaspoon almond essence
- 8 oz. dark [semi-sweet] cooking chocolate
- 1 to 2 tablespoons lukewarm water
- 10 canned pineapple rings
- 10 stemmed maraschino cherries
- 1 teaspoon cornflour [cornstarch]

Preheat the oven to fairly hot 375°F (Gas Mark 5, 190°C). Line a baking sheet with non-stick paper.

In a medium-sized mixing bowl, cream 4 ounces [$\frac{1}{2}$ cup] of the butter and all of the sugar together with a wooden spoon until the mixture is light and fluffy. Add the flour, ground almonds and almond essence and knead the mixture with your hands until it forms a soft dough.

Lightly flour a wooden board. Turn the dough out on to the board and roll it out thinly. With a 3-inch round pastry cutter cut out about 20 circles. Place the circles on the lined baking sheet.

Prick the surface of each circle with a fork and bake them in the oven for about 20 minutes, or until they are lightly brown. Transfer to a rack to cool.

In a small saucepan melt the chocolate and the remaining butter over very low heat, stirring constantly with a wooden spoon until the mixture is smooth and thick. Add 1 to 2 tablespoons of lukewarm water to the mixture to thin it slightly. Spread the chocolate mixture generously over each biscuit [cookie]. Sandwich 2 biscuit [cookie] rounds together while they are still moist.

Drain the pineapple rings, reserving 4 tablespoons of the can liquid, and place one ring on each of the biscuit [cookie] sandwiches before the chocolate has set. Put a cherry in the middle of each pineapple ring. Set the rings aside.

In a small saucepan mix the cornflour [cornstarch] with the reserved pineapple juice. Over moderately high heat bring the syrup to the boil, stirring constantly. Cook until it has thickened. Remove the pan from the heat and allow the syrup to cool to room temperature. With a pastry brush spread the syrup over the pineapple rings. Let the syrup glaze set for 10 minutes before serving.

Chocolate Pudding

This is a traditional English baked Chocolate Pudding. Quick and easy to prepare, it may be served with chocolate or custard sauce.

6 SERVINGS

- 4 oz. [$\frac{1}{2}$ cup] butter
- 6 oz. [$1\frac{1}{2}$ cups] flour
- $\frac{1}{2}$ teaspoon salt
- 1 teaspoon baking powder
- 4 oz. [$\frac{1}{2}$ cup] sugar
- 2 oz. [$\frac{1}{2}$ cup] cocoa
- 2 eggs, lightly beaten
- 5 tablespoons milk
- $\frac{1}{4}$ teaspoon vanilla essence

Preheat the oven to fairly hot 375°F (Gas Mark 5, 190°C).

Using 1 tablespoon of the butter grease a medium-sized pie or soufflé dish. Set the dish aside.

Sift the flour, salt and baking powder into a medium-sized mixing bowl. With your fingertips, rub the remaining butter into the mixture. Stir in the sugar and cocoa.

With a wooden spoon beat in the eggs and milk and continue beating until the mixture is smooth and of a dropping consistency. Add the vanilla essence.

Pour the mixture into the greased pie or soufflé dish and place it, just above centre, in the oven. Bake for 30 to 40 minutes, or until a skewer inserted into the pudding comes out clean.

Remove the pudding from the oven and serve from the dish.

Chocolate and Rum Fondue

This is a very unusual dessert to serve at a dinner party and one that is sure to delight your guests. The fondue should be served with a selection of fresh fruit such as pears and bananas or cake cut into small pieces. The fruit or cake is speared on dessert forks and dipped into the hot chocolate.

6-8 SERVINGS

- 8 oz. dark [semi-sweet] chocolate, broken into small pieces
- 6 tablespoons double [heavy] cream
- 2 tablespoons rum
- 2 oz. icing sugar [$\frac{1}{2}$ cup confectioners' sugar], sifted

In a small bowl set over a pan of hot water or in a double saucepan, melt the chocolate with the cream, stirring constantly with a wooden spoon. As soon as the chocolate has melted, remove the bowl or pan from the heat.

Stir in the rum and the sugar.

Pour the mixture into a fondue pot or a small flameproof dish set over a small spirit lamp.

Ignite the spirit lamp and serve the fondue with the fruit or pieces of cake.

Chocolate Rum Truffles

A delicious and elegant party sweet, Chocolate Rum Truffles take a very short time to prepare. Brandy can be substituted for rum if you prefer the taste.

ABOUT 30 TRUFFLES

4 oz. dark [semi-sweet] cooking chocolate, broken into pieces
3 tablespoons dark rum
2 oz. [¼ cup] unsalted butter, cut into small pieces
3 oz. icing sugar [¾ cup confectioners' sugar], sifted
3 oz. [½ cup] ground almonds
1 tablespoon cocoa

In a bowl placed over a pan of hot water or in a double saucepan, melt the chocolate with the rum, stirring occasionally. As soon as the chocolate has melted, remove the pan from the heat. Gradually add the butter, sugar and ground almonds, stirring constantly with a wooden spoon until the mixture becomes smooth and very thick.

Set the bowl or pan aside to allow the chocolate mixture to cool to room temperature. Then place it in the refrigerator to chill for 30 minutes. When the mixture is cool and firm enough to handle, make approximately 30 small balls by rolling spoonfuls of the mixture between the palms of your hands.

Sift the cocoa on to a sheet of greaseproof or waxed paper. Roll each truffle in the cocoa so that it is generously coated. Store in the refrigerator until you are ready to serve.

Chocolate Sauce

This is a semi-sweet chocolate sauce, suitable for using on ice-cream, sorbet, puddings, meringues and cakes.

JUST OVER 1 PINT

6 oz. dark [semi-sweet] cooking chocolate, broken into pieces
14 fl. oz. [1¾ cups] canned evaporated milk
1 teaspoon vanilla essence
¼ teaspoon almond essence

In a bowl placed over a pan of hot water or in a double saucepan, melt the chocolate with the milk, stirring occasionally. As soon as the chocolate has melted, remove the bowl or pan from the heat. With a wooden spoon or wire whisk, beat the vanilla and almond essences into the chocolate-and-milk mixture. Continue beating until the sauce is smooth. Serve warm.

An unusual and exciting dessert for a dinner party, Chocolate and Rum Fondue is served with fruit and cake.

Chocolate Soufflé

Light and delicate, this hot Chocolate Soufflé is an elegant dessert to serve for a luncheon or dinner party.

4 SERVINGS

3½ oz. dark [semi-sweet] cooking chocolate, broken into pieces
2 tablespoons water
15 fl. oz. [1⅞ cups] milk
3 tablespoons vanilla sugar or 1 teaspoon vanilla essence and 3 tablespoons castor sugar
3 tablespoons arrowroot
1 tablespoon butter, cut into small pieces
1 tablespoon butter, softened
3 egg yolks, lightly beaten
4 egg whites
1 tablespoon icing [confectioners'] sugar

Put the chocolate and water in a heavy, medium-sized saucepan. Melt the chocolate over low heat, stirring occasionally.

Put the milk in another heavy, medium-sized saucepan and scald it over low heat (bring to just under boiling point). Spoon out about 3 tablespoons of the milk, put it in a cup and place to one side. Add the vanilla sugar or vanilla essence and sugar to the milk in the saucepan and stir well with a wooden spoon. When the sugar is dissolved add the melted chocolate and stir well. Remove the pan from the heat.

Add the arrowroot to the reserved 3 tablespoons of milk and mix to a smooth paste. Add the dissolved arrowroot to the milk and chocolate mixture in the pan and stir well. Replace the saucepan on moderate heat and bring to the boil. As soon as boiling point is reached, remove the pan from the heat. Dot the surface of the mixture with the pieces of butter, cover the pan and leave to cool to room temperature.

While the chocolate mixture is cooling prepare the soufflé dish. Grease a medium-sized soufflé dish with the softened butter. Tie a piece of greaseproof or waxed paper around the outside, projecting 2 inches above the rim of the soufflé dish.

Preheat the oven to fairly hot 375°F (Gas Mark 5, 190°C).

When the chocolate mixture has cooled, add the beaten egg yolks, a little at a time, and stir well to mix.

Put the egg whites in a bowl and with a rotary beater or wire whisk beat them until they form stiff peaks. With a metal spoon lightly and quickly fold the beaten whites into the chocolate mixture. Pour the soufflé mixture into the prepared dish and place in the centre of the oven. Bake for 30 minutes or until firm and risen.

After 25 minutes remove the soufflé from the oven and quickly dust the top with the icing [confectioners'] sugar. Slide the soufflé back into the oven and cook for a further 5 minutes. Serve immediately.

Chocolate and Sour Cream Cake

This impressive, very rich chocolate layer cake may be served as a dessert or for afternoon tea. The sour cream filling contrasts deliciously with the chocolate cake.

ONE 9-INCH CAKE

- 6 oz. [¾ cup] plus 1 tablespoon butter
- 8 oz. [2 cups] plus 3 tablespoons flour, sifted
- 7 oz. dark [semi-sweet] cooking chocolate, broken into pieces
- 1¼ lb. [2½ cups] castor sugar
- 4 eggs
- 1 teaspoon vanilla essence
- 1½ teaspoons baking powder
- ¼ teaspoon salt
- 8 fl. oz. [1 cup] milk

ICING

- 1½ lb. dark [semi-sweet] cooking chocolate, broken into pieces
- ¼ teaspoon salt
- 16 fl. oz. [2 cups] sour cream
- 12 whole walnuts, shelled and halved

With 1 tablespoon of the butter, grease three 9-inch round sandwich tins and sprinkle a tablespoon of flour into each. Tip and rotate the tins to distribute the flour evenly round the bottoms and sides. Shake out any excess flour. Set aside.

Preheat the oven to fairly hot 375°F (Gas Mark 5, 190°C).

In the top of a double saucepan or a small bowl placed over a pan of boiling water, melt the chocolate, stirring constantly with a wooden spoon. As soon as the chocolate melts, remove the pan from the heat and place to one side.

In a medium-sized bowl, cream together the remaining butter and the sugar with a wooden spoon until the mixture is light and fluffy. Beat in the eggs, one at a time. Beat in the melted chocolate and the vanilla essence.

Sift the remaining flour, baking powder and salt together into another bowl. Beat half the sifted dry ingredients into the chocolate mixture, then add half the milk and beat to mix. Beat in the remaining dry ingredients. When well blended add the rest of the milk. Beat the batter until it is smooth.

Pour an equal amount of the batter into each cake tin. Bake in the centre of the oven for 15 to 20 minutes or until a skewer inserted into the centres of the cakes comes out clean. Remove the tins from the oven. Run a knife around the edge of each cake and reverse them on to a cake rack. Leave them to cool.

To make the icing, melt the chocolate in the top of a double saucepan or in a small bowl placed over a pan of simmering water. As soon as the chocolate has melted, stir in the salt and sour cream with a wooden spoon. Set the chocolate and sour cream mixture aside for 20 minutes or until it cools to room temperature and thickens to a spreading consistency. Place one cake on an attractive serving dish and spread the top with a ½-inch layer of icing. Place a second cake on top of the first and spread it with a ½-inch layer of icing. Cover with the remaining cake and spread the top and sides of the complete cake with the remaining icing. Decorate the top of the cake with the walnut halves.

This light and airy Chocolate Sponge Cake may be served as a luscious dessert or for afternoon tea.

Chocolate Sponge Cake

This light, fluffy Chocolate Sponge Cake may be served sprinkled with icing sugar [confectioners' sugar] *or for a richer cake coat it with vanilla or chocolate flavoured buttercream icing.*

ONE 8-INCH CAKE

- 2 oz. [¼ cup] plus 1 tablespoon butter, softened
- 2 oz. [½ cup] plus 2 tablespoons flour

$3\frac{1}{2}$ oz. dark [semi-sweet] cooking chocolate, broken into pieces
2 tablespoons prepared coffee or water
3 eggs, separated
3 oz. [$\frac{3}{8}$ cup] plus 1 tablespoon castor sugar
$\frac{1}{8}$ teaspoon salt
4 oz. plain or chocolate flavoured buttercream icing (optional)

Preheat the oven to moderate 350°F (Gas Mark 4, 180°C).

Using 1 tablespoon butter, grease a shallow 8-inch square cake tin. Sprinkle in 1 tablespoon of the flour and tip and rotate the tin to distribute it evenly. Shake out any excess flour and set the tin aside.

Place the chocolate and coffee or water in a small saucepan over very low heat. Melt the chocolate, stirring occasionally. As soon as the chocolate has melted, remove the pan from the heat and with a wooden spoon gradually beat in the remaining butter. Allow the mixture to cool to lukewarm. Meanwhile, in a medium-sized mixing bowl lightly beat the egg yolks with a wire whisk or rotary beater. Gradually beat in all but 1 tablespoon of the sugar. Continue beating until the mixture is pale yellow and will make a ribbon trail on itself when the whisk is lifted.

With a wire whisk or rotary beater beat the egg whites and salt together in another bowl. When soft peaks are formed add the remaining sugar and beat until the egg whites are stiff.

Blend the chocolate mixture into the egg yolk-and-sugar mixture. With a metal spoon carefully fold in one-quarter of the egg whites. When partly blended sift in one-quarter of the remaining flour and continue blending. Add another quarter of the egg whites followed by one-quarter of the flour. Repeat until all the egg whites and flour have been added and well blended.

Pour the batter into the cake tin. Bake in the middle of the oven for 30 minutes or until a skewer inserted in the centre of the cake comes out clean and dry. The cake will rise about $\frac{1}{4}$ inch above the rim of the tin and the top will split.

Remove the cake from the oven and cool in the tin for 5 minutes. The cake will sink slightly. To remove the cake from the tin, run a knife around the inside of the tin. Hold a wire rack, inverted, over the top of the cake tin, reverse the two and shake so that the cake slides out of the tin on to the rack. Allow the cake to cool for about $2\frac{1}{2}$ hours.

Serve sprinkled with icing [confectioners'] sugar or filled and topped with the buttercream icing.

Chocolate Swiss [Jelly] Roll

A sumptuous cold dessert, this rich Chocolate Roll is fragile and difficult to roll. You may need to turn it out on to a damp cloth instead of on to greaseproof or waxed paper for the preliminary rolling. For easier cutting, make the roll a day in advance and refrigerate it. Young people or those with a sweet tooth will appreciate your efforts.

6 SERVINGS

2 tablespoons butter
5 eggs, separated
6 oz. [$\frac{3}{4}$ cup] plus 1 teaspoon sugar
6 oz. dark [semi-sweet] cooking chocolate
3 tablespoons cold water
8 fl. oz. double cream [1 cup heavy cream]
$\frac{1}{2}$ teaspoon vanilla essence

Preheat the oven to hot 425°F (Gas Mark 7, 220°C).

With 1 tablespoon of butter grease a swiss [jelly] roll tin. Line it with a sheet of greaseproof or waxed paper large enough to overlap all four sides. Rub the remaining butter over the paper.

In a medium-sized mixing bowl beat the egg yolks with a wire whisk or rotary beater until they are pale and thick. Gradually beat 6 ounces [$\frac{3}{4}$ cup] of the sugar into the egg yolks.

In a small saucepan melt the chocolate in the water over low heat, stirring constantly. The moment the chocolate is melted take it off the heat.

Let the chocolate cool a little in the pan before pouring it into the egg yolk mixture. Mix well with a wire whisk.

In a separate mixing bowl beat the egg whites with a wire whisk until they form stiff peaks.

With a metal spoon lightly fold the egg whites into the egg-yolk and chocolate mixture.

Spoon the chocolate mixture into the swiss [jelly] roll tin. Place the tin in the oven and bake for 10 minutes.

Reduce the oven temperature to warm 325°F (Gas Mark 3, 170°C) and bake for a further 10 minutes, or until a skewer inserted into the cake comes out clean.

Remove the tin from the oven and cover it with a damp cloth. Leave it for 15 minutes. Turn it upside-down on to a fresh piece of greaseproof or waxed paper which has been sprinkled with a little icing [confectioners'] sugar. Place it in the refrigerator to chill for 30 minutes. With a sharp knife make a shallow cut across the sponge about $2\frac{1}{2}$ inches from the end to make rolling easier. With the help of the paper, roll the sponge carefully. Keep it rolled until it is cool.

For Chocolate Swiss [Jelly] Roll, beat the melted chocolate into the egg yolks and sugar mixture.

Remove the cake from the oven and turn it upside-down on to a sheet of greaseproof or waxed paper.

With the help of the paper, carefully roll up the sponge and keep it rolled until it is completely cold.

Unroll the sponge and spread it with the cream filling. Roll it up again and place it in the refrigerator.

In a medium-sized mixing bowl beat the cream, the remaining teaspoon of sugar and the vanilla essence together with a rotary beater or wire whisk until the mixture is stiff.

Unroll the sponge and with a knife, spread the cream mixture over the cake. Roll up the cake again, cover with aluminium foil and refrigerate until you are ready to serve it.

Chokladkaka

Chokladkaka (chock-lahd-kah-kah) *is a luscious Swedish chocolate cake that is rich enough to be served plain without icing. If you like, the cake may be accompanied by whipped cream.*

ONE 9-INCH CAKE

3 oz. [$\frac{3}{8}$ cup] butter
1 oz. [$\frac{1}{3}$ cup] dry white breadcrumbs
6 oz. [$\frac{3}{4}$ cup] sugar
2 eggs, separated
1 teaspoon vanilla essence
6 oz. [$1\frac{1}{2}$ cups] flour, sifted
1 teaspoon baking powder
3 oz. sweet chocolate, melted
4 fl. oz. single cream [$\frac{1}{2}$ cup light cream]

Preheat the oven to cool 300°F (Gas Mark 2, 150°C).

With 1 tablespoon of the butter, grease a deep, round cake tin. Sprinkle the breadcrumbs into the tin. With your fingers or a table knife press the crumbs on to the bottom and sides of the tin so that it is completely lined. Set the tin aside.

In a medium-sized mixing bowl, cream the remaining butter with the back of a wooden spoon. Gradually beat in the sugar and continue beating until the mixture is light and fluffy. Then beat in the egg yolks, one at a time, and add the vanilla essence.

Sift 2 ounces [$\frac{1}{2}$ cup] of the flour with the baking powder into the butter-and-sugar mixture and beat well. Blend in one-third of the melted chocolate and cream and add another 2 ounces [$\frac{1}{2}$ cup] of the flour. Continue adding the chocolate, cream and flour until all of it has been incorporated.

In another bowl, use a wire whisk or rotary beater to beat the egg whites until they will form stiff peaks. With a metal spoon, gently fold the egg whites into the chocolate batter.

Pour the batter into the tin and bake in the oven for 50 minutes or until a skewer inserted in the centre comes out clean. Turn the cake out of the tin on to a cake rack to cool.

Chop

A chop is a slice of meat, generally lamb, mutton, pork or veal, and usually including a rib or section of bone. It may also be cut from the chump or tail end of the loin, when it is known as the chump or loin chop, or from the neck, when it may be called a cutlet.

Chorizo Patties

Hot and spicy, Chorizo sausage patties are an unusual and tasty main course for a family lunch, accompanied by tomato salad and crusty bread.

4 SERVINGS

2 lb. belly pork, coarsely minced [ground]
2 fl. oz. [$\frac{1}{4}$ cup] red wine vinegar
2 teaspoons dried marjoram
3 garlic cloves, crushed
2 tablespoons mild chilli powder
1 teaspoon freshly ground black pepper
2 teaspoons salt
$\frac{1}{2}$ teaspoon ground cumin
$\frac{1}{2}$ teaspoon red pepper flakes
$\frac{1}{2}$ teaspoon tomato purée
2 tablespoons butter
1 tablespoon vegetable oil

In a large mixing bowl, combine the pork with the vinegar, marjoram, garlic, chilli powder, pepper, salt, cumin, red pepper flakes and tomato purée. Stir to blend the ingredients well together.

With your hands, form the sausage mixture into patties about $\frac{1}{2}$-inch thick and 2-inches wide.

In a large frying-pan, heat the butter and oil over moderate heat. When the butter foam subsides, add the sausage patties to the pan. Cook them for 10 minutes on each side. Remove the patties from the pan and transfer them to a warmed serving dish. Serve immediately.

Chou au Gratin

CABBAGE CHEESE

Cabbage, often regarded as a dull vegetable, is interesting and tasty when served as Chou au Gratin (shoo oh grah-tan) *and goes well with any roast meat or grilled* [broiled] *sausages.*

4-6 SERVINGS

1 teaspoon salt
1 medium-sized cabbage, washed and shredded
$\frac{1}{4}$ teaspoon grated nutmeg
8 to 10 fl. oz. [1 to $1\frac{1}{4}$ cups] béchamel sauce
2 oz. [$\frac{1}{2}$ cup] Gruyère cheese, grated
4 tablespoons fresh white breadcrumbs, fried in oil

Put enough water into a large saucepan to make a 1-inch layer. Add $\frac{1}{2}$ teaspoon salt and place the pan over high heat. Bring the water to the boil. Add the shredded cabbage and reduce the heat to moderate. Cook the cabbage for 15 minutes. Remove the pan from the heat, drain the cabbage in a colander and return it to the saucepan.

Add the remaining salt and nutmeg to the béchamel sauce and pour the mixture into the pan.

Preheat the grill [broiler] to high.

Place the saucepan over low heat and simmer the cabbage mixture gently, covered, for 5 minutes. Add three-quarters of the cheese, stirring well with a wooden spoon, until it blends into the sauce and the sauce is smooth.

Remove the pan from the heat and turn the mixture into a flameproof dish. Sprinkle the top with the remaining cheese and the breadcrumbs.

Place the dish under the grill [broiler] and cook for 2 to 3 minutes, or until the top is brown.

Remove the dish from the heat and serve at once.

Choucroute Garnie

A typical regional French dish, Choucroute Garnie (shoo-kroot gahr-nee) *is one of Alsace's contributions to French cuisine. It is a meal in itself and is excellent if accompanied by one of those beautiful white Alsatian wines, such as Traminer.*

6 SERVINGS

2 lb. sauerkraut
2 oz. salt pork, diced
3 tablespoons vegetable oil
1 medium-sized onion, finely sliced
1 medium-sized carrot, scraped and thinly sliced
2 garlic cloves, crushed
3 parsley sprigs
1 bay leaf
8 peppercorns
10 juniper berries
7 fl. oz. [$\frac{7}{8}$ cup] dry white wine
8 fl. oz. [1 cup] chicken stock
6 knackwurst sausages
6 slices smoked ham

Soak the sauerkraut in a bowlful of cold water for 10 to 15 minutes to get rid of excess saltiness. Drain the sauerkraut in a colander and dry it on kitchen paper towels. Set aside.

In a small saucepan, bring 1 pint [2½ cups] of water to the boil over high heat. Add the diced salt pork and reduce the heat to moderate. Cook the salt pork for 5 minutes to remove excess saltiness. Drain the salt pork and dry it on kitchen paper towels.

In a large frying-pan, heat the oil over moderate heat. Add the diced salt pork and fry for about 10 minutes, or until the dice are well browned and resemble small croûtons in shape. Add the onion, carrot and garlic to the pan and cook for a further 5 minutes or until the onion becomes transluscent, taking care not to let it brown.

Tie the parsley, bay leaf, peppercorns and juniper berries together in a small cheesecloth bag and put the bag in the mixture in the pan. Add the sauerkraut to the mixture. Pour on the wine and chicken stock, and mix well to blend all the ingredients. Bring the liquids to the boil, cover the pan and reduce the heat to very low. Simmer for 2½ hours, stirring occasionally to prevent the sauerkraut from sticking to the pan.

Add the knackwurst sausages to the pan and continue simmering for 30 minutes. Discard the cheesecloth bag before serving (although, if you like, the juniper berries may be added to the sauerkraut mixture).

Pile the sauerkraut in the centre of a large, fairly deep serving dish, cover the top with the ham slices and place the sausages around the sides. Serve immediately.

Chou-fleur en Casserole is a tasty and colourful dish of cauliflower, tomatoes and cheese.

Chou-fleur en Casserole

CAULIFLOWER WITH TOMATOES AND CHEESE

An elegant dish requiring minimal preparation, Chou-fleur en Casserole (shoo-fler on) *may be served with steaks, chops or roasts. It is also a delicious and light luncheon dish on its own.*

4-6 SERVINGS

1 tablespoon butter
1 large cauliflower, cleaned and separated into flowerets
6 tomatoes, blanched, peeled, seeded and roughly chopped
½ teaspoon salt
¼ teaspoon black pepper
4 oz. [½ cup] butter, melted
2 tablespoons fine white breadcrumbs
2 tablespoons grated Parmesan cheese
2 tablespoons grated Emmenthal cheese

Preheat the oven to fairly hot 375°F (Gas Mark 5, 190°C).

Lightly grease a large shallow casserole with the tablespoon of butter and set aside.

In a large saucepan, cook the cauliflower flowerets in boiling salted water over moderate heat for 9 to 12 minutes, or until they are tender. Drain the flowerets.

Place the flowerets in the buttered casserole. Arrange the chopped tomatoes on top and sprinkle with salt, pepper and half of the melted butter.

In a small bowl, combine the breadcrumbs with the Parmesan and Emmenthal cheeses and sprinkle the mixture over the vegetable pieces. Spoon the remaining melted butter over the mixture and bake in the oven for about 30 minutes, or until the top is golden brown. Remove the dish from the oven and serve immediately.

Chou-fleur avec Sauce Crevette

CAULIFLOWER WITH SHRIMP SAUCE

A versatile dish, Chou-fleur avec Sauce Crevette (shoo-fler ah-veck soss kre-vet) *can be served either as an hors d'oeuvre, a vegetable accompaniment to a main meal, or on its own as a light luncheon dish.*

6 SERVINGS

1 medium-sized cauliflower
6 oz. small fresh or frozen and thawed shrimps
8 fl. oz. [1 cup] mayonnaise
$1\frac{1}{2}$ tablespoons tomato purée
1 teaspoon salt
1 teaspoon white pepper

Clean and wash the cauliflower but leave it whole. Place it in a large saucepan, head down, and cover it with water. Put the lid on the pan and cook the cauliflower over moderate heat for 15 to 20 minutes, or until it is tender when pierced with the point of a sharp knife.

Drain the cauliflower in a colander and place it in a serving dish. Put the dish in the refrigerator to chill.

If using fresh shrimps, place them in a saucepan, cover them with water and cook over moderate heat for 3 to 4 minutes. Remove the pan from the heat and drain the shrimps, discarding the cooking liquid. Peel the shrimps and slice them in half lengthwise. Set them aside in a cool place.

In a medium-sized mixing bowl combine the mayonnaise with the tomato purée, stirring briskly with a fork or spoon to blend well. Add the sliced shrimps, salt and pepper and mix thoroughly.

Pour the sauce over the cauliflower and replace in the refrigerator. Serve cold.

Chou Rouge à la Flamande

BRAISED RED CABBAGE WITH APPLES

A hearty winter vegetable dish, Chou Rouge à la Flamande (shoo rooj ah lah flah-mahn) *provides a particularly excellent accompaniment to the classic Belgian dish Lapin à la Flamande or jugged hare.*

4 SERVINGS

2 tablespoons butter
1 small red cabbage
$\frac{1}{8}$ teaspoon grated nutmeg
$\frac{1}{2}$ teaspoon salt
$\frac{1}{4}$ teaspoon black pepper
3 tablespoons vinegar
4 tart cooking apples, peeled, cored and quartered
1 tablespoon brown sugar

Grease a medium-sized flameproof casserole with the butter. Quarter the cabbage. Wash it and remove and discard the core, stem and outer leaves. Shred it finely.

Put the shredded cabbage into the casserole and mix in the nutmeg, salt and pepper. Sprinkle with the vinegar and cover the casserole. Cook over low heat for $1\frac{1}{2}$ hours, stirring occasionally to prevent the cabbage from sticking to the bottom of the pan.

Add the apple quarters and brown sugar and mix well. Continue cooking for a further 40 minutes, stirring occasionally. Serve hot.

Chou Rouge à la Limousine

BRAISED RED CABBAGE WITH RED WINE AND CHESTNUTS

Chou Rouge à la Limousine (shoo rooj ah lah lee-moo-zeen) *is a marvellous vegetable to serve with roast goose, duck, pork or venison.*

6 SERVINGS

2 tablespoons butter
4 bacon slices, cut into thin strips
1 small carrot, scraped and finely sliced
2 medium-sized onions, sliced
2 lb. red cabbage, washed and shredded
2 garlic cloves, crushed
1 small bay leaf
$\frac{1}{8}$ teaspoon ground cloves
$\frac{1}{8}$ teaspoon grated nutmeg
$\frac{1}{2}$ teaspoon salt
$\frac{1}{4}$ teaspoon freshly ground black pepper
5 fl. oz. [$\frac{5}{8}$ cup] dry red wine
5 fl. oz. [$\frac{5}{8}$ cup] beef stock
24 dried chestnuts, soaked overnight and boiled until almost tender

In a large flameproof casserole, melt the butter over moderate heat. When the foam subsides, add the bacon, carrot and onions. Reduce the heat to low, cover the casserole and cook for 10 minutes.

Preheat the oven to warm 325°F (Gas Mark 3, 170°C).

Stir the cabbage into the bacon and vegetable mixture and continue cooking, uncovered, for a further 10 minutes. Add the garlic, bay leaf, cloves, nutmeg, salt, pepper, wine and stock.

Increase the heat to high and bring the mixture to the boil. Remove from the heat, cover the casserole and place it in the oven. Braise for $1\frac{1}{2}$ hours.

Remove the casserole from the oven and add the chestnuts. Re-cover and return the casserole to the oven to braise for 1 hour, or until nearly all the liquid has been absorbed.

Remove the casserole from the oven and serve at once.

Choux Pastry

This is special light pastry that is used mostly for éclairs, cream puffs and cheese savouries, but it is also used in such classic French desserts as Gâteau St. Honoré and profiterôles. French in origin, it was named choux (shoo) *because it puffs up during baking and sets in the shape of a cabbage. For savoury hors d'oeuvre or appetizers, fill the puffs with finely diced chicken salad, mixed seafood or finely sliced mushrooms mixed with sour cream, fresh chopped parsley and cayenne pepper.*

12 CHOUX BUNS

5 fl. oz. [$\frac{5}{8}$ cup] water
2 oz. [4 tablespoons] butter or margarine
$\frac{1}{4}$ teaspoon salt
$2\frac{1}{2}$ oz. [$\frac{1}{2}$ cup plus 1 tablespoon] flour
2 eggs
$\frac{1}{8}$ teaspoon vanilla extract [essence]
extra butter for greasing

In a large heavy saucepan, bring the water, butter and salt to the boil. Meanwhile, sift the flour on to a piece of greaseproof [waxed] paper. Place the eggs in a basin and whisk together. When the butter has melted, remove the pan from the heat and beat in all the flour at once.

Return the heavy-based saucepan to low heat and beat vigorously for 1-2 minutes until the mixture forms a smooth ball and pulls away from the sides of the saucepan.

Take the pan off the heat and let the mixture cool for 2 minutes. Beat in the eggs a little at a time, beating after each addition until the mixture is well blended. When the eggs have all been completely absorbed and the mixture is thick and glossy essence add the vanilla extract [essence].

Preheat the oven to hot 400°F (Gas Mark 6, 200°C). Grease two baking [cookie] sheets and lightly sift the flour over both of the greased surfaces.

Spoon or pipe the mixture on to the baking sheets, leaving plenty of space between them to allow for expansion. Place the baking sheets in the middle of the oven and bake for 20 minutes, then reduce the temperature to fairly hot 375°F (Gas Mark 5, 190°C) and bake for another 10-15 minutes. Do not open the oven door during the first 15 minutes otherwise the pastry will shrink and lose it's lightness.

Take the pastry out of the oven and make a small slit in the side of each bun, to let the steam escape and allow the pastry to remain crisp while it cools. Carefully place the buns on a wire rack and set aside to cool completely before filling.

To fill the buns, gently cut off the top with a sharp knife and spoon in the chosen filling, savoury or sweet. Replace the top, gently pressing the two halves together. Arrange the puffs on a serving dish and serve as soon as possible after filling.

Choux Puffs

PROFITEROLES

The perfect dessert for an extravagant dinner party, these Little Choux Puffs are filled with whipped cream and then coated with chocolate icing. The chosen filling can be prepared in advance and refrigerated until needed. The puffs can also be prepared in advance, but should not be refrigerated because they would lose their crispness. The profiteroles should be filled and iced as close as possible to serving time.

6 SERVINGS

Basic quantity of choux pastry as above

FILLING

15 fl. oz. [$1\frac{7}{8}$ cups] **whipped cream**

CHOCOLATE ICING

1 oz. castor [2 tablespoons superfine] **sugar**

5 tablespoons water

3 oz. [3 squares] **plain** [semi-sweet] **chocolate**

Preheat the oven to fairly hot 400°F (Gas Mark 6, 200°C). Lightly grease 2 baking sheets.

Make the choux pastry as above. Place the pastry in a large piping bag fitted with a $\frac{1}{2}$-inch plain tube and pipe approximately 30 puffs on to the baking sheets; they should be at least 1 inch apart. Alternatively, use a teaspoon to drop the mixture on to the baking [cookie] sheets.

Bake the puffs in the top of the heated oven for 15 minutes. Reduce the oven temperature to fairly hot 375°F (Gas Mark 5, 190°C) and bake for a further 10 minutes.

Remove the puffs from the oven and make a slit along the side of each bun. Remove any uncooked pastry from the centre of the buns with the end of a teaspoon, if necessary. Set aside and leave the puffs to cool completely on a wire rack.

To fill the puffs, use a teaspoon or piping bag with a plain tube and carefully fill the centre of each puff with the whipped cream.

To make the chocolate icing, first make a sugar syrup. Dissolve the castor [superfine] sugar in the water and bring to the boil over high heat. Boil steadily for about 2 minutes without stirring.

Meanwhile, melt the chocolate in a bowl over hot water, stirring frequently. When the chocolate has completely melted, stir in the sugar syrup and stir until well blended.

To coat the top of each puff, carefully dip the top of the filled puff in the icing. Allow excess icing to drip off and leave the puffs on the wire rack until the icing has set completely.

Serve immediately.

Profiteroles filled with whipped cream and topped with chocolate icing are a dessert to remember.

Chow-Chow

A Chinese preserve, chow-chow consists of ginger, orange rind and sometimes other fruits preserved in syrup. It is also the name given to a mixed vegetable pickle flavoured with mustard.

Chowder

A chowder is a thick soup, generally containing seafood. The name is a corruption of the French *chaudière*, a heavy pot used by farmers and fishermen to cook soups and stews. The best-known French chowder is BOUILLABAISSE.

This traditional old English Christmas Cake is really rich with raisins, currants, cherries and spices.

Christmas Cake I

Adapted from a 19th century Christmas cake recipe — the original called for several bushels of flour and 30 eggs — this cake is rich, moist and filled with fruit and nuts. Like other rich fruit cakes, it improves with keeping and should be baked at least 2 to 3 months before Christmas. Before storing the cake, pierce the top and bottom with a skewer or fine knitting needle and dribble 4 to 5 tablespoons of rum or brandy over both surfaces. Wrap it in aluminium foil and store it in an airtight tin.

Because of the long slow cooking the cake tin must be properly lined. Do this before you start mixing the cake. First, lightly grease the inside of the cake tin and then line it, base and sides, with a double layer of greaseproof or waxed paper. Cut a strip of heavy brown paper 1-inch wider than the depth of the tin and long enough to fit round the tin twice. Tie the brown paper around the outside of the tin firmly with string. Place a double thickness of brown paper or newspaper on a baking sheet wide enough to hold the cake tin.

Halfway through the cooking time check the cake to make sure that the top is not browning too quickly. If it is, place a piece of aluminium foil over the top of the cake and continue baking for the required time.

ONE 10-INCH ROUND CAKE OR
ONE 9-INCH SQUARE CAKE

$2\frac{1}{2}$ lb. raisins
1 lb. currants
6 oz. [$\frac{3}{4}$ cup] chopped candied peel
4 oz. [$\frac{3}{4}$ cup] glacé cherries, halved
4 tablespoons finely chopped crystallized ginger
6 oz. [$1\frac{1}{2}$ cups] blanched slivered almonds
1 lb. [4 cups] flour
1 teaspoon salt
$1\frac{1}{2}$ teaspoons grated nutmeg
1 teaspoon ground allspice
1 teaspoon ground cinnamon
12 oz. [$1\frac{1}{2}$ cups] butter at room temperature
14 oz. [$2\frac{1}{3}$ cups] dark brown sugar
8 large eggs, lightly beaten
1 tablespoon treacle [molasses]
5 tablespoons rum or brandy

Preheat the oven to cool 300°F (Gas Mark 2, 150°C). Prepare the cake tin and baking sheet.

Put the raisins, currants, candied peel, glacé cherries, ginger and almonds into a large bowl and add 4 tablespoons of the flour. Mix well together, making sure all the fruit is lightly covered with flour. Set the bowl aside.

Sift the remaining flour, salt, nutmeg, allspice and cinnamon into a medium-sized bowl and set aside.

In a large mixing bowl beat the softened butter and sugar together with a wooden spoon until the mixture is smooth and creamy. Pour in half the beaten eggs and stir well to mix. Pour in the remaining beaten eggs and stir until the ingredients are blended together. Stir in the treacle [molasses] until the mixture is an even brown colour.

Gradually add the flour-and-spice mixture, folding it in with a wooden spoon or spatula. When all the ingredients are well combined, add the fruit, a little at a time, stirring to make sure that no traces of flour can be seen on the fruit. Pour in the rum or brandy.

Spoon the mixture into the prepared cake tin, smoothing it down with a spatula, and make a hollow in the centre. This will stop the cake from rising too much in the middle. Place the tin on the lined baking sheet and put it in the oven on the shelf just below the centre. Bake for 5 hours.

After 1 hour, lower the temperature to 275°F (Gas Mark 1, 140°C) and bake for another hour. At this stage check the cake and if necessary place the aluminium foil over the top, without removing the cake from the oven. Continue to bake for another 3 hours. To test if the cake is cooked insert a skewer into the centre. If it is done, the skewer will come out clean.

When the cake is cooked, take it out of the oven and leave it to cool in the tin for $1\frac{1}{2}$ to 2 hours. Turn the cake out on to a large wire rack and when it is almost cold, remove the greaseproof or waxed paper from the bottom and sides.

Leave the cake on the rack for at least 12 hours before wrapping in aluminium foil and storing.